ETHICS FOR APOCALYPTIC TIMES

Ethics for Apocalyptic Times
Theapoetics, Autotheory, and Mennonite Literature

DANIEL SHANK CRUZ

The Pennsylvania State University Press
University Park, Pennsylvania

Library of Congress Cataloging-in-Publication Data

Names: Cruz, Daniel Shank, 1980– author.
Title: Ethics for apocalyptic times : theapoetics, autotheory, and Mennonite literature / Daniel Shank Cruz.
Description: University Park, Pennsylvania : The Pennsylvania State University Press, [2023] | Includes bibliographical references and index.
Summary: "Examines the writing of Sofia Samatar, Samuel R. Delany, Casey Plett, Miriam Toews, and others to theorize theapoetics, a queer feminist decolonial reading strategy"—Provided by publisher.
Identifiers: LCCN 2023024930 | ISBN 9780271095653 (pb)
Subjects: LCSH: American literature—Mennonite authors—History and criticism. | Canadian literature—Mennonite authors—History and criticism. | Ethics in literature. | Theology in literature. | Theapoetics
Classification: LCC PS153.M35 C78 2023 | DDC 810.9/9212897—dc23/eng/20230712
LC record available at https://lccn.loc.gov/2023024930

Copyright © 2024 Daniel Shank Cruz
All rights reserved
Printed in the United States of America
Published by The Pennsylvania State University Press,
University Park, PA 16802–1003

The Pennsylvania State University Press is a member of the Association of University Presses.

It is the policy of The Pennsylvania State University Press to use acid-free paper. Publications on uncoated stock satisfy the minimum requirements of American National Standard for Information Sciences—Permanence of Paper for Printed Library Material, ANSI Z39.48–1992.

This book is for Miki with love.

CONTENTS

Acknowledgments (ix)

Introduction: Theapoetics and Apocalyptic Times *(1)*
1. Sofia Samatar's "Request for an Extension on the *Clarity*," Queer Objects, and Theapoetics *(26)*
2. Theapoetics in Mennonite Poetry, Then and Now *(36)*
3. Conversing with the Other in Sara Stambaugh's *I Hear the Reaper's Song* *(61)*
4. Secular Mennonite Ethics in Miriam Toews's *Summer of My Amazing Luck* *(76)*
5. The Theapoetic Ethics of Speculative Fiction *(87)*
6. Samuel R. Delany's Surrealist Anabaptist Ethics *(115)*

Epilogue: Theapoetics and Other Traditions (124)

Notes (129)

Bibliography (148)

Index (161)

ACKNOWLEDGMENTS

Ethics for Apocalyptic Times: Theapoetics, Autotheory, and Mennonite Literature was written in Utica, New York, and Jersey City, New Jersey, the ancestral lands of the still living, still sovereign Oneida and Lenape peoples.

Many people have helped to make *Ethics for Apocalyptic Times* a reality.

First, huge thanks to M. L. DeLaFleur, James Henry Knippen, Suzanne Richardson, and Elizabeth Threadgill for being my chosen family, for writing encouragement, and for helping me get through the pandemic.

The inspiration for *Ethics for Apocalyptic Times* as a book came in the early days of the pandemic, but in some ways it expresses ideas that I have been struggling to articulate since my very first attempts to write about Mennonite literature as a student at Goshen College two decades ago. Major thanks to those of you who read and commented on part or all of the manuscript through the years of its gestation: Ervin Beck, Todd Davis, Lauren Friesen, Jeff Gundy, Anita Hooley Yoder, Ann Hostetler, Maxwell Kennel, Dennis R. Koehn, Kathleen Williams Renk, Mark Van Wienen, J. Denny Weaver, and two anonymous peer reviewers.

This book would be impossible without the 2018 Poetics of Place writing retreat at Laurelville Mennonite Camp and the fellowship that happened there. Thanks especially to Kirsten Eve Beachy, Jeff Gundy, Anita Hooley Yoder, Julia Spicher Kasdorf, Britt Kaufmann, Eileen Kinch, Michael A. King, Becca J. R. Lachman, and Cheryl Denise Miller for that wonderful, generative time.

In addition to those already mentioned, many others gave important support for this project in various ways, among them Torey Akers, Anita Anburajan, Arya the cat, Kelsie Baab, Bella the cat, Alexis Cheung, Christina Cruz, Jesus Cruz, Miriam Cruz, Andrew Harnish, Raylene Hinz-Penner, Jaydra Johnson, Julia Spicher Kasdorf, Ariana Krieger, saahil m., Nan the cat, Jessica Penner, Casey Plett, Becca Price, Sofia Samatar, Saïd Sayrafiezadeh, Mychal Denzel Smith, my tattoos, Hildi Froese Tiessen, Paul Tiessen, Yamilette Vizcaíno Rivera, my writing altar, Yao Xiao, and Robert Zacharias.

Thanks to all the writers whose work I discuss for your work and, in many cases, friendship.

A Utica College Faculty Sabbatical during the spring 2020 semester provided valuable writing time.

Thanks to Maddie Caso, Kathryn Yahner, and the rest of the team at Penn State University Press for believing in this project and helping it to come to fruition.

Some segments of *Ethics for Apocalyptic Times* have been published earlier in rather different form:

This book is derived in part from an article, "Mennonite Speculative Fiction as Political Theology," published in *Political Theology* 22, no. 3 (2021): 211–27, copyright Taylor and Francis, available online: https://doi.org/10.1080/1462317X.2021.1905332.

The book also includes portions of "Mennonite Literature's Queer Decolonial Anabaptist Vision" in *Anabaptist ReMix: Varieties of Cultural Engagement in North America*, edited by Lauren Friesen and Dennis R. Koehn (New York: Peter Lang, 2022), 287–305.

Parts of two essays first published online, "Narrative Ethics in Miriam Toews's *Summer of My Amazing Luck*," *Journal of Mennonite Writing* 5, no. 1 (2013), and "Fiction, Theory, Memoir: Sofia Samatar's 'Request for an Extension on the *Clarity*,'" *Journal of Mennonite Writing* 11, no. 1 (2019), are also here, as is a portion of "Learning to Listen in Greg Bechtel's 'Smut Stories,'" in *Education with the Grain of the Universe: A Peaceable Vision for the Future of Mennonite Schools, Colleges, and Universities*, edited by J. Denny Weaver (Telford, PA: Cascadia, 2017), 213–22. Thanks to the editors of these publications for their feedback on these pieces and their willingness to let them be reproduced here.

Miki, this book is for you!

Introduction

Theapoetics and Apocalyptic Times

On Saturday, 14 March 2020, I turned forty. My partner had a full day of festivities planned for us: brunch at Ocean Blue, my favorite restaurant; a relaxing afternoon on the couch perusing the books I received as gifts; and then dinner with our three closest friends back at Ocean Blue, with a session of Dungeons & Dragons and homemade whoopie pies for dessert. But there was an edge of uneasiness accompanying the day. I was on sabbatical and had been having a calm semester, but our friends, all fellow professors, were dreading the upcoming spring break week because our institution had just announced that it was moving all courses online in response to the COVID-19 pandemic. They would have to spend the week scrambling to adapt their courses to the new environment. On Sunday, I spent the day recovering from the previous evening's debaucheries. On Monday, I realized that the pandemic would affect everyone's lives when then governor Andrew Cuomo closed all schools and various kinds of businesses, including restaurant dining rooms, statewide. On Friday, Cuomo ordered the closure of all nonessential businesses.[1] In hindsight, as I write this in April 2021 (and still, as I do a round of revision in January 2022, and still, as I do another round of revision in July 2022, when numbers are again spiking and monkeypox has entered the mix, and still, as I do my final edits in December 2022 during another spike before turning the manuscript in to my publisher), my birthday feels like the last "normal" day.

A few months earlier, as I was finishing the semester and wondering what I would work on during my sabbatical, I received two invitations four days apart to contribute essays to theological projects, one on Anabaptist vitality in the twenty-first century and one on Mennonite political theology.² The timing of these requests may have been coincidence, or may have been a sign of something deeper, perhaps an act by what Sourayan Mookerjea identifies as "the animist agentic magic lying in the deepest recesses of antecapitalist life that the colonial project sought to drive from the face of the earth."³ Either way, they felt like a definite call from the theological Mennonite community, which I have had a vexed relationship with for twenty years. I said yes to both because I was happy that the editors felt I would have valuable ideas to contribute, but I also felt perplexed because I do not consider myself a theologian. I decided to write both essays about how you can read Mennonite literature theologically because it has often acted as theology for me since I left the church in 2002. As I began writing the essays, it became clear that a significant strain of Mennonite literature has always been concerned with ethics and therefore can be read as a kind of secular theology.

At the same time, I was working on a paper proposal for the 2020 Mennonite/s [sic] Writing conference (subsequently postponed to 2021, and then 2022) about how Mennonite literature should respond to the nefarious tag team of the 2017–21 White House occupant's administration in the United States and the global climate catastrophe that is already manifesting itself in terrifying ways. I have had an interest in apocalyptic literature since 9/11,⁴ and was using my proposal to intertwine this interest with my work on Mennonite literature for the first time. I was going to focus my paper on the future, but when the pandemic hit, more immediate, direct thinking about apocalypse became necessary.

Of course, a sense of impending doom is not new for some of us. Apocalyptic times have been present for people of color in the Americas since 1492. In other words, the idea that apocalyptic times have just begun is a product of white privilege. Much Mennonite literature remains flawed in its lack of engagement with this fact due to its lack of engagement with the lives of people of color in general, though the works of Sofia Samatar, Casey Plett, Abigail Carl-Klassen, Becca J. R. Lachman, and Ken Yoder Reed that I examine later are notable exceptions, as are Rudy Wiebe's novels *The Temptations of Big Bear* and *The Scorched-Wood People*.⁵ I am a Puerto Rican with Taíno and African ancestry, so this ongoing apocalypse has shaped my paternal family's history. My maternal Mennonite ancestors took part in settler colonialism when they settled what is now Lancaster County, Pennsylvania, in the early 1700s.⁶ However, after my birthday the interrelated symptoms of the 2017–21

White House occupant's administration and the pandemic felt especially close and oppressive. The current apocalypse affects everyone.

As I joined the wave of people turning to literature for comfort, panic-buying stacks of books to ensure that I would not run out of reading material, I began thinking about an old, old topic in literary discourse, that of literature's role in society. The pressure cooker of the pandemic led me to the intersection between looking at Mennonite literature theologically and looking to literature as a balm in terrible times. I realized that rereading the Mennonite literature I was writing about for the three essays offered my generally secular self spiritual comfort. This realization surprised me, and I decided to explore it further.

Ethics for Apocalyptic Times: Theapoetics, Autotheory, and Mennonite Literature is the result. The book argues that literature is an essential ethical resource for all of us, secular and religious, as we navigate these terrible times that disability justice activist Leah Lakshmi Piepzna-Samarasinha calls "the triple pandemic" of COVID-19, fascist white supremacy, and climate change, all of which remain strong despite regime change in Washington, DC.[7] To make this argument, *Ethics for Apocalyptic Times* examines a specific literary tradition as an example while also showing that we can imbibe these ethics from whatever literary tradition we belong to. As a Mennonite, I revisit the question of Mennonite literature's role in the faith community, which is one that dates from the beginning of the field's critical discourse, as I recount below. Therefore, the book offers one retelling of the field's history like Julia Spicher Kasdorf calls for in a 2013 essay, "Sunday Morning Confession," that asks the field to abandon prescriptive themes of "transgress[ion] and exile" when telling its history in order to be more inclusive of the rich variety of work that creative writers have written and continue to write.[8] Scholars have offered more expansive versions of the field since that time in a number of venues, including the 2013 After Identity: Mennonite/s Writing in North America symposium, the LGBT Fiction panel at the 2015 Mennonite/s Writing conference, Robert Zacharias's 2016 essay "'A Garden of Spears'" and 2022 book *Reading Mennonite Writing*, Jeff Gundy's 2016 essay "Mennonite/s Writing," and Samatar's 2017 essays "The Scope of This Project" and "In Search of Women's Histories." My 2019 book, *Queering Mennonite Literature*, also does so by calling for a queering of transgression and exile to show that these values are Mennonite ones rather than antagonists to the tradition.[9] *Ethics for Apocalyptic Times* builds on all these efforts. The introductory note to Kasdorf's essay states that it is partially in response to three younger critics—Zacharias,

Anita Hooley Yoder, and me—who have taken Kasdorf's early transgressive work as a model, and to Kasdorf's "guilt" about perhaps leading us astray. Zacharias discusses the essay in *Reading Mennonite Writing* and responds to it in radical, thought-provoking ways, in part by examining texts "*about* Mennonites rather than *by* Mennonites" and asserting that "Mennonite literature is a mode of reading rather than of writing."[10] Although I appreciate Zacharias's emphasis on examining how we read Mennonite literature because I am arguing that one way to do so is theapoetically, I am not ready to fully abandon the field's transgressive narrative yet. Transgression is a necessity for me as a queer (I'm bisexual[11] and kinky) Latinx Mennonite who has had to face both institutional and personal Mennonite queerphobia and racism my entire life. Instead, I hope to strike a happy medium between Kasdorf's and Zacharias's calls for alternative histories and an advocacy of transgression, which sometime necessitates exile, to show that theapoetic Mennonite literature's power comes from its healthy transgression of the world's valorization of violence and transgression of institutional Mennonitism's overly zealous policing of its boundaries.

As I explain below, *Ethics for Apocalyptic Times* suggests one way to read Mennonite literature and offers its hybrid form as an example of the kinds of texts this reading strategy might produce. The book is not an argument for what Mennonite literature *should* be or do but what it *can* be or do. It does not engage the question of whether Mennonite literature should exist as an academic field because that is a vibrant conversation going on in other venues, most notably Magdalene Redekop's 2020 opus *Making Believe*, which asserts that "there is no such thing as Mennonite art" while also acknowledging the "contradiction" of spending over three hundred pages discussing such art.[12] Instead, like most critics, I think that the construction "Mennonite literature" is a helpful one, albeit imperfect, and I document how the field has developed since its first book of literary scholarship, John L. Ruth's *Mennonite Identity and Literary Art* (1978).[13]

THE LITERARY VISIONS OF JOHN RUTH AND AL REIMER

Previous discussions of the faith community question date it back to Ruth's book. The question relates to the broader one of how Mennonites should relate to the world. Ruth begins by establishing the importance of storytelling for individual and group identity, and lamenting the lack of storytellers other than historians in the Mennonite community.[14] He acknowledges that "most discussions of this topic [i.e., the role of writers and literature] begin by making impressive claims for the necessity of the autonomy of the artistic imagination" and then spends the rest of the book showing that such claims are not "impressive" because it is noble for writers to serve their community.[15] Ruth argues that Mennonite writers should devote their work to the church, calling for "the imaginative courage for the literary artist to become involved in the very soul-drama of [their] covenant-community."[16] He wants writers to help construct and portray the "Mennonite identity" of his title.[17] This work is theological and therefore limited by Mennonite orthodoxy instead of having the "autonomy" that Ruth rejects, as he rejects the unquestioned validity of writing by Mennonites who leave the community.[18] Ruth's argument's theological nature, which makes *Mennonite Identity and Literary Art* a work of theology as well as literary theory, is understandable considering that it was published by the denominational publisher, Herald Press, as part of the Focal Pamphlets Series, the purpose of which was to "interpret and discuss problems of contemporary life as they relate to Christian truth."[19] Ruth wrote the book on assignment, so it exemplifies its call to writers to serve the community.[20]

The other theological element of *Mennonite Identity and Literary Art*'s argument is one that most readers of *Ethics for Apocalyptic Times* will take for granted. This is unfortunately still not the case in some segments of the Mennonite community. Ruth argues that writing, and artmaking in general, is not sinful but has value for the faith community because creative talents are gifts from God.[21] His advocacy for what we now call Mennonite literature was revolutionary for the time despite the limitations he suggests. The continued Mennonite resistance against literature's validity is why storytelling about the field's origins has emphasized the transgressiveness that Kasdorf wants us to reconsider.

Even though its outlook is conservative, Ruth's book was groundbreaking because it created Mennonite literary scholarship as a field. Kasdorf explains that it also "cleared a path" for many creative writers. Jeff Gundy states that it "remains important for those of us who still care about the pursuit of truth and justice and beauty and God, not necessarily in that order."[22] All of the terms in Gundy's list are theological and political and thereby imply that literature functions in these realms. I will talk about how I feel about the fourth term later, but I care deeply about the first three and hope that my book offers tasty food for thought about how to find them, as Ruth's does.

Al Reimer's 1993 book, *Mennonite Literary Voices: Past and Present*, offers a sustained reply to *Mennonite Identity and Literary Art* from the perspective of a time when there was much more Mennonite literature available to discuss than when Ruth inaugurated criticism about it.[23] Aside from Herald Press's proselytizing tomes, Ruth had only a handful of texts, such as Rudy Wiebe's *Peace Shall Destroy Many* and *The Blue Mountains of China*, Warren Kliewer's *The Violators* (the only two Mennonite writers Ruth mentions),[24] Dallas Wiebe's *Skyblue the Badass*, and Merle Good's *Happy as the Grass Was Green*, to respond to.[25] The explosion of Mennonite literature in the 1980s that Reimer celebrates established a foundation that writers in the United States and Canada continue to build on prolifically. Ruth's book is proactive in its call for a Mennonite literature, whereas Reimer's is reactive because it has the luxury of the irrevocable establishment of this literature to respond to.

Mennonite Literary Voices also has a different theological orientation. Ruth's book looks inward, focusing on the Mennonite community, whereas Reimer's looks outward, focusing on how Mennonite literature has been shaped by the broader literary milieu and the outside world in general, and looking at how that shaping affects the literature's relationship to the faith community. In contrast to what Kasdorf calls Ruth's "sectarian poetic," Reimer argues for embracing Mennonite writers who want a "general readership" and who, in many cases, "are no longer [theological] Mennonites."[26] This embrace includes an acknowledgment that writers should write what they want to write instead of worrying about how their subject matter relates to religious orthodoxy.[27] Reimer includes critiques of Mennonitism as part of this aesthetic freedom. Whereas Ruth says in an interview that he "get[s] a lot of pleasure in having people jolted but not attacked,"[28] Reimer celebrates writers such as Di Brandt and Patrick Friesen whose work can definitely be said to "attack" their home communities in necessary ways. Reimer appreciates that these writers are still interested in conversation with the Mennonite community and argues that their critiques can play a "prophetic" role from their position on "the dissident frontier from which all good art and literature speaks."[29] Reimer is interested primarily in aesthetic excellence, a secondary concern for Ruth. However, Reimer does acknowledge a collective element of writing by contending that "the literary voice has to be heard in the community" for it to make a difference and that this hearing will not occur if the writing is not good enough to deserve it.[30] So both authors agree that the writers need the community and vice versa.

Along with writing in different eras, Ruth's and Reimer's different roles affected their perspectives. Ruth wrote as a minister who had been called by the lot, though he had a PhD from Harvard and had worked as an English professor before becoming a full-time historiographer and filmmaker for the church, all of which gave him significant "individual power" within the community despite his call for a communitarian writing ethic.[31] Reimer wrote as an English professor who was an important voice in Mennonite studies but who had no official theological authority. Almost all of Ruth's writing is historiography, whereas Reimer authored a successful novel alongside his criticism and thereby was familiar with a creative writing perspective. In *Mennonite Literary Voices*, he reveals that he did not publish his novel with Herald Press because they wanted to censor his language.[32] He tried to offer his fiction to the institutional Mennonite community as Ruth calls for, and it rejected him.

The field embraced Reimer's ideas about writers' relationship to the community almost immediately after they were published, and literary criticism on Mennonite literature has mostly focused on other questions since then, with the notable exception of Ervin Beck's 2015 defense of *Mennonite Identity and Literary Art*'s position from a reader-response theory perspective.[33] Ruth himself indicates sympathy with Reimer's outlook in several statements from the mid-2000s. According to Kasdorf, Ruth has said in conversation "that he would not write the lectures that became *Mennonite Identity* in quite the same way now" and that he appreciates how Mennonite literature developed in the intervening years. In a discussion with two Russian Mennonite writers, Jean Janzen and Rudy Wiebe, Ruth says to Janzen after she states that "I don't think we [herself and Wiebe] are speakers for the community" (i.e., that they do not take up the role that *Mennonite Identity and Literary Art* calls for), "that produces better art than our [Swiss Mennonite] way" of responding to the community's call rather than writing what one wants to write.[34] This statement acknowledges the importance of authors writing without worrying about community standards while also leaving room for the legitimacy of some authors writing explicitly in service to the community should they so choose, a reasonable compromise despite Ruth's outdated use of the Russian/Swiss binary to represent the two practices.

Although many critics recap the books' debate,[35] and my choice to retell it might seem like a repetition of the field's mythology that Kasdorf warns against, I do so to reframe it, partly by pushing it earlier, and partly by arguing that ultimately the literature itself—not literary critics or theologians—resolves the debate.

The relationship between literature and the faith community is one Ruth was thinking about since at least 1964. In a sermon entitled "Revolution and Reverence" that responds to controversy over the publication of a Lawrence Ferlinghetti poem in a "Mennonite youth magazine," Ruth argues that the church must converse with 1960s radicalism.[36] He calls for Mennonites to embrace the arts as a corrective to our refusal to engage the wider world because "the serious artist, Christian or not, is a seer."[37] Ruth takes literature's legitimacy as a resource for the faith community for granted, a stance that, as I say above, was heretical in 1978, let alone 1964. Ruth also argues that writers have a prophetic role to play nearly thirty years before Reimer. Unlike *Mennonite Identity and Literary Art*, "Revolution and Reverence" focuses solely on secular literature because almost no nondidactic Mennonite literature existed at the time. At most, there were a handful of texts in English for Ruth to examine,[38] though it is probable he only knew of one, Wiebe's *Peace Shall Destroy Many*. Mabel Dunham's *The Trail of the Conestoga* (1924) and *Toward Sodom* (1927) and Gordon Friesen's *Flamethrowers* (1936) had all already faded into obscurity, but Elizabeth Horsch Bender's 1957 article on Mennonites in literature in *The Mennonite Encyclopedia* mentions them, so it is possible that Ruth tracked them down.[39] Kliewer's *The Violators* was published the year Ruth preached "Revolution and Reverence," but it was probably not out yet considering that the sermon took place in February.[40] As a result of this lack, the sermon argues for the use of secular, "worldly" literature in the faith community, with Ruth mentioning Henry David Thoreau, the Beats (including Ferlinghetti), and *Moby-Dick* favorably.[41] Thus, "Revolution and Reverence" is more liberal than *Mennonite Identity and Literary Art*, closer to Reimer's thinking and Ruth's later thinking, because the book examines how Mennonites can represent themselves to the world rather than what they can learn from it. Like *Mennonite Literary Voices*, the sermon focuses outward, even though it asks the literature-and-the-faith-community question from a purely theological standpoint, not a critical one. The Mennonite roots of seeing theological value in secular literature stretch back to at least this time. "Revolution and Reverence" reminds us that the history of the field is less fixed than we may assume.

MENNONITE THEAPOETICS

In the last decade, a number of Mennonite writers and scholars have begun conversing with the field of theopoetics, pushing its boundaries away from its original task of examining theology as literature to examine literature theologically, and thereby restarting the conversation about literature's theological role from the literary side.[42] Instead of asking what role literature should play for the community, theopoets assume that literature written on its own terms as art has theological relevance and try to illustrate that relevance. Theologian Jeremy M. Bergen admits this usefulness, observing that traditional (in the academic disciplinary sense) theology is not enough, that the community needs something else, by naming the importance of literature for broader Mennonite thought. He acknowledges that "the discourse that most directly engages the complex relationships between Mennonite identity, culture and faith, including lack of faith, is that of Mennonite literature and its critics."[43] Gundy also wonders if Mennonite writers might help to bring "renewal to a tradition now threatened with bureaucratic ossification."[44] Anita Hooley Yoder concurs, asserting that poetry's ethical outlook "is a crucial element in the quest for peace, inside and outside of our churches."[45] These statements critique the faith community in that they argue that its theology is insufficient, but they also affirm the community via their willingness to converse with it.

Ethics for Apocalyptic Times joins this conversation to illustrate it from a secular point of view. By "secular," I mean what Maxwell Kennel calls in his definition of "secular Mennonite" a "broad and undefined [i.e., not necessarily synonymous with atheism] category of the world that exists apart from the bounds of Christian theology, its church, and the category of religion in general."[46] I show how Mennonite literature teaches ethics, which can be useful for readers within and without the Mennonite community, because, as Gundy, paraphrasing theologian Grace Jantzen, argues, "the question is not what we believe, . . . [but] how we act in the world." Similarly, Mennonite poet Connie T. Braun argues the theopoetic notion that poetry that "witness[es]" to "suffering . . . serves as an ethical act."[47] Read this way, Mennonite literature offers an example for how literature in general can act as an ethical force in this time of pandemic and apocalypse. These ethics are necessary because we may well need to put them into practice. Who knows what these times will require of us?

Ethics for Apocalyptic Times also argues that, although Mennonite writers did not heed *Mennonite Identity and Literary Art*'s charge to write intentionally in service to the community (nor should they have; I do not argue for literature as propaganda but show how it offers ethical arguments as art), if we read Mennonite literature through the lens of theapoetics—a term I define momentarily—many pieces of Mennonite literature actually accomplish what

Mennonite Identity and Literary Art calls for while also fulfilling the prophetic outsider role that *Mennonite Literary Voices* calls for by "reflect[ing] in the deepest sense what is actually happening in the Mennonite community, and not what we like to think is happening or hope is happening."[48] The literature's implicit choice to follow Reimer and interact with the world gave it the freedom to also answer Ruth's call, but on the writing's own terms. Therefore, thirty years on from Reimer's reply to Ruth, the literature has manifested the best of both worlds.

In a dinner conversation at a gathering of Mennonite writers at Laurelville Mennonite Camp on 9 June 2018, poet Britt Kaufmann asserted that the movement from "theopoetics" to "theapoetics" is necessary. Her call for an emphasis on the feminist aspects of the Divine through the use of "thea" ("goddess") liberates the field from patriarchal language and moves it away from the often-elitist realm of academic discourse into the broader public sphere that includes space for those inside and outside the academy. I therefore choose to use it because patriarchal religion also oppresses queer folx such as myself. Theapoetics happens at the margins because those of us there need new ways to relate to the Divine that are not disciplined by the institutional faith community.

None of us at the table had encountered the term before. However, theologian Molly Remer writes about it in a 2015 book, sharing Kaufmann's feminist viewpoint to define it as "experiencing the Goddess through direct 'revelation,' framed in language." Remer also writes that theapoetics views "lived experiences as legitimate sources of direct, or divine, revelation."[49] Simultaneously a practice and a theory, theapoetics makes space for both lived experience and literature as theology. It takes a low church view of how to relate to the Divine just as Mennonite theology does because it argues that encounters with the Divine can happen anywhere without the need for sacraments or priestly interlocutors or a church building. Its emphasis on individual experiences, on the personal being political, is a queer, feminist one. As queer writer Michelle Tea observes, "we may be having spiritual experiences, but we are having them in our bodies,"[50] so it is necessary to consider theology as an embodied endeavor, a project that many theologians have already taken up but one that still struggles with queer bodies, and especially queer of color bodies like mine.[51] Therefore, via theapoetics it becomes possible to examine Mennonite literature as a form of theology from the literary side of the connection, even though this literature is a secular enterprise in that its authors write it as art rather than rhetoric.

Indeed, Redekop declares that Mennonite writers "worked hard during the 1980s to establish the category 'secular Mennonite'"—that is, someone raised Mennonite who is no longer in the church—as a way of showing that being Mennonite does not always mean adhering to a certain set of beliefs.[52] Paradoxically, though, naming oneself as secular is a theological move, so in a sense Mennonite literature has always been theological even as it has fought against such a label. Kennel's theological definition of a "secular Mennonite" as "a person for whom the cultures, values, and identities of Mennonites are important in a way that cannot be captured by either straightforward acceptance or rejection of theological statements," and who is able to undertake the queer task of "serv[ing] as a challenge to dualistic thinking of all kinds" helps make space for this paradox because it acknowledges the validity of a position that draws strength from multiple communities, not just the Mennonite community or the world.[53] Mennonite literature's power comes from its willingness to search for the Divine everywhere, not just within the faith community.

I find the term theapoetics helpful because it looks at theological discourse slantwise like Kennel's definition. Theapoetics does not require writing to be systematic; it revels in the unruly just as queer theory does. Literature can illuminate a sideways path toward a healthier faith community. Instead of being stuck in an exclusionary vision of community like institutional Mennonitism's strictly defended boundaries, literature can help us move toward a relational community that includes humans, animals, and the environment. Literature reminds us that ethical responsibility does not end with other humans but extends to all of creation, a principle the ignoring of which has played a major role in getting us to our apocalyptic moment. Mennonite literature serves the broader Mennonite community because the field itself functions as a nurturing community and has done so since the 1980s. Zacharias observes that those in the field are frequently described as "family." In a 2004 essay, Ann Hostetler documents how the field has created a vibrant "virtual community" inclusive of Mennonites of all theological stripes.[54] This is even more so the case now. Aside from meeting at semi-regular Mennonite/s Writing conferences,[55] members of the field build community through social media venues such as the "Mennonite Lit. Writers" Facebook group run by Andrew Unger and Darcie Friesen Hossack,[56] informal dinner meetups at the Association of Writers and Writing Programs annual conference and other conferences, reading drafts of each other's work, and referencing one another in our creative writing, not just our scholarship.[57] The field fulfills Mennonite poet Nikki Reimer's hope for "dissident groups of writers operating in interconnected pods, holding each other accountable, and collaborating toward a more equitable community" of writers and in general.[58] Mennonite writers share Ruth's concern for the community from *Mennonite Identity and Literary Art*, but we do so in new ways that acknowledge the community can profit from the world's ideas, not just vice versa. The theological community can benefit from this knowledge by using a theapoetic approach that broadens its vision of what theological thinking can be. As I show in the chapters to follow, this path is a queer one politically (i.e., in the way queer theory often uses the term) in its visions of a radically new society, and sometimes sexually in its affirmation of all sexualities.

There is a mystical element that Jane Bennett describes as "weirder and more wayward [than merely aesthetic] energies flowing in and out of" literature that theapoetics names in a way that literary criticism does not.[59] Thus, theapoetics enriches the study of both literature and theology. Traditional God language does not work for me (nor, for that matter, does Remer's "Goddess" language, though it gets closer to what I am looking for), but theapoetics' model of viewing personal experiences as something more than just having to do with oneself does. Remer also writes that "*my thealogy is the earthy, the mundane, the practical,*" elements that Hooley Yoder calls "the poetry of life."[60] Although Remer happens to be writing from a spiritual framework, this is a philosophy that works in the secular realm. She cites Elizabeth Fisher's claim "'that the sacred and secular are one.'"[61] This is an idea present in the queer tradition since at least Walt Whitman's 1855 poetry collection *Leaves of Grass*. Writing about Whitman from a secular viewpoint, Mark Doty echoes Remer's religious language to name writers' call, avowing that "artists need to live as if revelation is never finished," which is a theapoetic statement if there ever was one because of its belief that writing always has something to teach us.[62] In his description of "Anabaptist theopoetics," Gundy uses similar language in his belief that "revelation is continual and ongoing."[63] So theapoetics queers theopoetics by doing secular theopoetic work, which becomes theapoetic work.

Mennonite theologian Melanie Kampen echoes Remer's emphasis on the importance of experience in her call for decolonial theology that asks "'Who is suffering? Who is experiencing violence and trauma? And why? How is power distributed?'" to counter the intersectional violence of colonization, which affects women, people of color, queers, and the disabled, among others. Kampen posits that "experiences of" the oppressed are "primary sites of knowledge" that theology must use.⁶⁴ Her argument amplifies Remer's to show that theapoetics is a decolonial endeavor as well as a queer, feminist one.

LITERATURE AND ETHICS

Although I choose to focus on Mennonite literature here, explorations of the intersection between literature and something bigger (whether you use theological language for it or not) appear frequently these days in the broader literary community, and my book's advocacy of the ethics present in the literature I examine is applicable to everyone, not just Mennonites. For instance, one of these appearances takes place at the end of Elizabeth Acevedo's novel *The Poet X*. The protagonist, Xiomara, whom poetry has rescued from an oppressive Catholic upbringing, says, "I think when we get together and talk about ourselves, about being human, about what hurts us, we're also talking about God. So that's also church, right?"⁶⁵ Xiomara understands the theapoetic idea that personal experience is connected to the Divine even if it takes place away from theologically sanctioned spaces. As Gundy posits, "The problem of 'the world' is the most pressing one we face—Mennonites, yes, but everybody else too."⁶⁶ We all must reckon with apocalypse, and theapoetics helps us do so by showing how to encounter the Divine in our everyday experiences of the world.

Doty's Whitmanic call to seek "revelation" in writing describes the spiritual, ethical importance of writing. Literature offers aesthetic entertainment and works for societal change simultaneously by fostering community. Just as prayer in a religious context is an attempt to bring the person praying closer to God, so too are the acts of reading and writing attempts to build relationships between readers and writers. In a discussion of Audre Lorde's well-known statement that "poetry is not a luxury," Redekop agrees that "we need it [poetry] in order to live,"⁶⁷ not just to teach us how to live. In these times, I think the same goes for literature in general. Redekop further contends that "art is not a frivolous pursuit in the midst of the crisis of our time. Talking *about* art is another matter altogether."⁶⁸ I agree wholeheartedly with the first sentence but disagree with the second. We need champions for the art to work alongside the artists themselves to help make the activist community writing engenders visible.

Although theapoetics is helpful for investigating all literary genres, and *Ethics for Apocalyptic Times* examines mostly fiction, poets are the writers currently making the most impassioned arguments for literature's relevance in our terrible times. But poetry is often under attack. Ben Lerner describes how "every few years an essay appears in a mainstream periodical denouncing poetry or proclaiming its death" because of its perceived irrelevance. Reimer plays with this critique in her 2014 collection DOWNVERSE [sic]. The book's epigraph reads "I hated your poem. / Your poem was so boring. / — inebriated audience member at a poetry reading."[69] Similarly, an untitled poem midway through the book includes a prose fragment that mimics something an online troll might type: "only a poet would say that the reason non poets don't like poetry is because they don't understand it. and therein lies the real problem. it's not the poetry that is disliked. it is the poets who deliver it in such a way that they think they are somehow better, fairer, superior creatures than the rest of us that turns the stomach. you wrote some words that may or may not rhyme. you memorized them. you said them in front of people. they clapped. or didn't. good for you. now go cure cancer."[70] The poem refutes this critique in a delightfully snarky way by embedding it within a collection of poetry, which is itself a response that validates poetry's importance. It is necessary for me to also respond because I make the same kind of lofty claims for theapoetic literature that poets are making for poetry.

Poetry's—and, by extension, literature's—detractors want it to do something. It is not enough for it to just be there as itself. Likewise, there is a long tradition of poets agreeing that poetry must act in the world. For instance, Amiri Baraka writes that "poetry has to be as functional as anything else in our lives" because "we're trying to change the world."[71] Poetry is political. As any poetry reader knows, it does do something, even if that something is difficult to name. Perhaps the most famous expression of this idea is found in the work of William Carlos Williams, who was actually a physician, though he did not cure cancer. He asserts: "It is difficult / to get the news from poems / yet [people] die miserably every day / for lack / of what is found there."[72] Literature offers us healing if we let it so that our everyday lives are not "miserable," in part by modeling the theapoetic principle of showing how daily existence is sacred. Matthew Zapruder picks up on this idea. He writes of poetry's "'news,'" which Williams acknowledges is there even if it is "difficult" to get, that it "is something more than mere information, facts and opinions," it is "'gospel'" or "'good news.'" It offers spiritual sustenance. Indeed, Zapruder considers himself a "religious person" because he reads and writes and teaches poetry even though he does not practice religion.[73] He claims poetry as its own religion with poems as its theology. So literature does something, it gives us sustenance, but we have to seek that something out. Theapoetics takes work.

Literature's "news" often has a teaching purpose. Whitman argues that poetry has an ethical function, claiming that it can give readers a "*good heart* as a radical possession and habit."[74] Poetry's intense, observant way of viewing the world teaches us to appreciate the world more and to treat it with kindness. Reading literature changes us, but often in gradual rather than instantaneous ways, so the change can be difficult to see just as our heart is hidden from our sight.

In recent times, writers advocate for this change to occur in service to societal rebirth as a response to our apocalyptic times. For instance, Willie Perdomo asserts that we are in a "moment" of revolution "and that poets might play a key role in that moment."[75] This is an ambitious claim that some might see as too utopian to be useful. However, I agree with Melva Graham's observation that this skepticism "is the voice of white supremacy" because it attempts to silence the work of writers of color such as Baraka, Graham, Perdomo, Lorde, Williams, and myself by telling us that our work does nothing.[76] It repeats the critique documented in Reimer's poem. Another queer writer of color, Alexander Chee, argues that the interaction between readers and books is so transformative that it is the "reason that when fascists come to power, writers are among the first to go to jail. And that is the point of writing."[77] Like the voice in Reimer's poem, some people might not find writing interesting, but politicians know that it is powerful, which is why they try to suppress it, whether through cutting arts funding or more drastic measures. Writers must use this power even if it leads to persecution.

Therefore, I reject the assumption that writing does nothing and argue that literature has a role to play in these apocalyptic times that will inevitably change North American society in some way. The US government's refusal to take climate change or COVID-19 seriously has terrifying implications for the entire world. In such a situation, it is difficult to be optimistic. This was especially the case when I first drafted this paragraph in July 2020 while the 2017–21 White House occupant's minions were kidnapping protesters into unmarked vans. In her recent book *Showing Up*, Mennonite Esther Stenson includes a poem, "Museum Afterthoughts," that acknowledges such despair in its depiction of war, environmental degradation, and the genocide of Indigenous Peoples in the United States. It ends "Perhaps it were better that we, like dinosaurs, / would fossilize while there is still time."[78] Even in a collection that consists almost completely of poems about nature or the virtuous lives of plain-dressing relatives, Stenson offers the sentiment that it is time for humanity to close up shop before we destroy the planet even further. But I believe that advocating for literature is one thing US citizens can do to reject these governmental actions and assert our citizenship in the global community so that the change will be positive. These poets' calls for transformation through the power of literature are politically queer because they want a completely new society rather than tweaks to the old one, and because they believe their vision is possible.

Revolution does not necessarily mean violent uprising, though. One of the reasons poetry can be such a powerful tool is that it often rejects mainstream beliefs in the inevitability of violence. Gundy speculates that "the percentage of committed pacifists and peace activists among poets is probably at least as high as it is among Mennonites." Rachel Tzvia Back's poem "What Use Is Poetry, the Poet Is Asking" exemplifies this pacifism. Recalling Williams, it directs its question to "the evening news" before arguing for poetry as an antidote to war. Again, we see belief in literature's ethical usefulness. Revolution can also bring healing. For instance, although Rebecca Lindenberg's poem "A Brief History of the Future Apocalypse" testifies to personal apocalypses such as earthquakes, plane crashes, and the deaths of loved ones, she reminds us in a note on the poem that aside from "destruction," "apocalypse" also "means revelation, renewal, transformation."[79] I use the term in both senses here. My use of the destructive sense is not a scare tactic—it's a little late for that—nor does it refer to the genre of spiritual writing whose most well-known example is the New Testament's Book of Revelation because *Ethics for Apocalyptic Times* is not a work of eschatology.[80] Instead, I mean the general, more pop culture sense (insert the title of your favorite alien invasion or giant meteor movie here) of a cataclysmic event that changes society irrevocably. I am also interested in the hope Lindenberg references by citing the second definition. We cannot avoid our ongoing apocalypses, but we can seek to live through them ethically. It is important to remember that all hope is not lost and that something good may be built out of the rubble of these times.

In *Making Believe*'s acknowledgments, Redekop writes about her family's "love," "[It] brings me deep joy and hope for the future, without which I would not have bothered writing this book."[81] Her statement strikes me because it illuminates something true that I had never articulated before I read it. Whatever else writing is, it is an act of hope that there will be a future and that readers in that future—even if it is just you rereading your journal—will read what you have written and will benefit from it. This hopefulness is why writing is especially important during our time of pandemic and apocalypse. In a note to her poem "You Are Your Own State Department," Naomi Shihab Nye observes that "sometimes the audience at a reading feels so supple and hopeful it breaks my heart. It's as if people think the poet might put things back in place. This is a tenderness beyond measure—a belief in the powers of language and metaphor—a dream of abiding meaning."[82] As a writer and reader, I share this belief in literature's power to "put things back in place," or, better yet, put them in a new, queerer configuration that makes the world better for all of us. *Ethics for Apocalyptic Times* participates in this endeavor.

THEAPOETICS IN MENNONITE LITERATURE AND BEYOND

In the first five chapters that follow, I narrow my focus to Mennonite literature, but I widen it again in the final chapter and the epilogue to offer more examples of how theapoetic principles exist in other traditions. Again, unlike Redekop, who "do[es] not believe that there is something called 'Mennonite/s Writing' that transcends inconvenient differences between Canada and the United States or between Swiss Mennonites and Russian Mennonites,"[83] I believe it is helpful to consider Mennonite literature coalitionally as a field that includes all of these different perspectives and acknowledges those differences but coheres because these perspectives share beliefs in nonviolence and the importance of community. With Gundy, I believe that Mennonite literature's variety is "its greatest strength,"[84] so I examine a miscellany of texts from the past forty years from Canada and the United States. This examination is an example of why the construction "Mennonite literature" is helpful. Naming the field makes pieces of literature available for the Mennonite community to interpret; it creates a usable archive. Redekop observes that "community" is "perhaps the most enduring of Mennonite values." It is part of what Hildi Froese Tiessen calls the "trace" of theological Mennonitism that remains in secular Mennonite literature.[85] The community can undertake this interpretation with any piece of literature it wants to, as Gundy does with writers such as Whitman and William Stafford in his theopoetic treatise *Songs from an Empty Cage*, or I do in chapter 6. But I do think it is no surprise that many pieces of Mennonite literature include aspects of "Mennonite thinking" by advocating for nonviolence, communal mutual aid, and the importance of politically queer thinking, even when they do not include Mennonite subject matter.[86] The field makes these "traces" that share what theologian Karl Koop calls "a hermeneutics of [Mennonite] tradition" visible,[87] albeit in unorthodox ways, serving the community by challenging it from theologically heterogenous positions. I include older and quite recent texts to show how a significant strain of the field (there are many, many texts that I do not examine, and not all of them fit this framework because the field is a diverse one) has been and continues to be theapoetic.

Although Ruth may not have only had "literary" writing—that is, fiction, poetry, and memoir written for adults for art's sake rather than as a teaching tool—in mind in *Mennonite Identity and Literary Art*,[88] I focus on such literature because work published by companies such as Herald Press obviously has theological elements. I am interested in the theological elements of works that are written as secular endeavors, not in writing created with any kind of didactic purpose.

I do not consider myself a theologian and write *Ethics for Apocalyptic Times* from a secular viewpoint. Nevertheless, my discussions of theapoetics and ethics makes the book a piece of theology alongside its status as a piece of literary criticism. I write it as a theological effort of the kind Stephanie Chandler Burns calls for in her advocacy of queer Mennonites' employment of "ordinary theology," which is "the type of theological reflection engaged in . . . within everyday life" whether one is an academic theologian or not. As she asserts, "Queer theology is queer people talking about theological concepts," so this book is queer theology regardless of my academic training.[89] I am not a "theological Mennonite" in the sense of following institutional Mennonite theological orthodoxy, and when I use this term, I refer to those who do. But within the framework of ordinary theology, I am a Mennonite who has a theology, the contours of which will become apparent throughout *Ethics for Apocalyptic Times*. Ordinary theology's emphasis on everyday experience dovetails with theapoetics' belief in experience as theological material. This belief results in the creation of multiple theologies that make room for groups that official Mennonite theology has traditionally oppressed, such as women, queers, people of color, and the disabled. Queer theory teaches that binaries like the one this paragraph sets up between theological Mennonitism and ordinary theology are usually false, so I hope it is clear throughout this book that I still think that Mennonitism has lots to offer. But when the institutional community constructs and enforces a binary that you are outside of, its existence feels very real. Institutional Mennonite theology has a lot to answer for.[90]

Therefore, in my work on Mennonite literature I continue to struggle with a question that Kasdorf asked toward the beginning of her career: "If one has gifts, what is one's responsibility to the Mennonite community?"[91] Regarding another aspect of responsibility to one's community, Ruth says that "a lot of times you recognize a call only in retrospect."[92] This is how I feel about *Ethics for Apocalyptic Times*. I was working on another book project when the idea for this one seized me, and the first draft poured out of me in about four months. The Mennonite community keeps pulling me back in despite my attempts to leave it behind. I thus find myself reluctantly agreeing with the speaker of Patrick Friesen's poem "A Kind of Longing" that "the longing [for spiritual sustenance] never leaves."[93] I go back to Mennonite stories because these are the narratives that have shaped me and taught me how to relate to the world, so it is necessary for me to wrestle with them and see what parts of them I must reject and what parts I still find helpful and can keep as I continue to build a new lens through which to view the world.

As a literary object, *Ethics for Apocalyptic Times* places itself in the realm of creative writing as life writing and in academic discourse as an intervention in literary criticism, Mennonite studies, queer theory, and theological discourse. I could not have written it without the goad of Mennonite literature that has helped me to revisit my spiritual life in recent years. Although I remain outside of Mennonite orthodoxy, I am much farther away from atheism now than I have been for most of the past twenty years. The autobiographical aspect of the book manifests itself in each chapter via some personal stories that relate to my own experiences with the texts under consideration. These stories go in tandem with my more traditional literary criticism of the texts.

The book inhabits a hybrid, messy genre that goes under various names: "anecdotal theory," "research-creation," "autotheory."[94] Although scholars have been slow to examine the genre, its history dates back to books by queer women of color such as Cherríe Moraga and Gloria Anzaldúa's *This Bridge Called My Back* (1981), Audre Lorde's *Sister Outsider* (1984), and Anzaldúa's *Borderlands/La Frontera* (1987).[95] The genre's queer, decolonial roots are why it fits with theapoetics. Some Mennonite writers are gaining notice in the field, so it is also a Mennonite mode. For instance, Lauren Fournier examines the importance of Samatar's term "life-thinking" for defining autotheory, and Simon Pope discusses Mennonite visual artist and writer Rachel Epp Buller's work as an important example of research-creation.[96]

I write in this genre because, as the title of Natalie Loveless's research-creation "manifesto" *How to Make Art at the End of the World* asserts, it is a practice that can help us navigate our apocalyptic times because the speculative visions and language of visual art and literature have the potential to reveal new ways of living. As a part of these visions, it is necessary to create "new, unruly, driven stories" to use as teaching tools. Therefore, as scholars and creators we must "move forward, one classroom, degree, article, book, conference, conversation, and artistic research project at a time" rather than giving in to despair and hopelessness as I am often tempted to do, wanting to just sit on the couch with my cats.[97] Hence my choice to write this book. Fournier declares that the genre "reveals the tenuousness of maintaining illusory separations between art and life, theory and practice."[98] Instead, according to Loveless, the genre "insists that . . . artistic production is no longer solely an *object* of scholarly inquiry but is itself a legitimate *form of research and dissemination*." It is embodied like theapoetics, "a practice of love . . . erotic."[99] Some of the texts I examine use autotheoretical strategies as part of their theapoetics by drawing on their authors' lives, exemplifying how the genre can be a form of "self-preservation."[100]

The self in the genre always "draws shared breath with communal bodies of knowledge." Its melding of personal experience with broader public questions of how to live offers the potential for new ways of thinking about ethics.[101] One way it does this is in its recognition that who writers cite in our work is "politic[al]."[102] Sandra Ruiz writes in an endnote that "endnotes . . . are pregnant with possibilities—stories and lives missing from dominant discourse."[103] Similarly, Sara Ahmed observes that who we choose to cite can either reinforce exclusionary academic conversations or expand them.[104] To participate in this expansion, the genre often includes what Vilashini Cooppan calls a "flood of quotation" as a way to establish affinity with other creators.[105] Citation is a kind of digging, an archival archaeology that finds the most fascinating bits of others' foundational work and puts them together into something new. Ahmed states that "citation is how we acknowledge our debt to those who came before; those who helped us find our way when the way was obscured."[106] For those of us who love the physical acts of reading and writing, citation is a way to pay homage to what adrienne maree brown calls our "personal pleasure lineage[s]," the gatherings of those who have taught us to love our bodies despite capitalism's constant body policing.[107] Naming these lineages is a creative act, what Fournier calls a queer "artist[ic]" medium.[108] This profuse, world-making citational aesthetic, which I employ in my main text, endnotes, and generous index, is an act of joyful community building rather than simply being an act of scholarly obligation. As Zefyr Lisowski says, "I speak in a footnote because it's the clearest way I know to not speak alone."[109] Our citations show gratitude to those who teach us. They also create an archive for others to peruse and take inspiration from.[110] So make sure to read the endnotes, not just the main text!

There is a common sexist, racist critique of authotheory and research-creation similar to critiques of memoir in general that views their genre as "narcissistic." But, as Chelsea Rozansky asserts, "It isn't narcissism, but a kind of badass move, to assert your presence in a discourse that marginalizes you."[111] I do so here in Mennonite discourse specifically and academic discourse more broadly, both of which people of color and queers still must fight to access.

A MAP OF THE BOOK

Chapter 1, "Sofia Samatar's 'Request for an Extension on the *Clarity*,' Queer Objects, and Theapoetics," examines Samatar's memoirish story "Request for an Extension on the *Clarity*" from her 2017 collection *Tender* alongside Ahmed's concept of a "feminist killjoy survival kit" from her 2017 book *Living a Feminist Life*. Inspired by Ahmed's work, I close-read a segment of Samatar's story about the narrator's library to help describe my own queer killjoy survival kit and how this archive offers me emotional support. My investigation of Ahmed's concept helps to illuminate more of theapoetics' queer underpinnings. Although the word "queer's" ideological advocacy of openness makes attempts to define queer somewhat paradoxical, I use it throughout *Ethics for Apocalyptic Times* in at least three ways that queer theory uses it. The first is as an adjective to describe someone (or writing that describes someone) who is LGBTQ2IA+. The second is as an adjective to describe a political stance that calls for radical societal change in all areas, not just sexuality. The third is as a verb to refer to the action of reinvestigating the foundations of something for the purpose of working toward this radical change. This book is a queer one, but it does not focus specifically on sexually queer Mennonite literature, which I write about elsewhere.[112]

The chapter is also an example of how a reader (in this case, me) can experience theapoetic teaching from a text. I draw inspiration for the chapter's autobiographical elements, as with those throughout *Ethics for Apocalyptic Times*, from those in Samatar's fiction and essays. Samatar tells Amina Cain in an interview that she has "sworn never to write another" traditional "academic essay." On a related note, in an interview with Alicia Cole, Samatar declares that she is "always trying to merge things, rather than balance them."

I want to create new things that are mixtures of genres or categories I've been told are incompatible."¹¹³ Although I am not quite ready to abandon academic writing myself, I appreciate how Samatar integrates the personal in her own work so skillfully and work to do likewise here.

Chapter 2, "Theapoetics in Mennonite Poetry, Then and Now," begins with a description of my faith crisis in college and how Mennonite literature, and especially Mennonite poetry, helped me to stay connected to my Mennonite self. In hindsight, I realize that this connection was possible because of the poetry's theapoetic aspects. I study these aspects in the early work of two writers who were the most important for teaching me how to stray from institutional Mennonitism while also remaining in conversation with the community, Jeff Gundy and Di Brandt. I read Gundy's poetry through the lens of his 1998 essay "In Praise of the Lurkers (Who Come Out to Speak)," which theorizes writers' relationship with the faith community. Gundy's poems consistently write against religious orthodoxy while at the same time reveling in the presence of the Divine in the world. I then discuss Brandt's 2018 essay "Paradigms of Re:placement, Re:location, and Re:vision: The Creative Challenge of the New Mennonite Writing of Manitoba (and the World)," which returns to the themes of Gundy's essay to urge the faith community to make space for its writers. I examine some of Brandt's poetry to show how it exemplifies the feminist, decolonial nature of theapoetic writing that the community needs.

The third part of the chapter shows how the theapoetic roots of Mennonite poetry as found in work by writers such as Gundy and Brandt continue to flower in the field. It does so by offering brief examinations of recent books by Becca J. R. Lachman, Abigail Carl-Klassen, Janet Kauffman, Julia Spicher Kasdorf, and Julie Swarstad Johnson.

Whereas the poetry in chapter 2 urges us toward contemplation as a strategy for learning theapoetic ethics, the fiction I examine in subsequent chapters teaches us theapoetic ethics via the examples of the actions of its characters. Writing about theopoetics' cousin, narrative theology, Martha Nussbaum observes that the field is interested in "supplementing abstract philosophical attempts at self-understanding with concrete narrative fictions, which are argued by the proponents of the project to contain more of what is relevant to our attempts to imagine and assess possibilities for ourselves, to ask how we might choose to live."¹¹⁴ To live an ethical life, it is not enough for an individual or community to be aware of abstract ethical guidelines such as "love thy neighbor" or "be nonviolent" because it is difficult to put these guidelines into practice without concrete examples of how we should apply them in real-life situations. It is therefore necessary to teach ethics via stories that model proper ethical behavior, or, conversely, that model behavior that readers should avoid as unethical.

Stories give us a world view to work from, and as a result they do not just shape our ethics, they shape our entire lives. When stories are shared among a group of people, these narratives shape communities, which in turn shape individuals via the stories they tell, whether for good or ill. Reading others' stories always affects us; the important thing is to be cognizant of how they affect us, how they teach us, to determine how or whether to implement this new knowledge into our lives. Mennonites traditionally engage in this teaching with texts such as the *Martyrs Mirror* and other more recent real-life accounts of sacrifices for Jesus.[115] Mennonites are excellent storytellers, and we already emphasize the importance of narratives for the community. Mennonites love to talk about ourselves (this book is a prime example!), as can be seen in the disproportionately large size of North American Mennonite print culture in comparison to the number of Mennonites living here.[116] Unfortunately, many of the theological texts previously used by Mennonites to teach ethics have been oppressive, urging a hurtful, joyless, self-sacrificial, and misogynistic approach to the world. This is why looking to literature for some sideways theological instruction is necessary.

Chapters 3 and 4, "Conversing with the Other in Sara Stambaugh's *I Hear the Reaper's Song*" and "Secular Mennonite Ethics in Miriam Toews's *Summer of My Amazing Luck*," respectively, are close readings that examine two sides of the same ethical coin in two older texts from opposite sides of the US-Canadian border. Stambaugh's novel takes place in Lancaster County, Pennsylvania, which is traditionally one of the most important US Mennonite locations, and Toews's novel takes place in Winnipeg, Manitoba, the city with the largest percentage of Mennonites in the world. *I Hear the Reaper's Song* gives an example of how Mennonite ethics are used properly in a Mennonite context, and *Summer of My Amazing Luck* gives an example of how they are used in a non-Mennonite context as a way of critiquing how the Mennonite community often fails to live up to its own standards. Both novels use the theapoetic strategy of writing from real-life experience to teach ethics. Stambaugh's book fictionalizes a railroad accident that occurred in Lancaster in 1896, and Toews's incorporates many autobiographical elements.

While chapters 3 and 4 examine two Mennonite hot spots, chapter 5, "The Theapoetic Ethics of Speculative Fiction," examines texts that often depict other-worldly locales or realities. I begin the chapter by describing how speculative fiction has become an important genre in my life because of its emphasis on queer hope. I use Sami Schalk's broad definition of the genre and Samatar's description of its queerness to show that it is an ideal space for a secular theological endeavor such as theapoetics.

Readings of some mostly recent pieces of Mennonite speculative fiction follow. Janet Kauffman's novel *The Body in Four Parts* is one of the first works of queer Mennonite literature and Mennonite speculative fiction. Its amorphous, hybrid, superhero-esque characters create space for queer narratives within the faith community. Greg Bechtel's three "Smut Stories" likewise focus on making space for multiple experiences within community by portraying an ethic of inclusive listening. Two more stories from Samatar's *Tender*, "Honey Bear" and "Fallow," also focus on communal ethics. "Honey Bear" offers strategies for how we can relate to the Earth in our time of climate catastrophe, and "Fallow" returns to the Mennonite question of how to be "in the world but not of it" by arguing that it is impossible to live ethically unless we are actually of the world to a certain extent, interacting with those outside of our small communities. Casey Plett's story "Portland, Oregon" also examines our relationship to nature via its narrator, a talking cat. Like Bechtel's work, it advocates an ethic of empathetic listening as a form of queer hope that can help us survive these times. Much like *I Hear the Reaper's Song* and *Summer of My Amazing Luck*, Toews's novel *Women Talking* uses a narrative based in real-life events to critique Mennonite hypocrisy, most notably the violence of Mennonitism's continuing misogyny.[117] As theapoetics does, the book argues for the importance of writing as tool for combating such violence.

Chapter 6, "Samuel R. Delany's Surrealist Anabaptist Ethics," begins by describing how Delany's writing became an important touchstone of secular ethics for me after I encountered it in graduate school. I then highlight the common Mennonite fascination with Delany's work and use Gundy's "Manifesto of Anabaptist Surrealism" to show how the ethical principles in Delany's writing are akin to those in Mennonitism. A reading of Delany's novel *The Mad Man* illustrates how his work has helped me to learn to enjoy my body and has thus opened a pathway for me to put my Mennonitism and my queerness into conversation. This reading serves as an example of how readers can transfer *Ethics for Apocalyptic Times*'s theapoetic principles to non-Mennonite contexts.

The epilogue, "Theapoetics and Other Traditions," continues chapter 6's exploration of texts outside of Mennonitism by showing how two practices that combine literature and the spiritual, haiku and tarot, are theapoetic as an example of how we can apply theapoetic ideas to any literary tradition. Haiku's emphasis on everyday experience, tarot's emphasis on ecumenism, and their shared emphasis on ethics epitomize how we can lead lives that draw us to the Divine. These two practices have helped me survive the pandemic emotionally. My hope is that analysis of the various texts *Ethics for Apocalyptic Times* considers will show you, dear reader, how reading literature theapoetically can help you navigate our apocalyptic times too.

CHAPTER 1

Sofia Samatar's "Request for an Extension on the *Clarity*," Queer Objects, and Theapoetics

There are autobiographical elements everywhere in Sofia Samatar's 2017 short story collection *Tender*. They include the narrator's part "African," part "German" ancestry in "Walkdog," which Samatar calls "basically an ode to my hometown, South Orange, N[ew] J[ersey]";[1] a character in "An Account of the Land of Witches" who is a graduate student at the University of Wisconsin–Madison as Samatar was (158); and the Mennonites in "Fallow," Samatar's only piece of explicitly Mennonite fiction. As I discuss in chapter 5, "Fallow" asks what Mennonitism would look like if Mennonites could actually leave the world and establish our own colony in space away from worldly influences. In a 2018 "Ask Me Anything" (AMA) session on the social media website Reddit, Samatar speaks about how her personal life intersects with her fiction, making statements that show that seeking the autobiographical elements of her stories is an appropriate critical task. She explains that the "inspir[ation]" for her fiction is "pretty equally split between reading and life experience."[2] It is ripe for theapoetical analysis because of how it archives this experience.[3]

"Request for an Extension on the *Clarity*," another of Samatar's autobiographically inspired stories, is the story from *Tender* that I find hardest to shake because of how it relates to my own experiences as a Mennonite of color. "Request" takes the form of a letter from the narrator, the one-person crew of the space station *Clarity*, to the head of the space program, requesting an unusual twenty-year extension of her already thirteen-year-old posting.

The story is science fiction because of these space elements, but it focuses less on the speculative or fantastic than most of the other stories in *Tender*. It is one of the most accessible stories in the collection because of its plethora of sensory details. I can hear the narrator's cats meowing, I can taste the key lime pie that the narrator's mother throws away when she finds out the narrator wants to stay in space, and I can feel the tattered pages of the narrator's books as she describes their "gray and musty" texture (180, 185, 181). The story is also accessible for readers unfamiliar with the genre because it reveals its speculative elements immediately and then mostly sets them to the side, focusing on the narrator's very real-world problem of needing to find refuge in an oppressive society instead. This problem dates back to the narrator's college days at a school that is a thinly veiled Goshen College, Samatar's alma mater.[4] The story sticks with me because Goshen is also my alma mater. "Request" feels as though it writes my experiences in some ways too.

The story's status as a Mennonite thought experiment akin to that in "Fallow" intrigues me. What would it be like if Mennonites could leave the world behind instead of needing to be "in the world but not of it?" Would such a journey result in the peaceful quietude Mennonites have sought throughout our history in our numerous migrations for the sake of religious freedom, most notably from Germany and Switzerland to the eastern United States throughout the 1700s, from what is now Poland to what is now Ukraine in the late 1700s, and then from Ukraine to Kansas and Manitoba in the 1870s and from Ukraine to various parts of Canada in the 1920s? "Request" gives the answer "Well, maybe, but probably not." This negative answer results from the story's depiction of how Mennonites are actually part of the problem with the world because the Mennonite community adopts negative worldly practices such as racism and sexism rather than embracing fulfilling worldly values such as love of artistic beauty.[5] The story thus urges readers to think of ways to fight such systemic violence in our communities.

The narrator's discussions of her college reading stand out to me. They are part of how the story offers strategies for living in the world in apocalyptic times even though in the narrator's case they are what convince her to reject the world. She describes taking every course the college offers about Africa so she can understand her African ancestry better. She realizes that these courses are not enough, that something is missing. She tries to remedy this lacuna through her reading, seeking out texts in marginalized spaces such as "junk shops," "old people's basements," and unsecured websites even though the texts are too eccentric, too queer to cite in her schoolwork (180–81). These books are necessary for the narrator despite their lack of academic legitimacy because she recognizes that the official history she gets from her white anthropology professor is incomplete. However, the unofficial history in the books gives her a conceptual home. Their "pages make a private space" where she feels safe (181). Mainstream discourse and mainstream Mennonite discourse at Goshen do not offer her space to exist freely. The community fails her. Considering this oppression, it makes sense that she wants to be in space, where she can live with books and cats, rather than on Earth. The extreme nature of this desire illustrates heartrendingly just how much the oppression weighs on the narrator. If her superiors grant her preferred twenty-year extension, it will bring her into her sixties and thus will quite possibly encompass the deaths of her parents and other loved ones. Her attempt to gain the extension is an attempt to renounce the bit of human community she has left. The narrator's rejection of her people is in some ways essentially Mennonite, as she literally rejects the world in defense of her beliefs. She successfully finds a hybrid, queer, nonhuman community with her books, her cats, and the *Clarity* itself. The station is a physical refuge that resembles the emotional refuge she finds in her books.

The books continue to sustain the narrator after college because she saves them and brings them into space (187). The decision to keep them with her might seem queer in the older sense of the word in that she has already read them and gleaned their knowledge, knowledge that is probably not helpful in space anyway because she only has cats for company and thus does not have to spar with racist anthropologists. It would make more sense for her to bring well-written books that would stand up to rereading better.[6] But it is a theapoetic act for her to bring her marginal texts along because they give her spiritual sustenance. They are her sacred texts despite their literary marginality.

Part of their sacredness stems from the Afrofuturist nature of the narrator's curating of them. She mentions Sun Ra as an inspiration in contrast to her anthropology professor (183). Ytasha L. Womack documents how Ra, one of the foundational figures of Afrofuturism, advocates for the reading "of underground alternative history books and African history books" as part of educating oneself.[7] The narrator recognizes that this education is not finished despite her life away from the world and that undertaking it offers her spiritual sustenance.

QUEER KILLJOY SURVIVAL KITS

The narrator's decision to travel with her library reminds me of Sara Ahmed's contention that physical objects, whether books or other mementos, are an essential part of living a revolutionary life because they provide emotional as well as intellectual support. Objects can act as conceptual shields against oppression. Although Ahmed's idea is not new in that many religious traditions view objects such as clerical vestments, physical copies of holy texts, and ceremonial objects as sacred,[8] it is important that Ahmed names how certain objects still carry emotional weight in a secular context. In doing so, she creates a secular queer spiritual archiving practice for theapoetics to draw on. Ahmed describes this practice toward the end of her 2017 book *Living a Feminist Life*, where she lists the items necessary for "a killjoy survival kit."[9] A "killjoy is one who does not make the happiness of others her cause" as the killjoy works against oppressions such as sexism and racism, in part by refusing to let others assume that such systemic violences no longer exist because of certain civil rights gained by oppressed groups.[10] Ahmed writes primarily about feminist killjoys and makes it clear that this feminism is explicitly queer and intersectional in mirroring Ahmed's status as a lesbian of color, so it fits with the story's Afrofuturism.[11] Books are the first item listed for the kit. Therefore, like "Request's" narrator, Ahmed writes of her books, "Wherever I go, they go."[12] Ahmed asserts elsewhere that "objects can be used to tell stories about all manner of subjects."[13] So the narrator's library contains three levels of storytelling: the stories within the books, the stories of the books as physical objects, and the story of the narrator's life and the books' part in it.

Ahmed's idea of queer objects that can hold healing, invigorating emotional power for us is a central part of my ad hoc belief system because it puts into words something that I feel in my book collecting but have been unable to articulate myself. It is a very un-Mennonite idea in the sense that Mennonite theology emphasizes simple living, so to accumulate nonutilitarian objects is to engage in idolatry. Of course, Mennonites would traditionally acknowledge that some books—the Bible, the *Martyrs Mirror*, hymnals—have utility, but owning three thousand of them (a number that seems paltry as I type it; I need more!) might be excessive. If we take Walt Whitman's theapoetic, queer-in-the-sense-of-odd and queer-in-the-sense-of-radical idea that the Divine is everywhere seriously, though,[14] then the Divine, however one chooses to define that term, is also in objects because they can act as conduits through which we get to the Divine. They become something more than themselves because, as atheist theologian Vanessa Zoltan argues, "lov[ing]" an object makes it "sacred." This act of loving is an ethical action because it is a relational one. These relationships with our objects can teach us how to relate to others, whether humans or elements of the natural world.[15]

Ahmed's idea helps me to understand my sudden consumerism over the two years just before the pandemic, which included books and clothing, a kind of object I almost never buy. I realize that my spending was a way to comfort myself in these terrible political times: retail therapy. Ahmed's idea shows me why my purchases are comforting. I use them as a form of queer armor to keep myself safe. I know and have accepted that living in the current US political situation is shortening my life, whether from the stress I feel because of it or because of all the comfort eating of unhealthy foods I do as a way of coping. But I can use my killjoy survival kit to help me get through the life I have left.

In a book published the same year as Ahmed's, Mari Ruti also writes about being emotionally devoted to certain objects even when such devotion is not logical, and she argues that this practice is a queer, anti-capitalist one because it rejects the mainstream "logic" that objects are always "easily replaceable."[16] The emphasis on objects as queer antioppression weapons is gaining currency. Similarly, when writing about the suit of Pentacles, the tarot suit associated with materialism, Cassandra Snow contends that for queer people "living our lives joyfully [is powerful.] Living a full life in a world that hates you *is* resistance."[17] Snow's argument is another way of seeing how curating queer objects that we draw strength from is a way to queer capitalism and fight oppression. Although it is an important queer act to resist the conformity of consumerism, Ahmed, Ruti, and Snow show that such resistance does not necessarily require walking around in the twenty-first-century equivalent of sackcloth and ashes.

Like "Request's" narrator, my library is a part of my survival kit because of how my bibliophilia is an integral part of my personhood. My passion for book buying is queer because "collecting is a code for" queerness, according to Wayne Koestenbaum.[18] The objects in our personal queer archives help make our queerness visible and tangible in a society that wants to deny it. I have always enjoyed shopping for books. Bookcases were always prominent in my childhood home, and their presence taught me that it was normal to own one's books rather than only getting them from the library. When I was a child, I would save my allowance to buy books from the Scholastic book flyers that my teachers would pass out several times a year. My family would often stop at the large Mennonite-owned Provident Bookstore on Lititz Pike during our frequent trips to Lancaster, Pennsylvania, and it was always excruciating for me to choose which books to buy and which ones to leave behind because I wanted so many of them. In high school, after we moved to Lancaster and Provident had gone out of business, I would scour the Borders by Park City Mall for chess books and my literary obsessions of the time, Chaim Potok, C. S. Lewis, and Fyodor Dostoevsky. In college my leisure-time book buying diminished because most of my funds went to purchasing textbooks, but the two years I lived in Manhattan afterward were a book-buying orgy because I lived a ten-minute walk from the Strand at Twelfth and Broadway and was reading as much as I could in preparation for graduate school. In graduate school, aside from my assigned reading, my high school reading habits reasserted themselves. Whenever I found an author I liked, I would buy their entire oeuvre and devour it. These authors included Don DeLillo, Philip Roth, Theodora Keogh, and Samuel R. Delany. I currently read as much queer literature and Mennonite literature as I can find and have time for. I became an English professor because I love reading. These days, it is difficult to tell the difference between when I am "reading for fun" and when I am "reading for work." My reading leads to my writing, and my writing inspires new directions in my reading. Indeed, biography scholars Sidonie Smith and Julia Watson argue that beloved objects such as those in my killjoy survival kit themselves become a kind of life writing because of the emotions that adhere to the objects every time I use them.[19] Similarly, Lauren Fournier names writers' "physical engagement with" books—acts such as writing in their margins, leaving them propped open on our desks, or Samatar's example of carrying them "around reverently in [a] backpack"—as a form of autotheory.[20] So "Request's" narrator keeps her library because it is a way of hanging onto herself.

 Since college, I have bought almost all the books I have read rather than borrowing them from libraries. This practice is partly because of my profession; it is helpful to have my own copies of books to reference when I prepare lessons and write scholarship. I also document my history by buying books. My books remind me of where I acquired them and what was going on in my life at the time. They are the center of my personal archives. Every time I move, I unpack them first. Nathan Snaza describes how smelling his copy of *Leaves of Grass*, feeling its pages, or remembering physical spaces where he first read it causes bodily affects that are inextricably intertwined with the experience's intellectual affects.[21] Therefore, to take a book off its shelf or to pull it out of a moving box to place it in its new home is always a cognitive experience that changes the book's owner, even minutely. This is why I hoard my books rather than reading a copy from a library or, horror of horrors, using an e-reader. At this time in my life, I am done with the white guy, *New Yorker*–type fiction of writers such as DeLillo and Roth, but I keep their books on my shelves because they remind me of who I was in graduate school and my journey as a thinker since then. Like "Request's" narrator's books, they are part of my community.

I also frequently think about my books' futures as objects once they leave my possession. Although I am otherwise gentle with them, I always write my name in ink on the front flyleaf to mark my part in their history. I hope that they can provide joy and sustenance to others once I am gone, that they can become a part of someone else's survival kit. Related to my obsession with their future, I am just as happy shopping at secondhand bookshops as I am at those that carry solely new stock because I enjoy imagining the books' histories and speculating about why the previous owner of each one chose to get rid of it. Did they dislike the book? Did they enter a relationship with someone who also had a copy and did not feel the need to have duplicates? Did they die? These histories are part of the affects that Snaza names as part of the reading experience.[22]

Samatar says in an interview with Amina Cain that she is interested in figures such as "the ridiculously bookish child, the passionate scholar surrounded by objects of affection." Samatar states further that "the right word [for these affinities, both for the objects and, I think, for Samatar's fascinations with the figures themselves] is obsession."[23] Likewise, C. E. Gatchalian notes that our book and music collections are "a reflection of [our] personal obsessions."[24] This is an important idea for me because it points to how my bibliophilia is a double obsession. My book collecting is an obsession that reveals a history of the other obsessions I have had throughout my life: chess, postmodern fiction, sports, Dungeons & Dragons, poetry, and so on. Writing about the books that I own and the books that I love, including the books I examine in *Ethics for Apocalyptic Times*, is also an obsessive act because of how my book's hybrid genre creates space for what Migueltzinta C. Solís calls "self-examination, self-reckoning, and self-obsession."[25] This self-attention is a necessary act of love in the racist society that Samatar, Solís, and I inhabit. Relatedly, Samatar expresses an "affinity for overambitious, unread novels" that results in "protective literary instincts that go into high gear when I hear of some writer's obsession chucked in the dustbin of history."[26] I share these protective instincts in my choice to examine older texts in *Ethics for Apocalyptic Times* such as Jeff Gundy's *Rhapsody with Dark Matter*, Sara Stambaugh's *I Hear the Reaper's Song*, and Janet Kauffman's *The Body in Four Parts* that risk being forgotten.

While reading a book that Samatar recommended to me, Catherynne M. Valente's novel *Palimpsest*, I came across a sentence claiming that "scholars of a certain obsessive disposition" are among "the folk who may pass into the kingdom of heaven."[27] This sentence struck me not only because it describes me perfectly as a scholar but also because it occurs on page 314, my birthday in the United States' shorthand date system (i.e., March 14, 3/14), and thus feels especially directed toward me by the universe. There is something more going on with my survival kit than just the objects themselves. The experiences I have with them are theapoetic because the Divine sometimes manifests itself to me through them.

Palimpsest's suggestion that obsessive scholarship is a heavenly activity is an argument for the communal value of such activity. It does not merely benefit the obsessive individual. It benefits everyone who encounters the resulting work. As Melissa E. Sanchez argues, "the figure of the scholar whose work is spurred by love rather than professional aspiration, submission to texts rather than mastery over them" is laudable.[28] This love is also a submission to the community through the scholar's willingness to put their gifts at the community's disposal, which is a Mennonite act as well as a queer one when viewed through the lens of BDSM (bondage, discipline, Domination/submission, sadism, and masochism), a practice that has relevance for thinking about relationships with the Divine because of its queering of issues of power.[29] Becca J. R. Lachman calls submission "the physical piece of what the self has made" that "is meant to give back to the world."[30] Her definition names a parallel between BDSM and writing, reminding us that both are bodily acts even though we tend to think of writing as a purely cerebral one. My writing's documentation of my obsessions is an act of autotheoretical queer archiving that itself may act as part of some readers' survival kits. As the narrator of "Request" pays witness to her library in her attempts to convince others that a new society is necessary, so, too, do I write about my objects.

Considering Ahmed's assertions about the power of queer objects and my own bibliophilia, the narrator's cultivation of her library in "Request" makes complete sense to me. She does not engage in a kind of conspicuous consumption or fetishization by keeping her books with her. Instead, the books about Africa's history give the narrator emotional support, support that she has not gotten from other humans. Ann Weinstone highlights "the oh-so-queer and excessively wasteful scene of s[cience] f[iction] *reading*,"[31] naming why no one understands the narrator's desire to remain in space or her devotion to her books, and naming why the acts of collecting and reading her books are so powerful. In capitalism's logic, any kind of reading for pleasure is wrong because it does not produce anything tangible, and reading speculative fiction, whether it is the narrator's Afrofuturist tomes or Samatar's work itself, is especially unproductive because to the uninitiated it does not even mimic the "real" world. But William Carlos Williams's assertion about poetry being necessary despite the "difficult[y of] get[ting] the news from" it is famous because it is true.[32] The emotional support reading gives exists unquantifiably in the queer decolonial space outside of capitalist logic.

The narrator's college book seeking and collecting of the texts she finds remind me of my own reading practices at Goshen. I did not realize that I was queer until after I graduated, but I got an inkling while taking a Religion and Sexuality course my senior year. The subject matter was exciting, but at the same time frustrating because it seemed like something was missing, like it was only scratching the surface.[33] I began supplementing the course reading with my own, working my way steadily through the college library's HQ section, the Library of Congress heading for subjects relating to sexuality.[34] Like the narrator in "Request," I assumed there had to be a book out there that would magically give me the answers I required even though I was not sure of the questions I needed to ask.

I began to find some clues to the answers when I stumbled upon Corey K. Creekmur and Alexander Doty's anthology *Out in Culture: Gay, Lesbian, and Queer Essays on Popular Culture*. Two essays stood out. Thomas Waugh's asserts that sex writing is an "indispensable" part of "sexual liberation," which itself is necessary for "political liberation." This was the affirmation I needed that my reading about sexuality was not wrong and that I should continue to pursue it. Nayland Blake's essay about the gay visual artist Tom of Finland includes pictures that are the first images of men that I can remember being sexually attracted to, although at the time I could not fully articulate why I found them attractive.[35] These essays stuck with me as I finished college and moved to Manhattan and led me to keep searching for texts that my Mennonite upbringing had previously taught me to find scandalous. I found some of them, books that I cannot even give citations for because underground publishers that probably no longer exist and whose texts libraries do not collect published them. They were mostly queer comic books that I bought from eroscomix.com, a site that no longer exists, and there were also some collections of written gay erotica that I bought from xandria.com, a sex toy website that also no longer exists. Unfortunately, while I now have my own copy of *Out in Culture*, unlike Samatar's narrator I did not keep all the books that helped me toward my liberation, though I desperately wish I had. I was able to conquer my Mennonite shame enough to read them but not preserve them. I stored them in a dresser drawer while I was working my way through them and threw them out when I finished, so their traces in my memory are all that remain. I do not need to reference the knowledge in them anymore because it is now a part of me, but I wish I had the emotional support of them on my bookshelves alongside all the other queer texts I have collected since then. These works showed me what Samatar's narrator realizes: just like "the meek ... shall inherit the earth" and "the last shall be first" (Matthew 5:5, 20:16), texts on the margins are the ones that have the most power.

I learned about the power of stories from growing up Mennonite. My parents read to my sister and me every night before bed, often from books about Anabaptist or Mennonite heroes published by Herald Press, so I always knew that both the telling of and listening to stories is important, that they are how to learn about the world. This theapoetic training helped me to realize that I needed to do my own research in college, and it is significant that "Request's" narrator already has this skill as well; perhaps she gains it in a similar fashion. But such training also taught me to sense when there are gaps in the narrative that the community will not fill and that must be investigated. My reading of "Request" highlights these gaps by claiming their existence and illustrating a strategy for searching for them.

The narrator reveals part of this strategy. Just as she reads on the margins, she also writes on them. Although she writes the story as a formal document for her employer, she uses this official space to tell a personal, otherwise-ignored story, giving much more information about herself than would presumably be necessary for institutional purposes.[36] In doing so, she offers a model for how to write in liberating, transformative ways by claiming narrative space wherever you may find it.

CHAPTER 2

Theapoetics in Mennonite Poetry, Then and Now

My interest in Mennonite literature as a field rather than in scattered individual texts began in Ervin Beck's 2001 Mennonite Literature course, which I took my junior year at Goshen College. Seeing Mennonite experience reflected in so many texts was a powerful experience.[1] I grew up in a house with numerous Herald Press books on the shelves, but I was excited to learn from the course that other, larger publishers also valued Mennonite stories. I enjoyed the fiction we read in the course. Rudy Wiebe's *The Blue Mountains of China* became my favorite novel for a while, and Janet Kauffman's feminist fiction inspired me so much that I gave copies of her work to friends as holiday and birthday gifts for years afterward. But my encounter with the course's poetry made the biggest impact on me because it was the first time poetry ever felt relevant to my life. Unlike the poems I read in my ratty gray British Literature textbook as a high school sophomore, Mennonite poems sounded like how people I knew talked, even when they were talking about having sex with Jesus or the sun.[2] These poems showed me how poetry could be a part of everyday life by depicting that life. As a result, I fell in love with it. I spent the summer after the course reading through the poetry anthology shelf in the college's library, and I began writing poems of my own.[3]

That fall, I began doubting my faith while taking a feminist theology course and hearing about some of my classmates' experiences with church misogyny. Since then, feminist theory has consistently been transformative in my life. It opened the door to queer theory for me and teaches me how to live nonviolently as a genderqueer person. But at the time, questioning the church and losing my faith was terrifying. On a professional level, I felt called to be a pastor. This call came intertwined with the call to attend Goshen that I received my junior year of high school. I had always wanted to attend a non-Mennonite college, partly because I envisioned going to a larger school (Goshen's enrollment at the time was around one thousand), and partly because most of the members of my extended family had gone to Mennonite schools and I resented the expectation that I would too. I grudgingly had Goshen on the list of colleges I was considering to appease my parents, but I did not seriously consider going there until I woke up one morning and simply knew that God was calling me to do so. I knew this just as I knew that the sky was blue. I had an incredible sense of peace that Goshen was where I belonged. Over the next year, I discerned that I was supposed to go to Goshen to train as a pastor instead of training as a journalist as I had planned. This call stuck with me until my senior year of college. I completed a pastoral internship after my sophomore year that I enjoyed deeply, and I loved my religion courses. I assumed I would go to seminary after I graduated, and my application to the one I wanted to attend was successful, so I did not think about other possibilities. As a result of this tunnel vision, when I had my faith crisis, I was about to graduate with no job training outside of a field where I no longer wanted to work and with the seemingly divine plan for my life in tatters. On a social level, almost everyone I knew was a Mennonite, and I wanted to stay connected with the community while also being true to my newfound convictions. The feminist theologians I read were inspiring, but not Mennonite, so their models of rebellion only felt like partial fits for me.

Mennonite literature was one of my few comforts during this time. The rebelliousness of both the writing itself and the characters it portrayed—including in the semi-autobiographical poetry of many writers—showed me that it was still possible to care about the Mennonite community when disagreeing with its theology. As I moved farther and farther from the church over the next decade, I continued to read Mennonite literature voraciously because I still saw some part of myself in it. I realize in hindsight that these reading encounters were theapoetic because the Divine was revealing itself to me through them, helping me to navigate my life even though I felt I had lost my spiritual mooring.

One can read many Mennonite poets' work as theapoetic. Willie Perdomo calls poetry "a decolonial practice" because of "its queerness, its nonbinary *they*, its sense of lineage, family, tradition."[4] These sensibilities are Mennonite traits as well. Like speculative fiction (see chapters 5 and 6), poetry is a queer kind of writing because of how it takes other genres into itself (the term "prose poem" is inherently queer because of its hybridity, for instance) and because of the space it makes for politically queer thinking through "its strong activist traditions," as I write elsewhere.[5] It is therefore a good illustration of how theapoetics incorporates queerness and decoloniality. In this chapter I examine two of the poets whose work helped me cope with my faith crisis, Jeff Gundy and Di Brandt. I focus primarily on their early work here because it is the work I was reading at the time. Although I did not know the term then, the theapoetic nature of their work helped keep me connected to the Mennonite community because it illustrates how to rebel against the community while also expressing love for it through writing. Their work made it possible for me not to reject the Mennonite community completely. After these examinations, I turn to a sample of recent Mennonite poetry collections to show how Mennonite poetry remains theapoetic.

A comparison of Gundy and Brandt is fascinating because there are many differences between them, and yet their work ends up at the same theapoetic place. Gundy is from the United States and teaches at a Mennonite college, thereby maintaining ties with institutional Mennonitism. Brandt is a Canadian who has been outside of the church for much of her adult life and who also now has a vexed relationship with the Mennonite literary community. However, their autotheoretical scholarship often calls for the faith community to pay attention to its writers,[6] and their poetry frequently offers ethical instruction for how to live in the world.

JEFF GUNDY'S THEAPOETICS

Although Gundy makes his most concentrated argument for theopoetics in 2013's *Songs from an Empty Cage*, his thinking has been theapoetic since at least the mid-1990s even though he was not yet using the term. In the Mennonite Literature course, we read Gundy's 2001 collection *Rhapsody with Dark Matter* and his 1998 essay "In Praise of the Lurkers (Who Come Out to Speak)," which was first presented at the "Mennonite/s Writing in the U.S." conference held at Goshen in October 1997. The essay was hugely important for me as I tried to figure out my relationship to Mennonitism while I underwent the process of becoming post-Christian during my final year of college. Gundy describes a model of the relationship between writers and their communities that places writers in the role of "lurker," someone who is "in their world—and often their religious community—but not quite of it." He states that writers occupy a "borderline position in their communities," so "are bound to be at least partly 'other.'"[7] In the Mennonite context, writers' lurking position has resulted from the community's theological fear that artists distort the truth. In Hildi Froese Tiessen's famous phrase, the faith community views writers as "liars and rascals."[8] Although Gundy writes in a Mennonite context, he asserts that all writers exist in tension with their traditions and that their position on the margins is valuable. Julia Spicher Kasdorf's charge in "Sunday Morning Confession" to find new ways to discuss Mennonite literature that do not emphasize conflict is important, but it is also important to acknowledge that writing is frequently a transgressive act, as Gundy does. This is especially the case in the United States' present apocalyptic state. Theapoetics' ethical outlook that expresses concern for others is a form of resistance in light of recent presidential regimes (including Joe Biden's) that have prioritized the stock market over human lives by refusing to take any substantive action to fight either the pandemic or climate change.

Gundy further observes that "lurkers find themselves outside the sanctioned channels, in the company of... Bad People," and these heretics change lurkers to the point where they cannot live without these new perspectives, which become an integral part of the writer's being, and come into conflict with earlier perspectives from the faith community.[9] Lurkers encounter these new perspectives through physical or mental journeys, such as those provided by reading. Once they return from their journeys, it is lurkers' job to share "their strange and sometimes dangerous visions" of what they have learned with the faith community before they leave on another segment of their travels.[10] Here, Gundy makes explicit another element of theapoetics. It is necessary to share what one learns from encounters with the Divine rather than guarding such knowledge selfishly.

Gundy concludes the essay with a heartbreaking description of what it feels like to be a lurker caught between the writing and faith communities: "To be a lurker is to walk the streets knowing at once that you are in the community, inseparable from it, and at the same moment in a world far away, one where strange voices whisper brilliant, frightening sentences and demands—the most frightening demand of all being that you listen even when you know that doing so will mean that you must change your life. It is to feel yourself a disgrace to both worlds, knowing that you really are at home in neither, and that you can never do justice to either one."[11] This passage is rife with theological undertones of call and martyrdom for doing what you must despite the community's censure of it. The sense of writers' inevitable isolation because we cannot ever give ourselves completely to writing because we must be part of the world is crushing. The community does violence to us simply by existing. Gundy gives voice to the despair caused by this reality in his 2018 theapoetic essay "The Fields Have Edges, but the Roads Keep Going," lamenting that "some days I don't even want to think about 'my tradition.'" However, he admits "I know that there's no escaping it, only contending with it."[12] Lurkers who are writers do this with our writing, and we are saved by it, though perhaps not in the soteriological sense. There is some hope when we choose to investigate how our writing can help others, how it can be an ethical act.

Gundy reaffirms his belief in lurkers' importance in *Songs from an Empty Cage*, observing that "the work of the tribe also happens on the edges."[13] Lurkers need the community because it gives us something to question, and the community needs lurkers for our prophetic role. Kasdorf, citing a term used by Lois Frey Gray, suggests the "'positive marginality'" of Mennonite "upbringing."[14] That is, for Mennonites of a certain age (born in 1980, I count myself in this group but wonder whether generations after mine share the experience), growing up on the margins of society taught us how to value the odd, the queer, the downtrodden, because we learned that the world's standards of value are faulty. Being a Mennonite means being a lurker in the broader world. Therefore, Mennonite writers are already trained in how to be on the margins of community.

Mennonite literature shows that there are multiple paths to the Divine just as theapoetics does. Gundy's concept of "Bad Mennonites" from another 2018 essay illuminates this reality. Such Mennonites "may fail to meet the expectations of those who think they know just what it takes to be a Good Mennonite, but their work helps to define and imagine the sort of Mennonites that I believe we need in the world."[15] These rebels are very similar to lurkers; they have become the "Bad People" themselves. However, whereas Gundy only cites writers and philosophers in the lurker essay, his later essay is more explicitly theapoetic because it reads the work of Kasdorf and Sofia Samatar in tandem with theologian Grace Jantzen's work to argue that Bad Mennonites, like lurkers, are necessary for the health of the Mennonite community.

Reading Gundy's work during my faith crisis, two lurker themes stood out to me. First, unorthodox notions about God and the faith community that gave me permission to question my beliefs and a model for doing so. Second, an openness about sexuality because my experience was that Mennonites did not like to discuss sexuality in the comfort of their own homes or local congregations, let alone in a forum so public as a collection of poetry. Although the portrayal of desire in Gundy's poetry is heterosexual, its joy in the body gave me language for exploring my own sexuality, which I soon realized is queer. The portrayals of these themes are rooted in everyday observations that show the overlap between a lurker perspective and a theapoetic one.

The title of Gundy's first full-length poetry collection, *Inquiries*, highlights lurkers' questioning outlook. One of its poems, "Inquiries into the Technology of Hell and Certain Rumors Recently Circulating," portrays God using the royal "We" to portray their laissez-faire attitude toward whether people have orthodox belief in them. They explain that "We don't expect sympathy. We don't expect / trust, faith, any of that, we know how long / we made our gestures and you yawned." The poem goes on to relate a story about a snowball freezing in Hell, which is described as having "medieval" technology, signifying the outdated nature of the Christian notion that a place of eternal torment exists alongside a loving God. This is why "We" does not worry about people's unbelief. They want humans to come to them of our own free will rather than doing so because of the threat of punishment. The poem concludes with an affirmation of this openness. God says "We do not / require or forbid you to gather at the river, / or kneel in the evening, or dust your shelves. / When you want to hear, we will tell you again."[16] This assertion by God that it is acceptable not to sing hymns such as "Shall We Gather at the River" or "kneel" to pray shows an acceptance for questioning faith, or, in Gundy's theapoetic lurker language, going on a journey. Whenever we are ready to encounter the Divine, it will be there waiting for us. This idea is reminiscent of what one of Gundy's and my favorite theapoets, Walt Whitman, says about "letters from God dropped in the street" that he leaves "where they are, for I know that others will punctually come forever and ever."[17] This idea was incredibly comforting to me when I first encountered it in Gundy's work, and it remains so.

Three poems from Gundy's second collection, *Flatlands*, express cynicism toward Christian faith. The first of these poems is "Knowing the Father." The "Father" in the title refers to God and to the speaker's biological parent. (The speaker is similar to, if not actually, Gundy himself, as is generally the case with most of his poems, which is part of why they are theapoetical and autotheoretical.) The speaker wonders how his faith is relevant to everyday life, describing the "film" of "sweat" on his "glasses" as "sticky and implacable as the religion / of my childhood," which he is unsure how to "connect to the way the eggs still had / to be gathered the next day."[18] The speaker knows that everyday activities have to have some kind of significance because they are necessary and he spends much of his time doing them, and he knows that his faith must make space for them, a theapoetic idea. The view of religion as a "sticky" conundrum from which to escape rather than a place of comfort because it fails to recognize the importance of these daily activities shows a longing for something that is found outside the faith community, a framework that will encompass the world and the Divine. Later in the poem the speaker wonders whether he is "saved" and wishes for a sign from God, but knows he "didn't deserve it." God does not respond other than to cause the speaker to reflect on the times he would play catch with his aging earthly father. The beautiful simplicity of the community created by throwing a baseball back and forth causes the speaker to remember it as another kind of church.

The prose poem "Worms" expresses a cynical attitude toward the story of the prodigal son, asserting that these kind of stories "leave us slack and defenseless, crippled and brain shocked," and that "The real story is that love is dirty."[19] Christianity is not as dry and clean-cut as the speaker's faith community makes it out to be because it has to interact with the world, it cannot dwell solely in the heavenly clouds. The speaker implies the questions What is the sense of living by the strict regulations of the faith community if there is forgiveness for the wayward soul anyway? Why not enjoy the world's pleasures occasionally to balance out the onerous chores we must engage in sometimes, such as cleaning the gutters like the speaker? As theapoetics shows us, occasionally these pleasures result in encounters with the Divine.

"Big Dog and Little Dog, or Where Is God," is less cynical than "Knowing the Father" and "Worms," but more ambiguous about the relationship between God and humans, as the title indicates. The speaker likens humans "without God" to stumps without preachers and trees without pillows. These are ambiguous, confusing metaphors because preacherless stumps and pillowless trees are by no means tragic occurrences. Indeed, coming across a tree with pillows in it would be rather surprising. As readers, we expect metaphors about being without God to be clearer, more threatening. The poem uses its unexpected comparisons to assert that humans without God in an orthodox sense are doing okay. This is because the poem portrays God as something embodied in static electricity or "In a pebble, maybe, / or a feather."[20] These images foreshadow the way Gundy ends "The Fields Have Edges, but the Roads Keep Going," which offers a reminder from the noncanonical Gospel of Thomas that "if we lift up the stone, if we break the stick" God is there.[21] Again, Gundy turns toward everyday occurrences and objects as conduits to the Divine.

Gundy's third book of poetry, *Rhapsody with Dark Matter*, which was the most important book for me as I went through my faith crisis, continues his previous books' questioning of religious orthodoxy, in part by its open portrayal of sexual desire. Writing of Gundy's early work, David Wright argues that "Gundy's poetics stand out in the [now perhaps post-] postmodern landscape precisely because of his poetic reverence for and groundedness in details."[22] Gundy's theapoetic attention to everyday experience and openness to how it can lead to encounters with the Divine encompasses experiences of sexual attraction. In "Rain," the first poem of the collection, the speaker reminisces about a "black-haired girl" he "saw long ago" whose carefree nature leads to a longing in him: "It's not beauty or nostalgia or even lust / that's got me, I don't know what it is, / justice maybe, prisons and churches." This causes him to think about how God touches humanity from "very far away."[23] The poem contrasts the concrete nearness of the girl with the "far away" nature of God and asks for a personal incarnation of God rather than the church's official, impersonal God, which is associated with "prisons." Similarly, the prose poem "Smile" tells of a woman the speaker meets in an airport who "absently stroked her perfect brown thigh" and gives him a smile that is "part defense and part weapon" in return for his voyeurism. As I reread these poems where the male gaze is prominent, I worry that they cross the line between observation and objectification. The speaker of "Smile" acknowledges this possibility when he describes journaling about the woman, saying, "I hoped she was not reading this," and he ends the poem with his return home to his wife.[24] However, when I first read the poems, they seemed revolutionary to me because of the bodily hatred my Mennonite upbringing taught me. It was shocking to see a fellow Mennonite naming sexual desire openly. In light of his problematic gazing and his wish to play God via his writing because of his desire "to write a ten-line poem as dense as a neutron star, / too heavy to move, so tightly packed it will glow with its own light," "Smile's" speaker asks "How can I hope to be forgiven?"[25] His desires alienate him from the faith community's norms of behavior, and he must struggle with this marginalization. Being a lurker is not easy.

"Many Strong Rivers: Words on the Way Home" is another prose poem about travel that examines issues that lurkers' journeys outside the faith community raise, and what it is like to return home. The poem describes a cross-country car trip where the speaker is "thinking about paths to the sacred" and considers the possibility of romantic love as one of these paths. The speaker calls himself "boringly monogamous" and wonders, "Is it possible to recognize that your desire will never be satisfied, and come to terms with that, without becoming merely bitter or merely resigned?"[26] This is the ultimate lurker question because the lurker's in-between nature does not allow them to ever be truly satisfied or at peace; the conflict between their different worlds is always present. However, the speaker is finally able to admit that the only thing "worth doing" is "trying to learn the gods. Trying to learn what it means to worship." He recognizes the importance of faith, but at the same time he urges readers to get there via theapoetic means rather than orthodox ones by naming "a hope: that living an everyday, frazzled, even frantic life like mine can also be a kind of spiritual discipline."[27]

Three other poems in *Rhapsody* echo this choice to advocate for unorthodox ways to the Divine by expressing ambiguous views of the faith community. In "The Little Clerk," the speaker tells another poet (presumably Li-Young Lee, the poem's dedicatee) that he has "stopped trying / to escape" church.[28] That the church community is something the speaker thinks of escaping from rather than as something he wants to embrace shows the pull of the writing world on him. Two poems that deal with the traditionally oppressive nature of the Mennonite community illustrate this desire. "Ancient Themes #1: The Martyrs and the Child" references the legacy of the *Martyrs Mirror*. The poem is dedicated to Brandt and uses the all-lowercase style of her early poetry. The speaker takes an ambiguous attitude toward martyrdom, calling Dirk Willems, the most popular Anabaptist martyr, "half full of pious shit." The speaker does not answer Jesus's call at the end of the poem to "follow me / follow me well are you coming or not," leaving the reader to come to their own conclusion as to whether the norms of the faith community are right for them.[29]

"Crow" is the second poem about the oppressive nature of the church. It tells of Mennonite women who "have been talking of their silences, their losses, their long walks / and bruises" at the 1995 Mennonite women's conference at Millersville University in Lancaster County, Pennsylvania. The speaker uses a group of crows that he sees while jogging as a metaphor for the patriarchal Mennonite leaders who peck the ground futilely, hoping to salvage the past, and with it their relevance and power. The crows "don't care if / the women gather to discuss the symbology of red, how they survived, who did / the work." They are blind to everything except their rigid view of what the community should be. As an alternative to this hurtful vision, the poem calls for fluid community boundaries that allow for self-expression: "Can you live in two worlds if you're / not ashamed of either? Let's be honest instead of good."[30] The speaker tries to solve the two-world nature of his lurking by imagining a faith community whose values are closer to those of his artistic community than the values of the Mennonite community still are.

"The Cookie Poem" also describes this hoped-for faith community. The poem names different kinds of cookies throughout history and then calls for an acceptance of cookies by the church that is parallel to God's acceptance of all cookies, or humans: "All cookies / God's cookies, strange sweet hapless cookies / marked each one by the Imago Dei, / . . . oh God loves us all."[31] The poem names the church's unethical, exclusionary membership policies, which continued to discriminate against queer folx for two decades after the poem's publication.

The questioning in Gundy's early work that I found so comforting continues throughout his poetry and is perhaps most pronounced in his 2019 collection *Without a Plea*. The book's title references a hymn that Mennonites of Gundy's generation sang often at revival meetings, "Just as I Am," which begins "Just as I am, without one plea."[32] The hymn describes one's hopelessness without God, but Gundy's collection uses the title as an indication of the book's heretical poetry, which is so far gone that it is beyond saving by the church. I was shocked when I first read it because of how its disillusionment with the faith community is so raw and prevalent. This is not to say that such disillusionment is a bad thing—the book is poetry, not theology, and I share its view anyway—but its confrontational nature is more direct than the rest of Gundy's poetic oeuvre. For instance, "Theodicy with Tents and Masonry" begins, "When my unemployed faith reappeared as boredom, / it seemed like a diplomatic triumph." The speaker's faith first disappears and then reappears as something that checks a box off, that is "diplomatic[ally]" necessary but does not give any sustenance or joy to him. The rest of the poem does not rehabilitate this state. Even nature, which the speaker appreciates early in the poem, ultimately fails to move him, becoming "a diplomatic triumph" as well.[33] The speaker is tired of religious orthodoxy and also has a difficult time finding the Divine elsewhere.

However, other poems reaffirm the theapoetic importance of small experiences. "Speaking Truth in the Most Human Way" celebrates "little possibilities for love, like those little // Reese's cups."[34] Just as the sensual expresses itself erotically in *Rhapsody with Dark Matter*, it expresses itself through food here. Even in the most human of activities, eating, the Divine is present. (Maybe church would be more appealing if they served chocolate for communion!) Similarly, the speaker of "Cold Day in the Provinces" is able to find the divinity of nature that the speaker in "Theodicy with Tents and Masonry" is not, calling "The sycamore, snow in its high branches, a revelation in white and gray and three more grays."[35] The poem makes one of the most depressing colors, gray, something that reveals the beauty of the natural world and thus the Divine. Therefore, although the collection expresses cynicism about the church, it is also an example of Gundy's use of his writing gifts in service to others.

Gundy's lurker metaphor remains helpful for me because of how it continues to symbolize my relationship with the Mennonite community. Indeed, for a while I felt like a lurker on the margins of the Mennonite literary community, let alone the theological one. Around the time I finished my PhD, I saw a call for papers for the 2012 Mennonite/s Writing conference at Eastern Mennonite University. I attended the 2002 conference at Goshen and had a wonderful time, and I considered going to the 2006 conference in Bluffton, Ohio, but did not because I was a desperately poor graduate student without travel funds. The 2012 conference looked like a good way to enhance my CV and get a free trip back east to see my family because the school in Salt Lake City where I was a post-doctoral fellow would pay for it. I was nervous about going because I had not been around a large group of Mennonites in almost a decade. The conference was a mixed experience. Several attendees complimented my paper, and I was surprised to find that many people whom I had not seen since the 2002 conference, including Gundy, were happy to see me even though I had wondered whether anyone would remember me. But I could not shake a feeling of displacement the entire time. I was depressed even though I enjoyed the panels and readings. I felt like an interloper, like I was only masquerading as a Mennonite because I had been trying to run away from my Mennonitism and therefore did not have a right to take part in Mennonite discourse. I also suffered from a heavy dose of impostor syndrome because it was difficult to believe that I deserved a place alongside other presenters who seemed larger-than-life to me despite my new PhD. I felt bereft when the conference ended and assumed that it would be my last professional involvement with Mennonite literature.

Unexpectedly, though, a few months later I received an email from Kasdorf inviting me to the After Identity: Mennonite/s Writing in North America symposium that she was organizing the following summer at Penn State. I decided to accept the invitation, and she suggested that I write something queer-related because the goal of the event was to examine how Mennonite literature could converse with other areas of study. I initially assumed that I would do a queer reading of a few of the racier straight sex scenes in Mennonite novels. However, as word got around among the other eleven symposium participants that I was working with queer themes, several people told me about some novels with queer characters. I was surprised to hear about these books. I had previously pondered the lack of queer Mennonite literature and was happy to discover that this absence was not as glaring as I first thought, but I was also frustrated that I had not heard about these texts before even though Lynnette Dueck published the first queer Mennonite novel, *sing me no more*, back in 1992![36] I tried to keep abreast of publications in the field, but Mennonite journals did not generally review these books, and literary critics likewise ignored them.[37] To counter this censorship, my essay morphed into an examination of three of these texts as examples of what queer Mennonite literature has to offer to the broader field. Happily, reviews of queer Mennonite literature now appear in Mennonite journals regularly. The stream of recent queer Mennonite literature from the past decade is too strong to ignore.

As I worked on my essay, and after it got a good response at the symposium, I started to realize that I could serve the Mennonite community from its theological margins by being a much-needed visible queer Latinx voice within Mennonite studies. My scholarship could be a sideways answer to the call to ministry I felt in college by highlighting queer and anti-racist messages in Mennonite literature for Mennonites and other readers. Since then, much of my scholarship has been about queer Mennonite literature.

The After Identity symposium was the doorway to the Mennonite literary community that made me feel like I belong there and within the Mennonite community in general despite my continued rejection of Mennonite doctrine. The 2015 and 2017 Mennonite/s Writing conferences welcomed my queer work and that of other queer Mennonite writers, and the *Journal of Mennonite Writing* invited me to edit a special issue on "Queer Mennonite Writing" in 2018.[38] Mennonite literature is now a space where queer literature flourishes. The former field's strong feminist history, which dates from the 1980s, cleared a path for the latter. This feminism is a major reason why the field was a refuge for me during and after my faith crisis. It always pushes the faith community's boundaries, calling it to be more just.

DI BRANDT'S FEMINIST, DECOLONIAL THEAPOETICS

Di Brandt's work was important for me during my faith crisis because of its explicitly Mennonite feminist critique of the faith community.[39] The feminist theologians I read in my religion courses at Goshen were not Mennonite, but Brandt's poetry showed and continues to show me what a prophetic Mennonite voice can look like. Magdalene Redekop contends that the Mennonite literary "renaissance" of the 1980s reclaimed the goodness of the body for Mennonite thought through semi-autobiographical and autobiographical work by writers such as Brandt and Sandra Birdsell.[40] Therefore, feminist Mennonite literature has been theapoetic for close to forty years, so it is no surprise that *Ethics for Apocalyptic Times*'s theapoetic Mennonite canon consists primarily of women's writing. Brandt asserts that in her work she is "writing for [her] life" against the silencing might of patriarchy.[41] In her writing, and especially in her poetry, Brandt carries on her struggle to speak out against oppression in an ethical mode that encompasses personal experiences and global issues. This wide scope includes poems about her childhood in Reinland, Manitoba, as well as poems about violence in Palestine and Israel and about the destruction of the North American environment. According to Ann Hostetler, this mode is an "ethic of care" that includes "a compassionate witness of oppression, an ecological awareness of the human impact on the planet, and a commitment to share resources and live responsibly with others in the world."[42] Although at least one Mennonite writer (a man, of course) questions the anger in Brandt's work,[43] Hostetler's concept shows that this anger is productive, that it comes from a place of love for the community. Brandt's direct approach is a necessary complement to Gundy's subtler one, and both fulfill John Ruth's call in *Mennonite Identity and Literary Art* for writers to take their relationship with the faith community seriously.

Although this approach is present in her early work that I discuss below, Brandt's 2018 essay "Paradigms of Re:placement, Re:location, and Re:vision: The Creative Challenge of the New Mennonite Writing of Manitoba (and the World)" is a helpful framework through which to view it because the essay contextualizes Brandt's efforts to converse with the community within the broader efforts of Mennonite literature as a whole. The essay begins with a brief history of Mennonite literature's development in the 1980s. Just as Kasdorf questions the narratives that Mennonite literature tells about itself in "Sunday Morning Confession," Brandt warns of the "danger of constructing a false genealogy of our literary and cultural life," and she highlights the Mennonite myth of us as persecuted wanderers as an example of this danger because of how it erases Mennonites' role in colonial violence on both sides of the Canada/US border.[44] This is a theapoetic argument because of its call for decolonial examinations of writing. Brandt documents how when Mennonite writers such as herself have tried to name the violence perpetuated by Mennonites the community has attacked these writers rather than accepting their accurate critiques.[45] Such tactics are abusive, which is why Brandt's and Gundy's recent theapoetic work remains necessary. As Brandt says, Mennonite writers are "optimally situated to address these issues" because of our marginal position partly inside and partly outside the community as Gundy's lurkers, and we have a responsibility to engage in this "activism."[46] Brandt argues that theological Mennonitism needs to incorporate Mennonite literature to regain its health, echoing Al Reimer's call in the last chapter of *Mennonite Literary Voices* for the community to listen to its writers.[47] However, there is more of a sense of frustration in Brandt's essay than in Gundy's prose. The faith community has been more violent toward Brandt as a woman than to Gundy as a man, so there is more of a sense of her being ready to leave the community completely if it does not reform itself quickly than there is in Gundy's language of lurking with one foot out and one foot in. She documents this violence through a feminist lens in her poetry and her earlier prose.

One of the most prominent examples of Brandt's decolonial theapoetics is her essay "This land that I love, this wide wide prairie," which begins by recognizing the prairie on which she was raised as "stolen land, . . . Métis land, Indian land, Cree land," and recognizes that this "colonization" pollutes the "earthly paradise" her Mennonite community believes it has found.[48] Brandt realizes that she is complicit in this oppression of Indigenous Peoples. Along with whites' displacement of its original inhabitants, the numerous pesticides Mennonites and others use to farm the land also colonize and destroy it. Brandt writes that whites have decimated the prairie's wildlife population and that many people in her childhood community, including her father, have died early deaths from cancer caused by the chemicals they used to subdue the land.[49] Men have poisoned the land. Brandt recognizes that women's share of the stolen land has been denied them. It is "man's land," where women are "kept as servants and slaves" and face "endless disapproval" for their "bodies and dreams."[50] It is because of these oppressive acts that Brandt ends her essay by lamenting that she "cannot write *the land*" because she is "torn inside over it;"[51] she loves the land but must apologize to it rather than being able to embrace it. The issues Brandt raises in "This land that I love, this wide wide prairie" echo throughout her poetry.

These issues stem from Brandt's upbringing in Reinland, a conservative Mennonite village whose sectarian environment was akin to "gr[owing] up in the sixteenth century."[52] Brandt's work replies to her Mennonite community by choosing the middle ground between the two poles of giving into victimhood and abandoning her Mennonite identity completely. She attempts to rewrite Mennonitism to include places for women's voices and bodies.

Brandt depicts Reinland as a place ruled by men who use patriarchal interpretations of the Bible, which are often completely nonsensical, let alone inaccurate, to justify their colonization of women's bodies, minds, and voices. For instance, the prose poem "Diana" describes how "it was extremely hard to see for example how the point of a story like the multicoloured Joseph in Egypt being seduced by Potiphar's wife could possibly be that we shouldn't tell lies to our parents."[53] Brandt's Reinland is a place where no questioning of authority is allowed, even when contradictions exist within this authority. This is the case in the title poem of *questions i asked my mother*, which is written with Brandt's trademark first-person "i" like almost all the poems in the collection. Brandt notes on the verso of the book's dedication page that "some of this is autobiographical / & some of it is not." While it is not fair to assume that the speakers in Brandt's poems are always her, it is clear that her poetry is rooted in personal experience like Gundy's. Whether the experiences in their poems actually happened or not, the emphasis both writers place on personal experience is a theapoetic one. "questions i asked my mother's" speaker notices that after her grandfather's death "everybody said...he's in heaven now," but that "the minister" says her grandfather will be raised from the ground at "the final judgement." The speaker asks her mother about this contradiction, and her mother defers to her father, who accuses the speaker of "trying to figure everything out your own way instead of / submitting quietly to the teachings of the church."[54] Aside from denying the legitimacy of the speaker's individualized thought processes, this reply denies women a place in theological discourse, which is reserved for men and a masculine God.

The type of rigidity the father's belief in the church's infallibility espouses is also present in the behavioral expectations set by the church. These expectations haunt *questions i asked my mother* continually, as is evident at the end of an untitled poem: "i never meant to leave them / always tried to be good."[55] The poem's speaker is unable to fully escape the mores of her Mennonite upbringing. Despite her best intentions "to be good" and not to cause her community pain in her departure from it, she must leave to find a healthier place for herself.

Brandt's second collection, *Agnes in the sky*, continues to describe Reinland's religious oppressiveness. "scapegoat" details the sacrifices women are forced to make in the community. Reinland is not appeased by Jesus's crucifixion. Instead, "it had to be / repeated in every generation every / family someone had to die," and "the best deaths were the innocents / the babies the daughters with the / golden hair & most of all mothers."[56] The supposed beauty of women's deaths because of their spiritual purity is a false construct because it is built upon forced martyrdom. The community coerces women into a mold of "cheerful" sacrifice, which shows that the sacrifices are not made freely and are thus a form of oppression, because it is impossible for a sacrifice, even a supposedly necessary one, to be cheerful: note the anguish Jesus expresses in Matthew 27:46.

In her early work, Brandt also documents the struggle to obtain full use of language and her individual voice despite Reinland's censoring of women. This struggle for control over language can be seen in the almost exclusive use of lowercase letters and lack of punctuation in her first four collections. Brandt writes that the lack of punctuation in her poetry allows the writing "to speak the forbidden" because it is no longer constrained by "hierarchical constructions."[57] The release from these constructions gives her poems an oral quality that causes them to resemble the stories told by the women in her family,[58] and thus places her work firmly into a women's textual tradition.

Brandt's struggles with language are neatly outlined in "foreword," the first poem in *questions i asked my mother*. She writes that "learning to speak *in public* ... meant betraying once & / for all the good Mennonite daughter i tried so / unsuccessfully to become."[59] The conceptual place of the "public" here, which is akin to the "world" that Mennonites traditionally try to remain separate from, is a liberating space because it allows the speaker to use her voice, whereas Reinland does not.

Despite the language-reclaiming moves in *questions i asked my mother*, an untitled poem from *mother, not mother* asserts that the "fear of being silenced / isn't obsolete" because not only are the oppressive forces from Reinland still in existence throughout the broader Mennonite community,[60] but it is "hard ... to tell a story / so it can be heard" because of "how easily the reader climbs / on top of it, // pronouncing judgment."[61] The poem asserts that it is not enough for Brandt and other women to use their voices; the community must give these voices space to be considered carefully rather than being dismissed out of hand. Brandt recognizes the necessity for women to claim the small amount of space given to them by the patriarchy to exercise their voices in a way that creates more space for them by acknowledging the validity and power of those voices. As the aforementioned untitled poem says, "i stole the language / of their kings and queens, // but i didn't bow down to it."[62] Brandt subverts the oppressive use of language by "kings and queens," that is, those in power in Reinland and elsewhere, to use it as a tool against this oppression.

Jerusalem, beloved is another example of Brandt's decolonial work that focuses on a specific place. The book's first section, which gives its title to the entire book, consists of twenty-four untitled poems that recall events from a trip Brandt took to Jerusalem and occupied Palestine in 1991.[63] Almost immediately, the speaker recognizes the institutional guilt she carries because of her status as a Westerner and the inherent neo-imperialism of this position. She sees "soldiers on every corner, & i implicated / in it, a Canadian, North American, tourist, rich."[64] In a later poem, the speaker expresses further discomfort about her status as "another North American tourist." She feels "shame, shame at my innocence, / my stupid privilege, i never imagined such a place."[65] She feels guilt not only about the Palestinians' oppression and her role in that oppression but also about her previous ignorance of it. Here we see that Brandt's activism is valuable because it is not self-righteous. Her position of power as "a Canadian" is what allows her initial ignorance, but she attempts to fight against this potentially comfortable position by paying witness to the Palestinians' suffering via the poem.

Brandt also references the West's attitude of economic imperialism in a poem from *Walking to Mojácar*, "Guerra y Paz." While "Bombs are falling / on Syria and Lebanon," the North American "stock market / is holding its breath."[66] The poem's acknowledgment that what happens in one place affects another is significant because it emphasizes that we should have a global outlook. However, the poem's overall tone is a negative one because instead of worrying about the loss of life caused by the bombing, the West only cares about its own capitalist interests. There is no sense of awareness that the West's overconsumption of petroleum has any connection to the political volatility described in the poem. Instead, there is a singular focus on economic gain at any cost as those in power take advantage of their ability to ignore the oppression happening right under their noses. The economic imperialism in the poem dehumanizes both the colonized and the colonizers, as those in North America are no longer caring individuals but have been subsumed by the monolithic "stock market."

Brandt's anti-tourist stance in *Jerusalem, beloved* stems from a feeling that the Palestinians' oppression is trivialized by Westerners who view Israel and Palestine merely as a fetishized archaeological site rather than as a site where a slow but steady genocide continues to occur. By participating in the Israeli tourist industry, tourists are supporting the economy of the oppressors. Brandt expresses rage at this type of oblivious tourist in a poem about "a busload of silly Christians" who see "only / what the tour guide tells them to see" and would make Jesus weep "to / see them, how they walk blindly through the streets, / like stupid people, seeing, hearing nothing."[67] The tourists' ignorance parallels the speaker's previous ignorance, but now that she has uncovered the true reality of Palestine, she recognizes the oppressive nature of the tourists' ignorance and the necessity of the tourists' enlightenment. However, "that isn't what [they] want," they prefer the violence of "the crucifixion" and their "bloodthirsty Old Testament God."[68] Their North American privilege allows them to be content with the global status quo and to revel in "the pretence of sanctuary behind guns, & machines, / the romance of white American military might."[69] Brandt's condemnation of these unethical attitudes reminds readers how we should act instead.

At the end of another poem, Brandt goes on to recognize that the horrible oppression she sees in Palestine has a global presence. As Brandt explains elsewhere, she realized after her trip to Palestine that the Canadian prairie is "also colonized, occupied land."[70] The speaker of the poem explains that the bulldozing of Palestinian houses "is how we build parks, / in Israel, how we build them in Canada, too, it's how / we build them in Canada, too."[71] The Canadian parks in this poem symbolize the colonizing of Indigenous Peoples' lands by whites.

Walking to Mojácar angrily laments this colonizing in two poems, "Rodeo" and "The Phoenicians." The former asserts that "barbed wire prison camp / permits" are "whimsically referred to / in our history / as peace treaties."[72] The latter describes how Mennonites "thanked / the queen and / the Canadian government" for giving them land, but how the Mennonites did not "mention / the First Nations / and their wantonly / slaughtered buffalo herds."[73] Both poems pay witness to how colonialism and environmental degradation go hand-in-hand as livestock are displaced and their habitats are destroyed alongside those of Indigenous Peoples'. "Rodeo" boldly names this displacement as a form of genocide through its use of Holocaust imagery. It also illustrates how the violence of colonization is ongoing via the use of the oppressors' language, which sanitizes the horrors of imperialism under the guise of "peace." This insidious manipulation is likewise present in "The Phoenicians," as Mennonites are grateful to the ultimate colonial figurehead, Queen Victoria, who oversaw the British Empire at its most expansive stage, for letting them move to stolen land that they did not have to steal themselves in the 1870s. The Mennonites in the poem are just as complicit in the colonial project as the British soldiers who are its enforcers. The Mennonites do not acknowledge that true peace can only exist when all members of society are free from oppression.

Brandt goes on to express global concerns in *Now You Care*, which is written from Brandt's vantage point during the time of writing in Windsor, Ontario, just north of Detroit, Michigan. The destruction of the environment caused by Western industrialism is a primary subject of the collection.[74] *Now You Care*'s environmental activism is foreshadowed by an untitled poem from *Agnes in the sky*, which celebrates "the earth firm under / your feet" that welcomes the speaker like a caring mother. The speaker can smell "the sweet tufted truffula trees,"[75] and by doing so associates herself with the call to environmental activism found in Dr. Seuss's *The Lorax*, which tells the story of the destruction of the truffula trees and the need to rehabilitate their population.

Brandt sets the stage for the environmentalism that flowers in *Now You Care* in "Going Global," an essay on the state of Canadian literature at the turn of the twenty-first century. She references Jonathan Bate's assertion that "poetry is the most ecologically important genre" because of its traditional emphasis on the beauty and power of nature. Brandt believes it is essential for poets to continue to write about nature in the face of the techno-centric texture of Western society. While defending the environment in their poetry, Brandt argues that poets must also recognize their "complicity in the ravaging of forests through the use of paper and become much more active in the search for more sustainable writing materials."[76] In the midst of her prophetic writing, Brandt never loses sight of her own culpability. She realizes that her role in creating the change she calls for extends outside of her writing.

Now You Care's first poem, "Zone: <le Détroit>," recognizes environmental disaster as a biproduct of the colonization of North America. The speaker is "Breathing yellow air / here, at the heart of the dream / of the new world."[77] Humans have destroyed the land to make way for what is supposedly industrial progress but is instead a poison for its inhabitants, colonizer and colonized alike. Brandt continues to chart the casualties of this environmental genocide throughout the poem: "all those babies born with deformities... all those women's breasts / cut off to keep our lawns green / and dandelion free."[78] The poem recognizes that patriarchy's need for domination encompasses both women and the environment. Brandt depicts the earth as the giver of life rather than as a mere storehouse from which resources can be taken without cost, a realization that is absent in the minds of those she writes against. Just as they have done in Reinland, men have turned the Windsor/Detroit borderland into a place of pain.

Hostetler observes that Brandt's poems move "beyond the boundaries of ideology and tradition to empathetic engagement with the reader."[79] This is the case in Brandt's 2018 book *Glitter and Fall: Laozi's "Dao De Jing" Transinhalations [sic]*, in which she converses with a text that is completely outside of her Mennonite background. (This move resembles what I do with Samuel R. Delany in chapter 6.) *Glitter and Fall* is explicitly theapoetic because it translates (or transinhalates, breathes in, in Brandt's term) a religious text into poetry. In the book's "Foreword," Brandt recounts how writing the book became a spiritual encounter that helped her reconnect with her Mennonite "heritage."[80] Her story is an excellent example of how the Divine can surprise us when we think theapoetically. Brandt's home community would view her dalliance with another religion as blasphemous, but her actual experience proves the wrongness of such narrow-mindedness. In light of her encounter, Brandt writes that the intersection between spirituality and the poetic is necessary despite the frequent scholarly rejection of it. This idea is akin to the theapoetic hope Brandt expressed two decades earlier in "Going Global" that writers "remember the origins of literature in ritual and the living landscape, which includes our erotic, vulnerable bodies encountering one another in an erotic, living animal, vegetable, mineral, elemental world."[81] Brandt reminds us that the spiritual ("ritual") and the literary have always been entwined together and that this fusion manifests itself in physical, worldly existence. This is why theapoetics is relevant for our time.

Glitter and Fall explores theapoetic space by focusing on the "Queenly Divine Feminine," a move akin to Molly Remer's revisioning of theopoetics as theapoetics.[82] For instance, in "Ishtar, fish star," the speaker addresses this presence, observing how "You glitter in the sand. You shimmer / in the hills. You gleam in the scales" of fish.[83] The ecopoetics in Brandt's earlier collection are present here, as is Whitman's theapoetic celebration of the Divine in all aspects of nature. "Hole in the wall" portrays how daily human experience embodies the Divine Feminine. The speaker observes a woman who "makes poems out of images and sounds . . . carries vegetables home from the market . . . sews yellow curtains and hangs them."[84] The inclusion of writing in the poem's list of everyday activities is an argument that writing is a sacred act that can reveal the Divine just as the others can. Indeed, many of the collection's poems read like prayers even though they simply describe the world. These prayers include an emphasis on nonviolence, as in "Fried pickerel," which reminds us to "Refrain from harming yourself, or others. / This is how you will find comrades / who also seek wisdom and calm."[85] Through this element, *Glitter and Fall* reminds us that spiritual experiences are only meaningful if they lead to ethical actions.

RECENT THEAPOETIC MENNONITE POETRY

Just as some of the early roots of Mennonite theapoetics lie in poetry, recent Mennonite poetry by a new generation of writers and some first-generation writers continues to examine the theapoetic elements of what Molly Remer calls the "earthy," "mundane," "practical" parts of "lived experiences" by manifesting the ethics of care found in Brandt's work.[86] Anita Hooley Yoder argues that poetry teaches this ethic because it allows readers to inhabit "someone else's psyche and worldview and rich internal life," putting us in their shoes and enabling us to sympathize with them.[87] Even if we just read poetry for its aesthetic beauty, it makes us more humane.

Becca J. R. Lachman is a notable member of the second generation of Mennonite poets.[88] Aside from her own three collections,[89] she engages in the bridge-building act of anthologizing. Lachman's 2013 *A Ritual to Read Together: Poems in Conversation with William Stafford* is an example of poetry's queer archiving of "lineage" and "tradition" that Perdomo highlights.[90] *A Ritual to Read Together* is an exemplary blending of the Mennonite and the worldly because it treats a Mennonite-adjacent subject, Stafford, who was raised in the Church of the Brethren and was a life-long pacifist, and it includes poems by six Mennonite writers alongside canonical writers such as Robert Bly, Naomi Shihab Nye, and Maxine Hong Kingston.[91] Lachman's title emphasizes a Mennonite theme, community. Its inclusion of "ritual" names how the act of reading poetry includes a devotional element, creating a theapoetic cycle that documents everyday life, which brings one to the Divine, which gives one strength to live everyday life, and so on.

Abigail Carl-Klassen is another important member of the second generation. Her 2017 chapbook *Shelter Management* brings theapoetics into the explicitly activist realm through its portrayal of lives on the Mexico-US border, speaking about injustice there on personal and systemic levels. In a manner akin to Samuel R. Delany's novel *The Mad Man* (see chapter 6), *Shelter Management*'s title poem portrays people talking at a shelter for unhoused people in "El Paso, Texas." They complain about the hypocritical Christians who serve there, "Sunday saints and Monday / a'ints" [*sic*].[92] The poem simultaneously calls for an ethic of care toward the Other and calls out the faith community for faking this ethic by condescending to those it serves, failing to see their full humanity. "State of Texas Homeless Day in Count Survey, El Paso, Texas, 2011 (the Unofficial Results)" portrays this humanity by cataloguing different unhoused experiences in a Whitmanic, documentary fashion. Like Whitman, it celebrates activities such as sex work as being no less worthy of acknowledgment than any other professional activity one might name.[93] The poem argues that humane actions remain meaningful in seemingly hopeless situations. "Mandated Reporter" depicts a woman who is "not legal here" being raped by a US soldier. The poem is decolonial in its call for a demilitarization of the border on the US side as part of an end to US economic imperialism in Latin America in general. These three examples are representative of the rest of the collection's politically queer concern for the Other and hope for a new society that recognizes those it portrays as human. Although Carl-Klassen writes the pieces as poems, they read like sermons in the way they instruct readers how to live.

Likewise, poems from Carl-Klassen's 2020 chapbook *Ain't Country Like You* exemplify theapoetics' decolonial spirit. The title poem argues against the construction of the "country"—specifically, rural spaces, but by extension the United States in general—as white. The speaker shames the 2017–21 White House occupant and his followers for refusing to acknowledge either the "architecture of exile / and genocide" that they profit from or the work of immigrants in blue-collar jobs "in Wisconsin / and Indiana... Oklahoma... Texas / and New Mexico."[94] Part of theapoetics' belief in the importance of personal experience is an insistence that we witness to the experiences of those who society tries to erase. The poem does this by documenting a reality that many in the red states it lists want to ignore. Similarly, "Martin Luther King Jr. Day, West Texas, 2016" excoriates schools that still do not celebrate King's birthday and allow their students to wear "Confederate flag bandana[s]."[95] The poem asserts that both individuals and institutions have an ethical responsibility and that it is the responsibility of writers (among others) to name when those responsibilities are not met. Whereas the poems in *Shelter Management* are like sermons, those in *Ain't Country Like You* are like fire-and-brimstone revivalist admonitions that name sin and its wages of death (Romans 6:23). Indeed, they reveal the 2017–21 White House occupant's followers as "Apostates."[96] They show us that plain, direct language is necessary during these apocalyptic times, that we must speak "not as fools, but as wise, redeeming the time, because the days are evil" (Ephesians 5:15b–16). *Ain't Country Like You* takes on poets' prophetic role unabashedly.

Some recent books by first generation poets also express an ethic of care through the ecofeminist approach found in earlier texts such as Brandt's *Now You Care*. Janet Kauffman's 2017 collection *Eco-Dementia* documents humans' self-defeating destruction of the natural environment. "A Warring Machine" laments incursions into nature that seek to destroy it rather than celebrate it. The hunter's gun of the title shoots nongame birds for sport, not food, an act that "draw[s]" "lines" between the speaker and the hunter, "and not one is / nature / poetry."[97] The speaker argues that "nature poetry," which is an attitude, not just a genre, requires a theapoetic ethical outlook that views nature as something to respect rather than to dominate. The hunter might enjoy his day in the woods, but his violence epitomizes the hypocritical disconnect of the collection's title because of his failure to realize that the woods are his environment as well, and thus he should protect it instead of invading it. "The Blur Of" examines how such violence is connected to other forms of violence. "[T]he blast in granite" during mining is akin to "the bomb hitting the bush in the desert" is akin to "the blur of a hand slapping."[98] Again, degradation of the natural world degrades humans because we are part of nature. We must work against this destruction in personal and public spheres. The poem also ties such destruction directly to our politically apocalyptic times through its use of "bush," which reminds readers of the terrible environmental impact of George W. Bush's wars in Afghanistan and Iraq. In contrast to these two poems, "Glossed Over" offers some hope via its observations about how we can coexist with animals. Although the poem's speaker notes that "Every architecture // shatters sometime," which in the context of the collection causes us to consider how we are destroying the environment's "architecture" and how that abuse might cause society to "shatter," they also describe the joy of watching the spring thaw of a nearby pond, and how, "slow in love," they watch "silver green" fish play there.[99] The poem argues that our relationship with nature must be a loving one just as our relationships with other humans should be.

Similar to "The Blur Of," Kasdorf's 2018 documentary poetry collection *Shale Play* examines the impact of natural gas fracking in Pennsylvania. Like Carl-Klassen's work, it writes the experiences of those whose voices are often ignored through "their own words."[100] In her introduction to a special issue of the *Journal of Mennonite Writing* on "Documentary Creative Writing," Kasdorf contends that "documentary poets derive their authority . . . from evidence and empathy" and asserts that documentary writing offers a synthesis of John Ruth's and Al Reimer's visions for Mennonite literature because of this writing's bases in actual facts and literary truth-telling.[101] Therefore, documentary poetry is a theapoetic genre because of its belief in the ability of everyday experience to reveal the Divine.

Shale Play's entirety pays witness to the suffering fracking causes people and their landscapes through Kasdorf's poems and accompanying photographs by Steven Rubin. I discuss two examples here, one from the perspective of a resident and one from the perspective of a gas worker, because the collection acknowledges the humanity of those working in the industry despite its violence. "On a Porch Across from the Shamrock Compressor Station, a Tiny Lady Tethered to an Oxygen Tank Chats with a Stranger" shares the life story of the titular "tiny lady," who describes how she has lived in the same house for sixty years and how she watches the gas workers from her front porch. Her statue of the Virgin Mary keeps her company. It "used to be blue," but Rubin's photograph of it shows that it is now white because the paint has rubbed off.[102] The statue's frequent use symbolizes a daily theapoetic seeking of the Divine. Through the woman's spying, which she feels she needs to hide (the fracking companies' resistance to documentation recurs throughout the collection), the poem paints the gas company as an invader into the community, but it also acknowledges the region's history of unhealthy mining and steel production.[103] It reminds us that the climate catastrophe has been a long time in the making because of the repeated choosing of profits over people. "Happy Holds Forth at Fry Brothers Turkey Ranch on Route 15" documents a gas worker's feelings about his job. He says "It's government and Big Oil / in cahoots, like usual," and that "what we're doing / out here is not good" even though he is "not a bad person." He repeats this claim twice at separate times, as though to convince himself of it. The weight of his job makes him suicidal despite his nickname, so he "pray[s], *Take me now!*"[104] Happy does the job because he has a family to support, but he is also smart enough not to fall for his employer's lies about how their activities are safe. The presence of religion in both poems shows an awareness on the speakers' part that they have an ethical responsibility to something bigger than themselves, whether it is the Divine or the broader community. They fulfill this responsibility in part by sharing their stories.

Although most recent Mennonite literature performs theapoetics by examining experiences from the present or future, there is also a noticeable trend toward looking to past community experiences, as I examine in the next chapter. Just as Mennonites traditionally turned to stories from the *Martyrs Mirror* in times of war,[105] Mennonite literature's return to the past to reaffirm Mennonite values is one way of confronting apocalypse. Julie Swarstad Johnson is a third significant member of the second generation of US Mennonite poets. Her 2020 chapbook, *Orchard Light*, portrays pacifist experience during another apocalyptic time, the US Civil War. The book is a kind of documentary poetry because it uses "archival research," one of the genre's methods that Kasdorf names,[106] to retell true stories about a Brethren family, the Sherfys, whose farm was overrun by the Battle of Gettysburg. Johnson describes her research in *Orchard Light*'s "Notes" and "Acknowledgments."[107] The collection's basis in fact comforts me as I read it now in another time when warring ideologies divide the United States because the book's poems remind me that others have survived difficult times before by living out their principles. Indeed, *Orchard Light* tries to remind us of this fact immediately with its first poem, "Sleeping at Gettysburg," which takes place years after the battle and describes Joseph Sherfy working to come to peace with the trauma of it.[108] Living out a nonviolent ethic is not always easy, it takes a toll, but it remains the correct choice. We see this in "The Draft, August 24, 1863," when Rafael Sherfy's name comes up in the draft lottery and "he knows now he will refuse" even though there are rumors that other Brethren have been hanged for doing so and that paying a substitute will cost "A year's pay."[109] His ethical steadfastness is the kind that is necessary now in our times of deep political uncertainty.

When we examine these recent examples of Mennonite poetry, it becomes clear that they do something, just as the early work of first-generation poets such as Gundy and Brandt did and continues to do something. They offer us inspiration as pieces of art, and they offer us ethical training as examples of theapoetics. Carl-Klassen's, Kauffman's, Kasdorf's, and Johnson's choices to give us this training by portraying events from the news resemble that made in one of the early important pieces of US Mennonite literature, Sara Stambaugh's *I Hear the Reaper's Song*.

CHAPTER 3

Conversing with the Other in Sara Stambaugh's *I Hear the Reaper's Song*

Unlike the early work of Di Brandt and Jeff Gundy, which fits within the transgressive mode that Julia Spicher Kasdorf questions in "Sunday Morning Confession," Sara Stambaugh's 1984 novel *I Hear the Reaper's Song* is a story about an important historical event in the Mennonite faith community that affirms the community's ethics rather than seeking to critique them. Its examination of these ethics makes it a text we can read retroactively as theapoetic. I do so because the book is a prime example of work that fulfills John Ruth's call for writers to celebrate the faith community's beliefs while also being the kind that Al Reimer celebrates as prioritizing aesthetic issues rather than didactic ones.[1] As one of Stambaugh's publishers, Merle Good, notes in an obituary, she was "not much of a church person," but nevertheless wrote with a Christ-like kindness toward her characters.[2] Like Janet Kauffman, whose fiction I discuss in chapter 5, Stambaugh is an important writer from the 1980s flowering of Mennonite literature whose work scholars now ignore. Aside from her work being prominent enough for Reimer to mention it in *Mennonite Literary Voices*, her foundational status is such that she is one of only two writers from the United States included in Hildi Froese Tiessen's germinal anthology *Liars and Rascals*.[3] Stambaugh embodies the transnationalism that is now one of the field's trademarks, as she grew up in the United States but spent much of her writing life living in Canada. Therefore, I study her novel to show that its themes remain relevant to work in the field today and thus deserves renewed attention.

Another reason I investigate *I Hear the Reaper's Song* is that it is an early example of a text in the field that examines a historical event, a kind of narrative that is reemerging. Two recent fictional efforts examine historical Mennonite and Brethren responses to war as a response to the ongoing trauma of twenty-first-century US politics. Like Julie Swarstad Johnson's *Orchard Light*, Evie Yoder Miller's *Scruples on the Line* trilogy (2020–21) retells the story of real-life characters during the Civil War, including that of John Kline, the Brethren man rumored to have been killed in Johnson's "The Draft, August 24, 1863."[4] Ken Yoder Reed's 2016 novel, *Both My Sons*, focuses on the struggles of Pennsylvania Mennonites to define their nonviolent beliefs as they begin to understand the ramifications of their participation in imperialist violence against Indigenous Peoples. The book includes three scenes that highlight the *Martyrs Mirror* as an inspiration for characters' beliefs in nonviolence.[5] These references are metafictional moves that alert readers to the way the novel itself advocates pacifist principles. By doing so, it fulfills John Ruth's vision for Mennonite literature as work that serves the community, just as *I Hear the Reaper's Song* does. Indeed, Ruth is the author of one of the blurbs on *Both My Sons*'s back cover.

I also choose to examine *I Hear the Reaper's Song* because of its geographical setting. *I Hear the Reaper's Song* takes place in Lancaster County, Pennsylvania's sectarian Mennonite community at the end of the nineteenth century. Lancaster is an underexplored locale in Mennonite literary criticism despite being present in what is probably the field's earliest text in English, Mabel Dunham's *The Trail of the Conestoga*,[6] and despite Lancaster's important role in the theological Mennonite community as the locus of Mennonite conservatism up until Lancaster Mennonite Conference's decision to leave Mennonite Church USA in 2015. This lack of scholarly interest is odd considering that another early significant text in the field, Good's *Happy as the Grass Was Green*, takes place there, and it remains the only US Mennonite novel made into a film.[7] Kauffman's 1986 novel *Collaborators* also takes place there. But Jessica W. Lapp's 1998 essay on *Collaborators* is the last piece of Mennonite literary criticism to examine fiction that takes place in Lancaster.[8] Therefore, it is important to examine a representation of the area's theological impact in *Ethics for Apocalyptic Times*, a book about Mennonite literature and theology. *I Hear the Reaper's Song* is significant for fictionalizing an event of huge importance to the faith community that was still relevant to Lancaster in the 1980s when the book was published and remains relevant today.

I also admit that as someone who has had Mennonite family in Lancaster since 1711, including the characters in the novel, I have a personal stake in correcting the field's Lancaster lacuna. *I Hear the Reaper's Song* was brought to my attention by my mother, Miriam R. (Shank) Cruz, after her father, Lester C. Shank, found in his research on our family's genealogy that the novel's central character, Barbara "Barbie" Hershey (1878–1896), was my great-great maternal grandmother Anna Mellinger Kreider's (1848–1930) first cousin. Good notes that Barbie Hershey was Stambaugh's great-aunt,[9] so I am receiving the book's narrative and its ethic from a relative, albeit a distant one—third cousin twice-removed, I think.

This family connection exemplifies an important aspect of the theapoetic canon *Ethics for Apocalyptic Times* constructs. As chapter 6 and the epilogue show, we can each have our own canon because readers can read any literary tradition theapoetically. I choose to do so primarily with Mennonite literature because I am a Mennonite and happen to have close affinities with authors of many of the texts I examine. Aside from my relation to Stambaugh, Sofia Samatar and I both attended Lancaster Mennonite High School and Goshen College and have Swiss Mennonite mothers who married men they met doing mission work, Jeff Gundy is also a Swiss Mennonite who went to Goshen, Kauffman and I have deep Lancaster roots, and Casey Plett and I are both queer and have lived in New York City for significant stretches of time.

However, Patrick Friesen observes in an oft-cited essay, "I was born into this [i.e., Mennonitism]. I could have been born in Spain."[10] We don't choose the birth contexts that shape us. This reality highlights an important distinction between Mennonite ethnicity and Mennonite theology, which has always emphasized the importance of choosing as an adult to follow Jesus and participate in the faith community. In other words, Friesen likens Mennonite ethnicity to being baptized into a state church: it is of questionable value. We can choose to use our unchosen community's stories well to shape ourselves and others, though. Theapoetics and autotheory both do this. I also could have been born in Spain, but I wasn't; I was born in the Bronx to a Mennonite family who attended churches that belonged to Lancaster Mennonite Conference. As this book makes clear, I still find some value in this upbringing even though I have left theological Mennonitism behind. Therefore, I work with Mennonite stories here just as Stambaugh does in *I Hear the Reaper's Song*, and just as Miriam Toews does in *Summer of My Amazing Luck*, which I discuss in the next chapter. These novels' ethics are Mennonite because of their Mennonite settings and their Mennonite authors. But the ethics they teach are not inherently Mennonite; they are also available for readers to encounter in other traditions.

I Hear the Reaper's Song also fits in this project about ethics for apocalyptic times because the railroad's prominence in it makes me think of a railroad-related experience I had near the beginning of what I consider to be the start of this apocalyptic era in the United States, George W. Bush's presidency, and especially its response to 9/11. In October 2002, I observed an example of the government's resulting crackdown on immigrants. I was traveling via Amtrak from Manhattan to Goshen to attend the third Mennonite/s Writing conference. The train's early-evening departure was delayed for over two hours at New York's Penn Station. While I waited, I chatted with a fellow passenger, a young Senegalese man who was taking the train to Chicago, the end of the route. We parted ways once boarding finally began, but I noticed later that we obtained seats in the same car only a few rows apart. I settled into my seat and fell asleep soon after the train left the city. Midway through the night, I awoke to find that the train had stopped in the middle of a field somewhere. I began looking around and saw that two men wearing dark jackets with "INS" printed in large white letters on the back had entered the car and were asking each passenger where they were born. When they got to my conversation partner and heard that he spoke English with an accent, they asked him what he was doing in the United States. The man said that he was a student and had a student visa, but when he was unable to produce any textbooks from his luggage, I heard one of the agents tell the man that he did not believe the man's "story." The two agents forced him off the train along with several other passengers.

This was the most terrifying experience I had ever had. Even though I have lived in the United States my entire life, I was deathly afraid when the agent asked me my place of birth. I grew up with frequent bedtime stories about Russian Mennonites having their documents interrogated by border guards and sometimes being allowed to leave, and other times being sent to Siberia.[11] The stress of those stories jumped to life on the train. These agents had power that they could wield as they chose without any concern for justice. I was outraged that representatives of my government were using these Gestapo-like tactics, and especially that they did it so lightly, ruining people's lives without showing any emotion. Whether the people the agents removed from the train were "illegal" immigrants or not is beside the point. The point is that the agents did not hesitate to designate fellow humans as Other; they seemed to be doing their job with glee. This adversarial world view was hurtful to everyone involved that night—if they are human, I am sure those agents must have nightmares about what their job requires them to do—and is not helpful in any situation I can think of. Of course, such actions have become much more frequent in the United States in the two decades since this experience because of ICE's creation and the 2017–21 White House occupant's administration. I return to this problem later in the chapter.

I HEAR THE REAPER'S SONG'S HISTORICAL THEAPOETICS

I Hear the Reaper's Song fictionalizes historical events that caused the Lancaster Mennonite community to become even more separatist and conservative because it felt that its young people were becoming too worldly. The book thereby embodies theapoetics by attempting to illustrate lessons from actual experiences. The railroad symbolizes this encroachment of worldliness in the novel and as a result resides in the position of Other in relation to the Hershey family, the farmers whose story the book chronicles. However, the adversarial relationship between the Hersheys and the railroad heals by the end of the novel because Peter Hershey does not use violence, whether physical or judicial, to relate to the railroad but converses with its representatives as individuals rather than faceless company men instead. Stambaugh's choices about how she fictionalizes this conflict reveals the advocacy of a nonviolent ethic for interacting with those who are in the position of Other, especially because of how, according to Good, she writes ethically by choosing not "to take revenge" against any of the book's characters who treat the characters based on her ancestors unkindly.[12] Kasdorf asserts in an interview that "all art identified with Mennonite makers . . . is deeply influenced by conversations with others."[13] This conversing happens in multiple directions. As Gundy's lurkers, Mennonite writers interact with the broader literary world, and our work often also advocates for the Mennonite ideal of communal conversation that is willing to hear and respect the voice of the Other. We see this in *I Hear the Reaper's Song*'s portrayal of the Hersheys' interactions with the railroad. The stories the Hersheys know about the nonviolence practiced by their Mennonite forebears teach them how to relate to the railroad. In turn, Stambaugh's retelling of their story teaches readers how to relate to those in the position of Other.

Reviews on the back cover of *I Hear the Reaper's Song*'s paperback edition from newspapers such as the *Washington Post* ("A fine performance by a writer of considerable ability") and the *Philadelphia Inquirer* ("a genuine find") laud it, and it was popular enough to remain in print until its publisher's demise in 2013 (and an ebook is still available). However, there is no scholarly work on it. Therefore, a summary of it is necessary here because of its obscurity. The book tells the story of Barbie Hershey's death in a railroad accident in 1896 and the after-effects of her death on her family and their Mennonite community. Historian James C. Juhnke writes that the accident portrayed in *I Hear the Reaper's Song* occurred near midnight on Saturday, 25 July 1896, in Bird-in-Hand, Pennsylvania.[14] Hershey and her escort, Enos Barge, were returning from a party when Barge's horse was startled by a train whistle as they were crossing tracks owned by the Pennsylvania Railroad. Stambaugh's retelling references the tracks' dangerous reputation: "The Bird-in-Hand crossing had a bad name.... The crossing scared people, because the tracks curved behind a rise just before they crossed the road, so you couldn't see if anything was coming. Instead, you stopped and listened for the engineer to whistle and let you know if a train was on its way from the West, but before they went across most people said a little prayer that if one was coming, the engineer would remember and do his job."[15] On the night of the Hershey-Barge accident, the train's engineer forgot his job until it was too late, blowing his whistle when he was just about to cross the road, not leaving enough time for traffic on the road to react. Barge's horse froze at the sound of the whistle, and the oncoming train hit the buggy before he and Hershey could jump to safety. Stambaugh writes that the train hit the buggy with such force it "'ripped off all [Hershey's] clothes'" (169–70), and Ruth's account in his history of Lancaster Mennonites says that the train "cut [Hershey] to pieces" and severed Barge's right arm from his body.[16] Hershey died instantly, and Barge died the next day after being taken to the Lancaster City hospital on the next train through.

I Hear the Reaper's Song recounts that "more than two thousand" people went to Barbie's funeral (147), and "three thousand" went to Enos's (156). We see from these large numbers that the accident touched the Lancaster Mennonite community deeply. Historian Mark Aldrich documents how such train accidents were fairly common at the time.[17] The novel reinforces this frequency by mentioning another accident that happened the same week in New Jersey (164). However, the Hershey-Barge accident was significant because it sparked a religious revival among Lancaster County Mennonites. A traveling Mennonite evangelist, Amos Wenger, who was in Lancaster at the time of the accident, claimed the tragedy was a warning from God to the County's young people that they should repent of their worldly, party-going ways and get baptized into the church.[18] Hershey and Barge were not baptized when they died because of the Mennonite belief in adult baptism. Wenger implied that the two youngsters had gone to hell as a result because he felt they were old enough to make the decision whether to join the church or not.[19] Wenger's preaching was effective. Ruth reports that approximately five hundred young Mennonites joined the church during the rest of the summer after the accident.[20]

A longer-lasting effect of the post-accident revival was Lancaster Mennonites' adoption of plain dress. When Wenger came to preach from Indiana, he was already wearing the plaincoat, a suit jacket without lapels that buttons up to the neck, but plain dress had not taken hold in Lancaster. Ruth describes the worldly dress worn by some Mennonites up through the 1890s, such as wedding dresses "requiring fifteen yards of lace."[21] Hershey and Barge dressed fashionably during their short lives. Stambaugh's memoir includes a photograph of teenage Barbie and her sister Martha wearing dresses with elaborate ruffled sleeves and intricately stitched bodices. There is also a drawing of Barbie wearing a white dress with a large ruffled collar and puffy sleeves and a photograph of Barge wearing a lapeled suit jacket and wide, bright tie.[22] However, after Wenger's and other revivalists' sermons against worldliness, which included exhortations calling for the rejection of ostentatious clothing items such as neckties, frilly dresses, and fashionable women's hats, a wave of plainness overtook the County's Mennonites.[23] As Stambaugh highlights in her memoir, this plainness was a sexist tool the church used against women because women's dress regulations were much more extensive and "strict" than men's.[24] Thus, her novel argues that the accident is a tragedy because it affects the faith community negatively, not only because of Hershey's and Barge's deaths.

I Hear the Reaper's Song portrays the plain revival in its description of Barbie's sister Martha and her mother Barbara sewing plain cape dresses (a dress with a large triangular flap on the front which hides the bosom) and head coverings (small gauze caps usually worn toward the back of the head) for themselves after attending a revival meeting (196). Stambaugh's memoir reprints a photograph of Martha sometime after the accident wearing a covering so large that it nearly covers her entire head.[25] Even the worldly Minnie Hoffman, who is visiting Lancaster from New York City and teaches the Mennonite young people songs about women who are "Not too timid, not too bold, / Just the kind you'd like to hold, / Just the kind for sport I'm told" (108), rejects her "fancy" clothing in favor of plain attire (170). Ruth reports that by 1900 Lancaster Mennonite Conference began to regulate how its members could dress and that by 1911 all members were required to wear the plaincoat if they were men or cape dresses and head coverings if they were women.[26] Although plain dress is no longer a requirement for church membership, and was beginning to be abandoned as early as the 1960s,[27] some Lancaster Conference Mennonites, mostly women, continue to dress plain, so the effects of the Hershey-Barge accident still resonate. This long shadow is why Stambaugh feels the accident is a significant enough subject for a novel.

Barbie's brother Silas Hershey, *I Hear the Reaper's Song*'s narrator, describes how the revival movement divides the Hershey family in half.[28] Martha and his mother accept the revivalist preachers' claims that Barbie's death was a warning from God for the community to reform itself, but Silas, his father Peter, and his brothers Hen and Mart do not go along with the revival and are outraged that the preachers use Barbie's tragic death to further their own ends. Hen stops going to church (165), and Peter is especially disgusted that Martha and his wife follow the preachers' lead and begin dressing plain, telling them, "'I never knew godliness could be judged by the clothes people wore'" (197).[29] Martha's attempts to cajole the rest of the family into going to revival meetings with her also anger Peter. He yells at her that he will not forbid her from "'hear[ing Barbie] set up for an example [by the revivalists] and racked into more pieces than the train knocked her into,'" but he will not stand for her trying to convince the rest of the family that Barbie was not saved simply because she was not baptized (177). Later, Hen accuses Martha of turning against Barbie by agreeing with the revivalists, and he calls her a "'stupid bitch'" for believing that Barbie did not go to heaven, to which she retorts that Hen will "'be damned in hell'" (183). Silas also mentions that he is unable to "forgive Martha" for going with the revivalists (202). During this time, the Hersheys forget that their Mennonite ethic teaches them to love one another even though they may have disagreements with each other. However, they are reconciled at the end of the book when they visit Barbie's gravesite together and all agree that the inscription on Barbie's headstone that claims she is in heaven is correct (211–14).

The division in the community caused by the revivalists is also evident in a metaphor from the second verse of a hymn sung at one of the revival meetings, from which the novel's title comes:

'Tis the harvest time, 'tis the harvest time,
Oh! who will go along?

See the fields for harvest now are white;
I hear the reaper's song. (195)

Although the "reaper" here is Jesus calling his followers to "harvest" souls for him, which is a positive metaphor for those who agree with the revival, there is a sinister undercurrent for Silas and his family in the hymn's reaping imagery because the reaper has cruelly cut Barbie down while still in her teens. Although the Hersheys believe that worldly events are subservient to God's will, the revivalists' claim that God killed Barbie to send a message to the community creates too much cognitive dissonance in the Hersheys' minds for them to accept the claim, so the hymn's reaping metaphor sounds like a cruel mocking of their pain. The hymn's imagery is powerful enough that, according to Silas, "thirty-nine" young people join the church right afterward, the most "ever at one time before" (196).

Silas also narrates how the accident tests the Hersheys' belief in loving their enemies because they blame the railroad for Barbie's death. *I Hear the Reaper's Song* portrays the railroad in mixed terms before the accident occurs. During the novel's historical setting, Mennonites in the United States were still a sectarian community that urged as much separation from the outside world as possible. Before the accident the railroad functions both as a physical boundary aiding in the separation of Mennonites from the outside world and as a conduit to that world.[30] Its tracks serve as a property line for some Mennonite farms, including the Hersheys' (5, 30). But it also serves as a means of escape from the close-knit Mennonite community. For instance, Hen takes the train to Atlantic City to visit his sister Lizzie (29), who represents the secular world because she is married to a non-Mennonite and follows worldly fashions; she arrives for Barbie's funeral "looking like the fanciest pages from the Sears-Roebuck catalogue" (139). Silas also says that the train leads to "the end of the world," even though he is merely describing the "eight mile" distance between his home and Lancaster City, which is "so different from [Mennonite] life, with the rich people who ran things and all those Catholics" (62). Mennonites are not the ones who "run things" because they separate themselves from political power, although they are not above discussing politics: the Hersheys talk about the 1896 presidential election throughout the novel (103–5, 176, 181, 192).

The Hersheys and their fellow Mennonites view the railroad's power to take people away from the community with ambiguity. This power is dangerous because it carries people into the unfaithful world. At the same time, it can also bring them back into the safety of the community, such as when Mart, who leaves Lancaster to work the harvest in the Dakotas for a Lutheran farmer, is able to make it back to Pennsylvania in time for Barbie's funeral because of the railroad's speed (144).[31] Mart then decides to remain with his family for the winter instead of returning to his job (162). The railroad also connects the Lancaster Mennonite community with other Mennonite communities. Silas notes that Amos Wenger arrives on the "train" just as previous Mennonite evangelists from the Midwest had (89–90). These Mennonite connections do more to hurt the community than to help it, though, because of Wenger's divisive preaching.

After Barbie's death, the Hersheys understandably begin to view the railroad negatively. This view provokes reactions from the Hersheys that do not fit in with their peaceful Mennonite faith. The Hersheys begin to react toward the railroad with hatred several days after the accident. Silas is praying at the train station while he waits to see if Mart will arrive in time for the funeral, but he realizes that after he hears the incoming train whistle and begins to think about how the train that killed Barbie did not whistle in time, he "[i]sn't praying any more" (144). The railroad is now something that leads to ungodly thoughts for Silas and his family. These thoughts continue to be evident when Silas says that every time he rips a worm in half when weeding the family's tobacco fields, he thinks "of Barbie torn up by the train and hate[s] the railroad for doing that to her" (162). Likewise, Peter's "pain" from losing Barbie transforms "into hate against the railroad. [He exclaims] 'God damn that engineer'" in a rare moment of anger (164). Peter dehumanizes the engineer by thinking of him as a monster who belongs to the unfeeling class of "railroad engineers... wild men who didn't care how many people they killed" (165). At this time, the Hersheys are unable to think about the humanity of the engineer and how he might feel about killing Barbie because their anger over Barbie's death prevents such empathy. As a result, they view the engineer and the railroad as Other. Silas becomes especially aware of the adversarial relationship between the Hersheys and the railroad when he learns that the train that killed Barbie was a troop train, because one reason Mennonites came to Pennsylvania from Europe was to escape compulsory military service (139). A train that represents the antithesis of everything Barbie's family stands for kills her, and this cruel coincidence mocks them.

The Hersheys' anger at the railroad stems in part from the fact that the railroad does not suffer any consequences for committing what the family views as a crime. Peter bitterly states that the railroad "'murder[s his] child and get[s] out from any blame for it'" (142). Mart concurs with this statement, lamenting that the railroad "'get[s] off scot free'" (157). He later remarks that "'the railroad killed [Barbie], and the railroad should have to pay, but we know the railroad doesn't give a damn. They have the government under their thumb and can get away with whatever they please'" (163). The railroad, representative of big business and the city, is able to oppress the farmer because it speaks the language of worldly power and can thus manipulate the government, the official wielder of that power. It is therefore necessary for the Hersheys to look somewhere other than the law for restitution and some sort of reconciliation with the railroad that will heal their conflict with it and allow them to move on with their lives.

We see the railroad's ability to manipulate legal procedures in its favor through the novel's portrayal of the inquest held about Barbie's death. The court exonerates the railroad from any blame because the engineer blew his whistle, which the law views as an adequate warning. This excuse angers Silas's cousin Hon. He is frustrated that the inquest happens in the city on the railroad's turf because "'all those city men who run things don't know what's going on [in the country landscape through which the railroad runs], so they decided as long as [the engineer] said he whistled, he wasn't to blame'" (138). Hon's brother Sam chimes in, noting that the train was speeding around the curve at "'better than fifty-five miles an hour'" and that the inquest "'never asked when [the engineer] blew [the whistle], ... whether it was in time to warn them or just in time to spook the horse so Enos couldn't move if he wanted to'" (138). Hon asserts in reply that "'those city men don't care about things like that. . . . All they care about is running things'" (138). In Hon's view, those with worldly power exercise it without any concern for justice. The cousins portray the railroad as an unfeeling machine that can manipulate the strings of truth as it wills to serve its own interests without concern for the rights of those less powerful than itself.

Even when the court does not completely exonerate the railroad in the inquest on Enos's death, it does not assign the railroad responsibility for the accident. It merely suggests that "'the Bird-in-Hand crossing should have a watchman, as if a watchman could look through the hill more than anybody else to see a train that doesn't whistle till it's too late to stop from killing someone,'" as Dave acidly reports (141). The law cannot control the railroad with any effectiveness, so the Hersheys are required to find another channel through which to gain resolution in their conflict. However, even though the Hersheys hate the railroad right after the accident, they are eventually able to remember their nonviolent ethic and start to try to relate to the railroad in a nonadversarial manner. Because they have heard stories about practicing nonviolence as the most ethical way to live for all their lives, the family internalizes this ethic and is able to act according to its principles in a time of crisis. They begin conversing with the railroad when it offers them compensation for Barbie's death. When the railroad sends its representative, Ira Winters, to the Hershey's farm to reach a settlement about the accident, Peter is initially unwelcoming. He is civil to Mr. Winters but does not do anything to make Mr. Winters feel comfortable while he explains the railroad's offer. Peter does not invite Mr. Winters into the house, preferring to remain in the "barn" to talk, which is Peter's turf (172). The railroad offers the Hersheys "'five hundred dollars'" because it is "sorry" about Barbie's death (172). This offer makes Peter "smile," and Mr. Winters is glad that the family and the railroad agree that there should be some sort of compensation for Barbie's death (172). A common goal for the conversation is established that begins to change the relationship between the Hersheys and the railroad from an us-them dynamic to a partners-working-together dynamic. At this time, though, the railroad still refuses to accept the blame for the accident (172–73). This refusal outrages Peter because he thinks the railroad is trying to "buy" his silence about what really happened, so he cuts the conversation short and tells Mr. Winters to leave (173).

I HEAR THE REAPER'S SONG'S ETHICS

However, Peter refrains from using violence against Mr. Winters to gain a small amount of revenge. Instead, he recognizes the railroad's right to have its say even though he disagrees with its stance. By letting the railroad present its view of the accident, and therefore entering into dialogue with it, Peter begins to break down the hurtful barriers between his family and the railroad that cause the Hersheys to designate the railroad as Other. When the Hersheys begin to dismantle these barriers, they begin to focus on healing themselves rather than spending all their emotional energy hating the railroad. The family needs some kind of closure to their conflict with the railroad so they can move on with their lives. Without this closure, their anger will kill them slowly emotionally just as Barbie was killed physically.

The railroad continues to "sen[d] letters" to the Hersheys offering them money, and Peter files the letters away after reading them without sending a reply (192). After its letters are unsuccessful, the railroad sends another representative to visit the Hersheys, this time "a vice-president real high up... all the way from Philadelphia," according to Silas (208). The conversation between Peter and the vice president goes better than the one with Mr. Winters, beginning with where the men meet. Peter hosts the vice president in the family parlor (212). By this point, Peter and the railroad have decided to compromise some so that the conversation can continue. The railroad's decision to send one of its executives to visit the Hersheys shows that it does care about the consequences of the accident and therefore is not as unfeeling as Silas and his cousins assumed. Silas is happily surprised that "the railroad could have a conscience" (213). This softer, more humane side of the railroad is only able to emerge because the Hersheys engage with it. They bring out the best in the railroad by no longer rejecting it as Other.

The result of the dialogue is a positive one for both sides. The vice president tells Peter that the railroad is willing to acknowledge that "'the train was going too fast and if the engineer had been more careful [the accident] wouldn't have happened,'" (212). The railroad also admits that it was at fault for Barbie's death even though it is innocent according to the law (213). The railroad meets its goal of avoiding legal sanction but is also able to satisfy the Hersheys' desire that it acknowledge its responsibility for Barbie's death. The railroad's vice president tells Peter that the engineer who killed Barbie has been filled with remorse since the accident and refuses to drive engines anymore (213). So the humans working for the railroad also need healing from the accident. Peter still refuses to take money from the railroad but accepts a free trip for the family to Niagara Falls instead (215). By doing so, he brings closure for both the family and the railroad; the family is appeased by the railroad's admission of guilt, and the railroad obtains the family's forgiveness.

We see *I Hear the Reaper's Song*'s ethic in the way the Hersheys interact with the railroad. The Hersheys are willing to converse with the railroad instead of rejecting all contact with it or acting violently against it. Even though they have easy access to the tracks on the edge of their farm, they do not attempt to get revenge on the railroad by sabotaging the tracks to cause a costly derailment, or by doing violence to the railroad's representatives when they visit the farm. This attitude contains a willingness to acknowledge the Other's right to existence, thereby redeeming the Other from their outsider status, and creating the possibility for peaceful coexistence between the two parties. This ethic of relating to one who was the Other nonviolently is the only option for the Hersheys because they have no hope of relating successfully to the railroad on its worldly, power-based terms. The railroad controls the law and has enough money to overcome the Hersheys in whatever other arena they might try to meet the railroad in, but the family's transferal of the conflict onto their own turf of nonviolent dialogue allows them to enjoy a successful resolution of the conflict despite the railroad's superior material resources, showing that nonviolence is powerful.

Importantly, the Hersheys' nonviolent ethic does not preclude anger. For dialogue with one who was Other to be successful, it must be honest; therefore it is necessary for injustices to be named when they occur along with the emotions they cause. Peter expresses his anger against the railroad by kicking Mr. Winters off the farm and refusing to answer the railroad's letters. However, Peter's anger does not prevent him from listening to the railroad's side of the story. After initially being full of rage against the railroad, Peter calms down and is able to work with it to reach a satisfying solution to the conflict.

Of course, the Mennonite community has often used its emphasis on nonviolence to silence marginalized groups such as women, people of color, and queers within the community, blaming us for creating conflict when we ask for an end to our oppression. This dynamic is also frequently visible in the public sphere, such as when people attack protesters for "rioting" instead of addressing the systemic injustices that cause protests' necessity. Although the Hersheys choose not to tear up the railroad tracks, such disruptive actions may be necessary sometimes.

However, the nonviolent ethic taught by *I Hear the Reaper's Song* is a helpful one because it offers benefits to both sides of a conflict via conversation that rehabilitates each side's view of the opposite side as Other. It offers an alternative to violence, which solves conflicts by destroying rather than healing. Nonviolent dialogue also creates a level playing field for the parties involved, whereas the use of violence to solve conflicts ends in victory for whichever side has the most power, not necessarily the side that should justly prevail. Trying to see the humanity of the railroad's agents in the nineteenth century as the Hersheys do is like trying to see the humanity of ICE agents now as we try to convince them to resist their orders on an individual level. It will probably be a long struggle to abolish ICE and other similar institutions, but we can chip away at them by breaking them down one agent at a time.

What would happen if more people questioned the routine Othering that creates adversarial relationships in all arenas of life and thought about trying to use the ethic of nonviolence and willingness to dialogue *I Hear the Reaper's Song* advocates instead? I do not mean to suggest that if everyone read the novel US immigration policy would magically be fixed and the capitalist oppression of the developing world by the West would cease, but I do think that the book presents an intriguing alternative. Maybe focusing on people's stories more often, and thereby revealing our humanity to one another, would help us learn how to create a better world. Miriam Toews's *Summer of My Amazing Luck* helps us do so by highlighting the stories of women on society's margins.

CHAPTER 4

Secular Mennonite Ethics in Miriam Toews's *Summer of My Amazing Luck*

In an interview with Natasha G. Wiebe, Miriam Toews remembers Rudy Wiebe's 1962 novel about violence in a Canadian Mennonite village, *Peace Shall Destroy Many*, being banned in her church and laments that this official reaction was "so *sad*, because the Mennonites have so much to offer."[1] Toews herself is explicitly aware of the power stories have to change lives. In her account of her father's life, *Swing Low*, Toews has him say that he "learn[s] how to live" by reading the biographies of famous Canadians and trying to apply their examples to his life, a theme that repeats throughout the book.[2] This practice embodies theapoetic ethics. Toews also recognizes the pedagogical nature of narrative in an interview with Hildi Froese Tiessen when she discusses how she uses her writing as a form of instruction. Toews says that she wants to convey "what's important in life . . . like being compassionate, having a sense of humour, not taking yourself too seriously. I would think of these things in terms of how I would want to raise my kids. A book would sort of be an extension of that."[3] With this acknowledgment from Toews that we may read her work as having real-world implications rather than merely existing on an aesthetic level, it is up to us as readers to determine the message that each of her books tries to send. Although all three of the "important" elements that Toews mentions are apparent in her first novel, *Summer of My Amazing Luck* (1996, revised 2006), "being compassionate" is the most significant and best shows the influence of Mennonite thought. *Summer of My Amazing Luck* teaches theapoetic ethics. This teaching continues in Toews's fiction through to a text I examine in chapter 5, *Women Talking*.

Despite her rejection of Mennonite theology,[4] Toews recognizes that the Mennonite community has much to teach the outside world. Toews repeatedly calls herself a "secular Mennonite," a term that, aside from acknowledging the impossibility of escaping one's Mennonite ethnicity, also argues that it is possible to hold on to the positive aspects of Mennonitism by separating its radical essence from the oppressive institutional church.[5] While the idea of a "Mennonite on the margins" is not new,[6] Toews's claiming of this status is important because it signifies a willingness to remain in conversation with institutional Mennonitism and also posits that there is a particularly Mennonite way of being secular. Literature offers a safe space for secular Mennonites to write frankly about Mennonite values. This open, welcoming space in literature is the kind of arena that secular and religious Mennonites need in order to keep communication with each other open. While *I Hear the Reaper's Song* teaches ethics by celebrating positive aspects of Mennonitism, *Summer of My Amazing Luck* critiques the community and offers it a narrative vision to aspire to by showing that Mennonitism echoes many oppressions found in broader society, such as classism, sexism, and queerphobia. *Summer of My Amazing Luck*'s ethic is relevant to non-Mennonites and Mennonites alike.

Summer of My Amazing Luck tells the story of a Winnipeg welfare mother, Lucy, and her infant son, Dill, as they try to adjust to life in public housing and as Lucy continues to work through the grief caused by her mother's murder. The novel meanders along in a realist style through seemingly unremarkable scenes, including Lucy's visits to the welfare office, her building's janitor's attempts to clean graffiti off a wall, and her building's rivalry with the welfare mothers from the house across the street. Weeks of constant rain and a brief road trip to the United States provide the only bits of narrative excitement.

But these scenes combine to offer a powerful, Mennonite-inspired, theapoetic message to readers about the necessity of relating to the poor as persons rather than as mere charity cases. As in all Toews's novels, the use of humor throughout *Summer of My Amazing Luck* helps draw readers into the narrative by making its characters more sympathetic. The book's humor helps to open readers up into a position where we can empathize with characters who are from a different socioeconomic stratum in most cases. The novel does not stop at merely describing its characters' difficult lives; it urges readers to act against the societal systems that cause these difficulties.

When I first read *Summer of My Amazing Luck*, its Mennonite nature kept striking me despite its lack of the word "Mennonite." I saw "the trace" of Mennonitism that Tiessen argues is present in nonexplicitly Mennonite work by Mennonite writers.[7] I recognized Toews's background forcing itself into her writing even though in her interview with Tiessen, Toews says she made a conscious decision not to write about Mennonites in the novel.[8] But small Mennonite markers that only other Mennonites will probably notice work their way in: one of Lucy's childhood neighbors has a common Mennonite surname, Sawatsky, and Lucy and her mother sometimes play Dutch Blitz together.[9] Because these Mennonite traces are invisible to most readers, the novel exemplifies how we can read theapoetically regardless of our literary tradition. I read the novel as Mennonite theapoetics, but a non-Mennonite reader could still read it theapoetically without knowledge of Toews's Mennonite heritage. *Summer of My Amazing Luck* acts as moral instruction for all readers. In my reading, the book epitomizes a secular Mennonite text via the ethic of helping the poor and oppressed that it espouses, and which becomes evident when viewing the novel as ethics. It offers clues as to how one may live an ethical life that is inspired by a specific faith tradition without having to be part of an oppressive organized religion. In articulating this vision, the book thus shows the value of Mennonite literature as a space for conversation between religious and secular Mennonites, and non-Mennonites.

Mennonites traditionally emphasize helping the less fortunate, from the *Martyrs Mirror* story of Dirk Willems rescuing a drowning Anabaptist-catcher to the present-day efforts of aid organizations such as Mennonite Disaster Service, even though this compassion is not always present in intra-Mennonite relationships.[10] *Summer of My Amazing Luck* teaches this ethic of helping the unfortunate by having its characters live it and by urging readers to work for social change by combating the institutional violence that the characters suffer under. This argument is relevant for all of North American society, and it is especially relevant for Mennonites because it implicitly begins Toews's critique of the Mennonite community that becomes explicit in *A Complicated Kindness*, *Irma Voth*, and *Women Talking*. Although Mennonites try to be "in the world but not of it," Mennonitism is not immune from participation in the broader forms of systemic violence found in "worldly" society. *Summer of My Amazing Luck* offers guidance as to the kind of steps Mennonites and other readers can take to minimize this oppressive participation more than we have in the past.

SUMMER OF MY AMAZING LUCK'S AUTOBIOGRAPHICAL THEAPOETICS

One of *Summer of My Amazing Luck*'s most engaging features is the vividness of its characters, a result of the book's semi-autobiographical aspects. These aspects include Toews's and Lucy's status as single mothers, Toews's and Lucy's mothers' love of travel, and Toews's and Lucy's fathers' affectionately calling them their "bombshell blonde."[11] Also, when Toews was writing the novel, her husband was a traveling street performer like the father of Lish's twins.[12] The novel successfully breaks through the barrier that stigmatizes welfare mothers as Other and portrays them as sympathetic characters instead because Toews experienced the struggles they face firsthand. She explains to Tiessen that she wrote the book because she wanted to pay witness to the difficulties of being a welfare mother since she "had been one," and she realized that a novel would bring more attention to this issue than a CBC documentary would; it would make welfare mothers "more real."[13] *Summer of My Amazing Luck* was born out of a wish to teach readers about oppression and how to combat it. It is an explicitly moral and political text, and its basis in real experience makes it theapoetic. These characteristics play an essential role in the novel's ethic. It writes back to broader society as well as to a religious tradition that silences women and those who do not fit easily into the mold of propriety. Echoing *I Hear the Reaper's Song*'s call to listen to others' stories, *Summer of My Amazing Luck* urges the necessity of hearing these stories as a way of acknowledging the humanity of their tellers and as a channel for hearing critiques of the community in order to create a better world.

The book also shows that it is important to share our own stories to help others learn from them, not just to listen to others' stories. *Summer of My Amazing Luck* is a form of testimony, showing how North American society oppresses women, and especially poor women, but also showing via the women's cooperation throughout the novel how this oppression may be overcome through collective action. The book's narrator, Lucy, shares her life with us for this reason. She affirms her value as a person by making herself and the other tenants of her public housing building visible through her narrative, teaching us as readers while at the same time learning more about herself.

This parallel learning creates a mutual community between Lucy and readers because we provide the audience that makes it possible for her to construct her narrative. The authority figures in her life, such as her father, welfare administrators, and even librarians, refuse to listen to her, so she is forced to seek an audience elsewhere. Even though she does not know what readers she is writing for, her decision to tell her story is a hopeful act that claims agency, affirming that there will be someone who cares enough about her humanity to read her manuscript. Our willingness to read her narrative is also a liberating act because it is impossible to learn ethics theapoetically without being open to the possibility that the stories we hear might change us.

Summer of My Amazing Luck acknowledges the importance of narrative as a device for structuring our lives and helping to shape our future actions in its first chapter. Lucy introduces us to her neighbor and fellow welfare mother, Lish, and explains that Lish loves telling the story of her night with a traveling fire-eater who departed before she awoke, stealing her wallet and leaving her pregnant with twins (2). This sounds like a sad story, but Lish tells it repeatedly because she focuses on its happy ending, her two youngest daughters. It is a foundational text for her. It reminds Lish that she has value as a mother and as someone worthy of erotic joy even though her economic position in society names her as worthless. The novel's refusal to condemn Lish for having sex out of wedlock is one way it critiques institutional Mennonite theology, which denies physical pleasure to everyone except those in heterosexual marriages. Like the other theapoetic texts I examine, especially Janet Kauffman's, Greg Bechtel's, Sofia Samatar's, Casey Plett's, and Samuel R. Delany's, *Summer of My Amazing Luck* offers an inclusive sexual ethic that views any act between consenting adults as permissible.

The story about the fire-eater also gives Lish something to hope for, because in her mind there is the possibility that the performer will come back for her. This hope keeps Lish from slipping into despair about her tenuous situation and, via her resultant cheery mood, helps her perform the role of an encouraging maternal figure to the rest of the tenants in her and Lucy's building, Half-a-Life. Lish's hopefulness rubs off on Lucy throughout the novel, giving her the strength to complete her narrative. Lish recognizes the necessity of telling stories about ourselves to help us remember who we are and what is important to us.

Similarly, Lucy affirms the importance of narrative by giving readers brief histories of each of her neighbors at Half-a-Life in chapters 2 and 4 of the novel before focusing on her own story in the remainder of the book. In doing so, Lucy makes her neighbors visible as well and acknowledges that her story does not make sense when it is divorced from the stories of those around her. In this sense, all the women's narratives are equally important even though we hear Lucy's in much more detail. Some men also live at Half-a-Life, though the women's stories receive much of the novel's attention. The most prominent male character is the house's caretaker, Sing Dylan, an undocumented immigrant from India (206). Like the women, he is a sympathetic character, and his story thereby urges readers to question whether current immigration laws are just or not.

Lucy's retelling of the other women's stories also causes readers to see them as human rather than as stereotypes who are on welfare because they are too lazy to get a job. Their heartbreaking backgrounds show that in many cases women are forced to go on welfare because of systemic violence or because of men abdicating their parental responsibilities. For instance, Naomi's husband molests her daughter, which is why she leaves him and moves into public housing. Despite his actions she is unable to get sole custody of her children (22–24). The justice system, controlled by men, throws her to the margins of society for being a disobedient wife and choosing her children over her husband instead of punishing the actual crime. Many of the other women at Half-a-Life also suffer at the hands of the legal system, which does nothing to enforce the payment of child support by the women's former lovers (25, 28). Society punishes the women by forcing them to deal with the "consequences" of their out-of-wedlock sexual pleasure alone, arguing that they should only be able to enjoy their bodies when men control them within the bonds of marriage.

Summer of My Amazing Luck further illustrates its ethic of concern for the oppressed via Lucy's description of the hardships present in the lives of Half-a-Life's residents. These hardships result from society's attempt to pretend that the women do not exist. Lucy states that the residents were put into Half-a-Life "because we were poor and had kids" (24). They are put into a ghetto for single mothers so that those more economically fortunate than they are do not have to see them and can pretend that their needs are met.

Lish concurs, explaining that she and her building-mates are denied access to various public places, which further cuts them off from "respectable" society. She asserts that "women and children" are barred from many businesses by "No Strollers" signs or made to feel unwelcome in them by their staff (78). Implicit in this practice is the stereotype that men earn and control money, therefore women unaccompanied by men are not serious customers but rather nuisances only interested in browsing and letting their children run wild. The women recognize that they are undervalued in the North American economic system, as both Terrapin and Lish state that being mothers, a role that is obviously essential to society, is their full-time job (55, 176), but they must stay on welfare because society does not value stay-at-home mothers enough to compensate them in a nonstigmatized way. Capitalism places no concrete value on this work, so it views the women as financial burdens.

Lucy reports how she and her neighbors attempt to combat society's oppression of them by putting up a façade of toughness in public. They "carr[y them]selves like gangsters, warriors, [they a]re just fine, d[o]n't need anybody" (12). This pantomime forces society to see them. The women claim their personhood by making themselves visible and therefore refuse to accept their oppression, even if they can only do this by projecting the image that others want to force on them. However, the language that Lucy uses to explain the mothers' rough public exteriors shows that there is a price for having to fight for this visibility. The women must adopt unhealthy, violent, stereotypically masculine roles as "warriors" and "gangsters" to survive because this is the only kind of assertiveness that society will respond to. They are unable to be authentic outside of Half-a-Life. *Summer of My Amazing Luck* calls for readers to help create a more understanding, helpful society that makes it possible for all its members to be themselves rather than being forced to fake it like the women do.

The women's tough circumstances are important for readers to see. Toews tells Claire Kirch that "writ[ing] about difficult and tragic situations . . . is 'how I make sense of my world'. . . . 'Fiction can be more true than truth.'"[14] It is necessary to pay witness to life's hardships in the most effective ways possible, which often includes the use of narrative. While the Mennonite community does a good job of appreciating narrative, it does a poor job of appreciating the power of fiction as a genre with life-changing potential. Therefore, aside from teaching broader society about the lives of welfare mothers and urging us to revise our attitudes toward them, *Summer of My Amazing Luck* also acts as a specific critique of the Mennonite community, calling for it to be more open in its definition of which texts are important and in its definition of who might be able to give wisdom to the community. While many Mennonite writers, including Toews, are no longer theological Mennonites, they still have insights that are necessary for institutional Mennonitism to consider.

The novel's ethic also argues for the necessity of political activism through its portrayal of society's begrudging help for the women, the welfare system. Lucy offers numerous examples of how the system is dehumanizing and in need of reform. In her description of the relationships with men that Half-a-Life's women are forced to conduct covertly so they can retain government support, she shows that the system marginalizes Half-a-Life's residents because of their gender through the system's advocacy of traditional gender roles. The system assumes that having a visible boyfriend equates to him providing financial support and thus causes the women to stick to one-night stands so that their liaisons are not revealed (87). The system insists on stripping women of their sexual agency in exchange for their monthly payments. It denies them humanity by attempting to control all aspects of their lives.

As Lucy observes, these welfare policies are sexist and heteronormative. She explains that a woman will lose all her welfare money if she is living with a man no matter what his financial circumstances, but if she is living with a woman who is her lover, she will only lose a part of her rent allowance even if her lover is wealthy (86). This example of the welfare system's ignorance of reality shows that it is not interested in the women as persons that it actually wants to help, but that it simply exists as a self-perpetuating bureaucracy. Frustratingly, Half-a-Life's residents, who best understand the system's brokenness as its victims, are the ones who have the least amount of political clout to try and change it.

Lucy also explains that the system polices welfare recipients as though they are children, being forced to provide death certificates if they claim to have missed an appointment as the result of the death of a loved one (34). Not only do the women have to combat society's stereotype of them, but they must also combat the system's stereotype of them as untrustworthy persons. Lucy is stunned when Lish explains to her how much many people hate those who are on welfare. Lucy does not understand it, telling us that if she lived disliking others for no reason she would "have an awful life!" (162). She recognizes that it is necessary to live out an ethic that sees the value in others no matter what their circumstances. Her positive attitude toward life and openness to listening to others' stories throughout the novel acts as an example for readers.

Lucy explains that the dehumanizing nature of the welfare system means that being on the dole "requires complete denial" of how bad one's life must be to have it get caught up in such an eviscerating bureaucracy (120). The system helps its recipients survive, but it does so at great emotional cost. It sees the women as case numbers rather than as persons. It can do this because of its recipients' powerlessness, economic and otherwise. The welfare workers can afford to be rude to Lucy because she can't do anything about it (35–36, 119). She has the unpleasant choice of accepting their disrespectful behavior or starving. *Summer of My Amazing Luck* urges readers to take note of this negative example of failing to serve the oppressed and strive to do the opposite.

THE PERSONAL IS THE POLITICAL

Aside from the rudeness the women must face in their regular visits to the welfare office, the novel shows how those in charge of funding the system use it as a political football rather than as a tool for positive social change. The government minister in charge of the province's welfare program, Bunnie Hutchison, wants to cut welfare mothers' child tax credit because they are on welfare (others would still get the credit), not considering how these cuts will drastically affect the women's lives. Lucy laments that the proposed cut of fifteen hundred dollars is just over a sixth of her income for an entire year (98–99). In this instance, there is a happy ending for the women because they find that Bunnie Hutchison is a tax fraud, and they use this information to blackmail her into not making the cuts (117, 141, 213). Despite their breaking the law, the book depicts the women's actions in a positive way because their actions are just in that they are undertaken out of a concern for the oppressed. The blackmail helps many more people than it hurts, and it is questionable whether Bunnie Hutchison is even hurt by it rather than simply being reminded that she is in office to serve her constituents instead of herself. The women show the importance of working together in community in this episode, which is another one of the novel's primary ethical emphases.

Lucy says at the beginning of her story that when she moves into Half-a-Life she is grateful to belong to a community. Although society stigmatizes welfare, being on the dole at least helps to give Lucy an identity, something she has been lacking. She tells us, "Lish and I were single welfare mothers. I was proud to be something finally, to belong to a group of people that had a name and a purpose" (8). Lucy's description of her community as having "a purpose" is essential. She realizes that the women must rise above society's hatred of them to do a good job of raising their children even though society does not recognize motherhood as a "job" and simply takes it for granted instead. The women draw inspiration from one another in this task emotionally and physically through helping one another out with advice and tasks such as babysitting. When Lucy moves to Half-a-Life, the women model good community behavior for her, and she in turn becomes a useful member in the community.

The residents build the sense of community at Half-a-Life via mutual aid, shared traditions, and a common ethic of social justice. In this way, it resembles Mennonite community, which is part of how *Summer of My Amazing*

Luck uses its narrative to call for change within Mennonitism as well as the broader world. Lucy writes that the women "stick together" even when they are not the best of friends because they realize that as members of multiple oppressed groups (women and the poor, and in some cases BIPOC communities and the queer community) they cannot get by on their own, but together they can be a formidable force (86). One example of this help is when Lucy allows the other women to use her brand-new stolen stroller as a grocery cart. In an episode of vigilante justice like that of the women's blackmailing of Bunnie Hutchison, Lucy steals the stroller for her son from Sears (43). The novel argues that society should provide mothers with the essentials for raising their children, and because it does not Lucy is ethically justified in taking the stroller. Once she acquires it, she uses it ethically. Lucy understands that objects are made to be used rather than coveted or fetishized, so she lets others use it in whatever way is the most helpful even though it gets "beat up" (153). In contrast to the begrudging sharing of wealth that society engages in through the welfare system, the women are happy to share what little they have. One of the striking things about the novel is that its worldview is a positive one despite the harshness of the characters' lives, and this outlook encourages readers to approach life with hope no matter what their circumstances at the same time as it calls for radical social change, rejecting the status quo that causes the residents' difficulties.

Rituals that help to build a collective identity strengthen Half-a-Life's community. Like an ethnic group, Lucy explains that it even has its own "national dish," pasta, which the women often eat together (95–96). These meals help strengthen the bonds of the community much like the Christian ritual of communion, but without all the sacrificial imagery. The women also hold frequent Scrabble tournaments (26, 212), which show the importance of building camaraderie via leisure-time activities, of the necessity of friendship in community to complement pragmatic exchange.

These communal activities help to create a collective ethic as the women learn from one another. They have a sense of social justice and concern for the oppressed that mirrors the novel's message to readers, which expresses itself in various ways. These include Betty's anger about the disproportionate number of African American men who are incarcerated in the United States (51), Mercy's insistence on reading only "feminist" authors (54), and Lucy's distress about the unjust economics of producing Nike shoes (198–99). The women recognize that their small community is a part of the global community and as a result refuse to be self-centered despite their day-to-day worries. They are often wiser in their view of the world than those who look down on them.

The women's awareness of the world is an important one for institutional Mennonitism to note. Books such as *Summer of My Amazing Luck* can help the institutional church learn how to better interact with the world that it claims to serve. Toews's novel is an effective witness because it focuses on ethics rather than dogma. The book's offering of an ethical vision to readers without the use of religious language makes it a more effective form of ethics than institutional Mennonite fiction, such as that produced by Herald Press, or theology because it is accessible to all readers as an instructive text, not just Christians. Anyone interested in literature can find the novel appealing. Similarly, because of its Mennonite-inflected ethics, the book may appeal to Mennonites who do not read much secular fiction.

Summer of My Amazing Luck illustrates why Mennonite literature is still important for the institutional Mennonite churches in North America despite its authors' frequent positions on the margins or completely outside of the Mennonite faith community. The novel acts as a prophetic theapoetic voice for all of North American society, not just the Mennonite community, and it shows the Mennonite community how to better share its message of social justice with the world.

CHAPTER 5

The Theapoetic Ethics of Speculative Fiction

Like *Summer of My Amazing Luck,* Mennonite speculative fiction interrogates how we relate to the world and offers real-world strategies for how to do so, even when it takes place in outer space. Queer scholar Sami Schalk contends that "*speculative fiction* [is] any creative writing in which the rules of reality do not fully apply, including magical realism, utopian and dystopian literature, fantasy, science fiction, voodoo, ghost stories, and hybrid genres."[1] I can only name a short list of experiences with texts that have fundamentally changed my thinking in my twenty-year scholarly career. Such epiphanies are rare and precious. My encounter with Schalk's definition in early 2019 was one such moment. It gave me a new, broader way of seeing a field that I had studied for the past ten years, showing me how speculative fiction and literature in general offer pathways for living during these apocalyptic times. Reading speculative fiction theapoetically is one of these ways.

It took me a while to experience speculative fiction's theological power. My mother introduced me to the work of C. S. Lewis and J. R. R. Tolkien when I was a boy, and it was clear that I was supposed to glean theological instruction from these texts. Aslan is Jesus and sacrifices himself to save Narnia, Frodo and his friends are willing to sacrifice themselves for the common good and their quest shows that good ultimately triumphs over evil, and so on. Combined with their status as bedtime reading alongside narratives of Mennonite persecution such as Elizabeth Hershberger Bauman's *Coals of Fire* and Barbara Smucker's *Henry's Red Sea*, emphasizing these books' theological aspects erased their speculative ones. I experienced them as realist parables akin to those in the New Testament because their fantastic aspects—talking animals, orcs, sorcery—had the purpose of teaching a specific lesson rather than offering new alternatives for what life might be.

When I became an adult, I continued to neglect speculative fiction because I bought into the literary snobbery that dismissed it as unserious, that said it was drivel for nerdy teenage boys. I cannot name where I acquired this bias, but it was culturally pervasive enough that even when I was actually a nerdy teenage boy (member of my high school chess team, spent most of my money at the local Borders bookstore, six feet tall but only weighed 140 pounds, deathly pale because I never spent time outside, et cetera), I thought it was beneath me. The ubiquity of this societal anti-speculative fiction stance is striking. It is a reaction against the radical ideas the genre often espouses, and a reaction against the anti-capitalist "wasteful[ness]" that Ann Weinstone argues reading the genre entails, as I discuss in chapter 1.[2]

I continued to encounter this bias during my first round of graduate school. My professors assigned a handful of speculative texts: Mary Shelley's *Frankenstein*, Angela Carter's *Nights at the Circus*, *Beowulf*, Margaret Cavendish's *The Blazing World*, and Toni Morrison's *Sula* and *Beloved*.[3] However, because the literary establishment considers these works canonical, class discussions glossed over their speculative elements, divorcing them from the broader context of speculative fiction and forcing them into incongruous relationships with mainstream literature.

But now I think speculative fiction is the most important fictional genre for two reasons. First, in some ways it benefits from its position in the literary hinterland because the lack of attention that results from this status also results in a lack of responsibility to propriety. Independent presses that are more interested in good writing than in mainstream marketability publish most of the books in the field, including all the speculative texts this chapter examines except for Miriam Toews's. This freedom allows the genre to flourish in exciting directions, making space for stories about characters on the margins that often get ignored in big publishers' literary fiction. Second, the genre is especially relevant in ways that realistic fiction is not as I write in a time of pandemic and potential societal collapse. These are times that defy previous notions of what reality can be. Speculative fiction offers models for how to live hopefully in dystopian contexts and visions of what a better, rebuilt society could look like. Whereas most theapoetic work takes daily life as its model, speculative fiction does this while also offering us models for what everyday life might look like once theapoetic ethics are put into place to create a better world. It gives us encouragement to live theapoetically by showing us what the rewards of such a choice might be.

My view of the genre began to change in 2009 when I had my first profound experience with it, which I now view as a theological one, and which is another of the textual epiphanies that has changed the way I see the world. I found Samuel R. Delany's work while studying for my PhD exams. Delany, a gay African American from my hometown, New York City, is the author of more than three dozen books that encompass the genres of memoir, literary criticism, queer theory, comics, and many of speculative fiction's subgenres. I describe my encounter with his work more fully in the next chapter, but for now it is enough to say that his writing affected me because of its consistent ethic of concern for the marginalized. Aside from sympathetically examining the lives of queers and people of color, it also portrays the working class, the unhoused, and those with disabilities as complete beings. It gave me a model for thinking about theological concerns outside of the religious framework I left behind after my college faith crisis. Delany was the spiritual teacher I needed at a time when I was struggling in an unhealthy marriage and getting ready to transition from graduate school to the outside world. I had often found myself thinking theologically in my graduate school papers, feeling compelled to cite various Mennonite theologians, while being frustrated that I was doing so. In hindsight, I realize that it made sense for me to do this because I was still thinking like a Mennonite, which is something I have since acknowledged that I cannot get away from even if I have left much of Mennonite theology behind. Ethics have always been central to Mennonite thought. Delany gave me a way to think ethically without the religious language that I could not reapproach at the time. This pathway made it possible for me to return to a conversation with spirituality in recent years. As a result of Delany's impact, I wanted to read writers that had influenced him, so I began reading speculative fiction seriously and writing about it.

It is no surprise that Delany's work is influential within both speculative fiction and queer theory because the two genres share a desire for a new society. Sofia Samatar draws on queer theory's vision of societal change in all areas to assert that "speculative fiction ... [is] writing queerly" because "it is the genre of change, of expansion."[4] Like poetry, as a queer genre, speculative fiction is also a political genre. Also using "queer's" multiplicity of meanings, Andy Buechel argues for the queerness of another genre, asserting that "*all good theology has always been queer*, even if this way of describing it is new. Christian practice and belief have always been somewhat bizarre."[5] Although

Buechel is not a Mennonite, his idea seems quite Mennonite in that we have always considered ourselves to be outsiders from both the world and other Christian traditions, and we have a long history of being persecuted because of this position. Mennonitism is a third way that is "neither Catholic nor Protestant," according to Walter Klaassen's famous formulation.[6] Following this line of thinking, theapoetics, theology that impacts everyday life, should be off the beaten track, incomprehensible to those who hold the mainstream values that speculative fiction resists. Examining the queer-theology relationship from the other direction, Melissa E. Sanchez speculates that queer theory can use "theology as a theoretical resource" to examine the "secular."[7] Rather than staying within the boundaries of theology, Sanchez suggests that queer theorists use theology as a method rather than a religious act, expanding its work in queer ways just as theapoetics does.

The hybridity Samatar's, Buechel's, and Sanchez's statements exemplify falls within Schalk's definition of speculative fiction and is also one of queer theory's most important concepts for revisioning society. Queerness is messy, it is skeptical of boundaries, it seeks space where new ideas can grow unencumbered by rigid restrictions. Therefore, I wonder what the hybrid space between autotheorizing and theologizing that *Ethics for Apocalyptic Times* tries to inhabit can look like. What of the "theo" in "theory"? Where are elements of the Divine ("theo") in academic prose? Although "theology" and "theory" do not come from the same root despite their shared first four letters, the *Oxford English Dictionary* (*OED*) gives one obsolete definition of "theory" as "a spectacle which has a spiritual effect or provides insight into spiritual matters."[8] Theory is a way of viewing the world just as theology is; it is a form of secular devotion. Or, from the other direction, theology is theory about the Divine. Speculative fiction is a kind of theory that can sometimes be a kind of theology, a theapoetics. Like bisexual me, it goes in multiple directions. It is interested in the fantastic kind of "spectacles" that the *OED* names. Like the rest of the genre, Mennonite speculative fiction occupies the space that Magdalene Redekop names when she argues that "the best art ... happens at the crossing places where ... different visions of community are contested."[9] These intersections are queer and speculative because they are sites where hybridity can occur.

Schalk writes that speculative fiction uses a strategy of "defamiliarization" to cause readers to see "familiar thing[s]" in new ways. This approach helps speculative fiction to function as theory by spurring readers to think about ways our reality could be different.[10] Regarding defamiliarization, Jeff Gundy writes that "art, poetry, and theopoetics dwell on this ground of making strange, bringing us back to the uncertainty and oddity of the most familiar things."[11] Once again, there is overlap between speculative fiction and theapoetics. Perhaps unexpectedly, Schalk's definition stretches to include spiritual practices via its inclusion of a particular faith tradition, voodoo, thereby embracing hybridity. She includes these practices under the broad term "creative writing." Therefore, she queers the genre of "speculative *fiction*" (my emphasis), opening it up to include other genres of writing within it. This definition gives us a pathway by which to consider speculative fiction as theology when we consider the theapoetic view of theology as a genre of writing.

THE BODY IN FOUR PARTS AS EARLY MENNONITE SPECULATIVE FICTION

Janet Kauffman's fiction is a good starting place for speculative Mennonite thinking. Robert Zacharias observes that "it resonates strongly with contemporary" Mennonite writing.[12] Kauffman was the first Mennonite writer from the United States to achieve prolonged success in the broader literary community, with her books finding homes at prestigious publishers. Alfred A. Knopf published her short story collections *Places in the World a Woman Could Walk* and *Obscene Gestures for Women* and her novel *Collaborators*, and Graywolf Press published her story collection *Characters on the Loose* and her novel *The Body in Four Parts*. Both Mennonite and non-Mennonite literary critics published essays on her work in the 1990s.[13] Unfortunately, as Zacharias notes, her work has disappeared off the radar in the last twenty years.[14] The time has come to reexamine it.

For instance, *The Body in Four Parts* portrays topics that are now important subjects in queer theory such as gender fluidity, interspecies interactions, and sexual pleasure through a feminist lens. The novel is queer-as-in-weird in general because its events are so hard to pin down. It is about four adult siblings, but very little of it is straightforward—there isn't really a plot—which give the queer-as-in-sexually-and-politically bits equal weight with everything else as the novel focuses on playing with language. It acknowledges its abstractness and the fallibility of language in general. The narrator, who is the book's main character in that she is present for all of its action, but who remains mysterious throughout because the book never names her and gives no details about her other than her relationship to her siblings, observes, "Words in the air, what are they? Words in the air! Suspended things, like stars.... They're outdated, old when the light reaches us, some of them already long gone."¹⁵ The novel's resulting lack of solidity makes it feel like a long prose poem. It queers genre.

The Body in Four Parts's treatment of gender mirrors its genre fluidity. The book frequently questions the gender of certain characters. These passages do not take up much space. They are tiny little openings for queerness that the text does not highlight, so they haunt it instead. For instance, a nonsibling character, Joseph, claims he has been reincarnated many times and says that he can remember some of his previous lives, including as a woman (56). Although he has apparently always been a man in his present incarnation, his memories of his multiple selves dissolve the boundaries of his corporeal body, queering it. One of the siblings, Jean-Paul, also has a gender that won't stand still. Four-fifths of the way through the novel, the narrator directly addresses readers about this issue, telling us that we ask, "Is he [Jean-Paul] a man?" This is "a good question. How can he be, as he is, housed in a body with girl breasts and woman-hard heart" (99–100). Regardless of the use of "he," the narrator's answer implies that Jean-Paul is queer in some way, whether he is intersex, or nonbinary, or trans, or some other term that he chooses not to give us. Part of the lack of plot is that the characters hardly get described, so we do not get a sense of what they might look like, whereas in most other novels the fact that someone named Jean-Paul has a woman's breasts would be stated early on as an important characteristic. The novel's lack of physical description means that its hints at queerness stand without further information in one direction or another. Jean-Paul, who is somehow listening to the conversation between readers and the narrator, dismisses our question, saying, "Mine is the body you dare not interrogate, dare not, without invitation, touch, and what you don't touch, sweetheart, you don't know anything about" (100). His statement reinforces the novel's opacity while at the same time asserting that knowledge begins in the body, a queer notion. The narrator then says that Jean-Paul does have a "penis, balls," and further complicates things by noting that he is not a native English speaker (although his siblings apparently are, or at least do not have his difficulties with English), so what he says about himself is ambiguous and we cannot trust it (100). Again, the novel leaves us with language's fallibility. This fallibility may induce feelings of helplessness in some readers, but from a queer perspective, it indicates an openness that offers space for radical change to occur.

The Body in Four Parts pushes the fluidity of its gender portrayals even further by giving some of its characters other-than-human attributes. The narrator tells us that her sister Dorothea is "a fluid thing" who may not be human and that "she had this swamp heritage, I suppose. She was a metamorphoser," implying that Dorothea might be a mermaid or some other hybrid water creature (3–4).[16] One way queer theory interrogates societal norms is by conversing with the field of animal studies to question traditional models of human relationship with other species, arguing for a kind of equality that recognizes the benefits of cooperative relationships between humans and other animals.[17] Viewed through this lens, Dorothea's mermaidishness does not make her monstrous, lower than human, but makes her an exemplar of queer hybridity, as she is able to inhabit the human realm on land and the piscine realm in water. Indeed, she has superheroic qualities that invite comparisons to Aquaman, as she can traverse even the smallest waterways with great speed, apparently by shapeshifting. Although the novel does not spend time analyzing Dorothea's hybridity, it is significant that the narrator names her aquatic characteristics on the first two pages because such naming alerts readers to the importance of queer themes throughout the book. We immediately see that we are reading an unconventional story.

The novel also blurs the human boundaries of two other siblings, Jack and Jean-Paul. Jack is like another superhero, the Invisible Woman, in that he "is invisible, entirely, he's nothing but air" (100). Like Dorothea's superheroic resemblance, Jack's crosses gender, yet another example of their queerness. Jean-Paul also resembles another member of the Fantastic Four, the Human Torch, because his hair is literally "fire" (114, 118). The brothers are hybrids like Dorothea, reminding readers that humans do not exist in a species vacuum. Although each sibling represents one of the basic elements (the "four parts" of the title; the narrator is earth),[18] and thus readers might be tempted to read the descriptions of Dorothea, Jack, and Jean-Paul metaphorically, they are described mimetically, so readers are supposed to understand them as being possible within the novel's world.

The novel's third queer theme is much more concrete than the first two. Its portrayals of sexual pleasure encompass its human and other-than-human characters as well as queer and straight sex. The narrator introduces the most significant nonsibling character, a fishmonger named Margaretta, early in the book as a sexual guru for the community. Margaretta "improve[s]" the town's "lovemaking" just by talking with her customers (8). Her own sex life includes partners of multiple genders, and the narrator describes her admiringly as "wholly sexual" because she acknowledges her body, unlike most people (35–36). Within the queer context of the novel, this is not an essentialist description that reduces her to a sexual object. Instead, it celebrates how she embraces her sexuality as a healthy part of life, refusing patriarchal notions of sexual propriety. Like Lish in *Summer of My Amazing Luck*, Margaretta seeks sexual pleasure freely. *The Body in Four Parts* celebrates this ethic.

There is also a sex scene in a short story by Dorothea (24–26). This scene is extra noticeable because of how it is printed. It is handwritten rather than set in type, which is another way the novel plays with genre expectations. Although the scene is between a woman and a man, it takes place in the belly of a whale, so it also replicates the queer human-animal hybridity Dorothea epitomizes and references other queer narratives that also play with genre, such as Herman Melville's *Moby-Dick*. The sexual elements of *The Body in Four Parts* might not seem remarkable now, but Kauffman was only the second Mennonite fiction writer to write frankly about sex, and the first to do so successfully, as Rudy Wiebe's 1983 attempt *My Lovely Enemy* received legendarily poor reviews.[19] They therefore represent an important touchstone in the genesis of the queer Mennonite writing that has flourished over the past decade or so. They exemplify Molly Remer's theapoetic "lived experiences as legitimate sources of direct, or divine, revelation," asking Mennonites to think queerly about gender and sexuality.

Even though speculative fiction often takes place in other worlds and is always in some way "unrealistic," just like queer theory it has a vision that directly relates to the real world because it believes the real world can be better. This is also a Mennonite ideal. When the first Anabaptists gathered to rebaptize each other in 1525, they did so because they believed it was possible to change society. The same kind of hope is present in *The Body in Four Parts*.

THE ETHICS OF LISTENING IN GREG BECHTEL'S "SMUT STORIES"

Just as *The Body in Four Parts* queers genre, Greg Bechtel's interrelated series of speculative short stories from his 2014 collection *Boundary Problems*, "The Smut Story (I)," "The Smut Story (II)," and "The Smut Story (III)," examines the nature of stories themselves and how we should encounter and interpret them. They offer a theapoetic example of how those on different sides of any fractious community issue might approach one another.

In an interview with Samatar, Bechtel, an ethnic Mennonite, acknowledges that "a Mennonite influence shows up" in his writing even though he is not a theological Mennonite. One way this background reveals itself in his writing is that he thinks about his work in ethical terms. He tells Samatar that having a "sense of uncertainty" when crafting stories is "an ethical necessity" to keep from "oversimplify[ing]" his characters and their perspectives.[20] The "Smut Stories" teach us that the sense of uncertainty Bechtel mentions is essential for us as readers or hearers of stories to maintain as well. Taking this approach allows us to be open to what we might hear instead of forcing narratives to fit our preconceived notions of them.

One helpful aspect of Bechtel's stories is that they model talking to a different tradition through their interaction with non-Mennonite speculative fiction. I first encountered Bechtel's book as a piece of Mennonite literature, but what draws me to write about it is that it takes me out of the tradition to other valuable texts that I have found in my continuing search for narratives that speak to me. "The Smut Story (III)" begins with an epigraph from the Canadian science fiction writer Candas Jane Dorsey's 1996 essay "Being One's Own Pornographer."[21] When I saw this epigraph, I got tremendously excited because Dorsey's essay, which I first came across while doing research on Delany for my dissertation, is one of the best pieces of literary criticism I have ever read. Dorsey devotes much of the essay to discussing some of Delany's sexually explicit fiction, especially his 1994 novel *The Mad Man*. *The Mad Man* is one of the most Mennonite texts I have ever read in terms of its insistence on paying attention to those on the margins of society, as I discuss in the next chapter. Dorsey's essay responds to Delany's willingness to confront seemingly taboo subjects, and Bechtel's stories respond to Dorsey's essay by also advocating this openness. "Being One's Own Pornographer" is also the title of the mysterious story by Bechtel's character Boop that I discuss below.[22] Bechtel's references to Dorsey and the Bechtel-Dorsey-Delany-Mennonite connection illustrate the theapoetic principle that we never know where stories that impact us will come from, so we need to have the openness that the "Smut Stories" advocate.

Bechtel asserts to Samatar that Mennonitism and speculative fiction share similarities because they both emphasize "a certain *in-the-world-but-not-of-the-world* . . . self-consciously alienated from the mainstream" outlook.[23] This is the case in the "Smut Stories" because their narrators all belong to groups on the fringes of their societies. One of speculative fiction's strengths is that it offers visions for what the world can be rather than of what it is. The "Smut Stories" do this in their narrative slipperiness, which functions as a kind of openness, and in their characters' insistence on loving actions, especially in "The Smut Story II" and "The Smut Story III." The stories are speculative in that they take place partly in the future, offering hope that society will develop into a more just environment than it is currently.

Bechtel sprinkles the three stories throughout *Boundary Problems*. There are two unrelated stories between each of the "Smut Stories." "The Smut Story (III)" is the third story in the collection, "The Smut Story (II)" is the sixth story, and "The Smut Story (I)" is the ninth story, the second-to-last one in the book. The placement of the stories at seemingly random spots in the book rather than side by side immediately teaches readers that encountering stories requires hard work for us to get their news. The "Smut Stories" do not make sense individually, but only when read as a whole.

The stories' misleading titles further complicate their larger narrative. "The Smut Story (III)" is actually the first of the stories printed, and its events take place before those in the other two stories even though it is numbered "III" rather than "I." Likewise, "The Smut Story (I)" is the last of the three stories printed in the collection and is the concluding one of the set plot-wise even though it is numbered "I." On the surface, this misnumbering of the stories might appear as an annoying postmodern gimmick. However, aside from being a subtle nod to the notion that "the last shall be first" and "the first shall be last" in one of the stories' numerous Biblical allusions (Matthew 19:30), it also suggests that sometimes stories reorder our world if we let them, and we need to be open to this possibility as readers. The process of piecing the three stories together is a reminder that we must be an active listener or reader to do a story justice.

The three stories illustrate the diversity that terms such as "narrative" or "story" signify because they each use the form of a different genre. "The Smut Story (III)" is a transcript of a 2010 press conference, "The Smut Story (II)" is a personal letter written in 2015 (recall that this date was in the future when the story was published), and "The Smut Story (I)" is an excerpt from an introduction to a new edition of a collection of scholarly essays called *The Smut Story* published in 2059. The varied generic nature of the stories teaches us that we need to keep an open mind about what a story might entail. We may think we know what the story will be, and this close-mindedness leads to an inability to have a theapoetic experience. But when we set aside preconceived notions, we allow room for transformation to occur.

The titles of the stories also play with readers' expectations because they are not actually explicitly "smut[ty]." At their core, the three stories are all about trying to determine what happened during the "Mother's Day Affair," an open mic reading at an Edmonton coffeehouse in 2009 (50). The press conference in "The Smut Story (III)" is about its aftermath, the letter that is the second story is an attempt by one of the audience members to describe the reading to his then-infant daughter, and the essay collection introduced in "The Smut Story (I)" examines how the events of that night have spawned a movement of people known as "Smutsters," who hold rituals that mimic the reading (169n). The central element of the reading is a story told by someone that the stories refer to variously as "T.," "Tia," or "Tio" Boop (50, 104, 166). Although there is general agreement that Boop's story included erotic elements—it is the "smut story" of the title—audience members are unable to agree about the content of the story. Therefore, Boop's narrative itself never actually gets included in the three stories. The hearers cannot reproduce a definitive version of the story because they are all awestruck by Boop's body, which is so dazzling that it transcends gender (53). Boop's uncategorizable body epitomizes speculative fiction's theapoetic queerness because its ambiguity allows all Smutsters to see themselves in Boop's image, just as feminist and queer theology insists that the Divine contains all genders and no gender. Boop's beauty and subsequent vanishing before any of the audience members can ask Boop about their story echoes Jesus's quick disappearance in Luke 24 after revealing himself to several followers on the road to Emmaus. No one ever sees Boop again, but Boop's story is so inspirational that some of its hearers decide to move in together and live in community (106). From this original community, which is reminiscent of the early Christian community in Acts 2, the Smutster movement develops over the next fifty years.

The Smutsters are very much like a faith community in two ways.[24] First, they hold meticulously choreographed rituals that commemorate and mimic the 2009 reading where Boop appeared. As a part of these readings, the group always leaves a spot open where Boop's story would occur with the hope that Boop will reappear (169–70n.). This practice alludes to the practice of leaving an empty chair for Elijah during a Passover Seder. This element of the "Smut Stories" is significant because it reminds us that we never know where or when a representative of the Divine might appear, so we must practice openness to others rather than being close-mindedly dogmatic.

Sadly, the second way the Smutster movement is akin to a faith community is that conflicts among Smutsters about the proper ways to observe their rituals lead to schisms within the movement (170n.). The "Smut Stories" are about trying to reconstruct a story that is central to a movement that it inspires and the conflict within the movement that result from squabbles regarding this reconstruction. The Smutsters are akin to Mennonites in that rather than bonding together over their belief in the importance of a founding event, they split up into factions who squabble about doctrine.[25] As John Ruth wryly observes in *Mennonite Identity and Literary Art*, one of the essential elements of the Mennonite "stor[y]" is "the apparently inevitable Mennonite schismatic process."[26] The question therefore becomes, if this fragmenting must happen, how can we do it in a healthy way? The model of open listening found in the "Smut Stories" might not lead to reconciliation in all cases, but it can at least lead to more peaceful breaking apart, or enable healthy conversation after the separations.

Aside from Bechtel's Biblical allusions evincing the stories' Mennonite character, these allusions reveal that the stories are, in a sense, a retelling of the Christian story. Their speculative nature encourages speculation about what the Christian community could be like if it were more open to present-day prophets. The name of the central character of "The Smut Story (I)," Eva, who is the addressee of the letter from the second story and the one responsible for the coagulation of the Smutster movement via her propagation of the story of the "Mother's Day Affair," is significant because it points to the possibility of a new beginning by referencing the first Biblical woman, Eve. Eva's farm symbolizes this new beginning. It includes "a spacious garden ... [with] fruit-bearing trees," and a lack of "fences" around it (168n.). The Smutsters and their primary antagonist, Peter Smith, reconcile there (174n.). The farm is like a revised, healed Garden of Eden, open to everyone. It reminds us as readers that a better future is possible despite our currently fallen state.

Similarly, two of Boop's possible names, "Tia" and "Tio," are Spanish for "aunt" and "uncle," which is significant in the stories because Boop's narrative leads to the creation of a family, the Smutsters. The "Smut Stories" do not offer a completely utopian vision because there are the schisms among the Smutsters, but they do argue that a more peaceful way of being in community is possible.

"The Smut Story (I)," the essay collection introduction that is the last of the three stories printed, also teaches through its form that true listening requires a willingness to offer a hearing to all perspectives on an issue. The story is ten pages long, but sixteen footnotes take up more than half of it. The main text takes up nineteen inches of page space while the notes take up thirty-six inches even though they are a smaller font size. Furthermore, the content of the notes is more interesting than the body of the story itself because they contain the history of the Smutster movement, an essential element of the stories. Without these footnotes, the three stories' shared narrative falls apart, so it is necessary for readers to take the time to peruse them. This deliberateness is a key component of the listening ethic the stories advocate. Similarly, Mennonite understandings of Jesus traditionally emphasize the necessity of being on the margins of society, of being in the world but not of it. "The Smut Story (I)" reminds us that being on the margins is an exciting place to be because it allows us to see the world in a way that those ensconced in the center cannot, as long as we are open to doing so. Bechtel's stories teach us the kind of deliberate listening that facilitates this kind of seeing.

SOFIA SAMATAR'S DYSTOPIAN THEAPOETICS

Speculative fiction's queer envisioning of a new society is especially relevant during a time of pandemic. Much dystopian speculative fiction works to warn readers what actions are necessary to prevent such dystopias from happening and thus might not feel relevant to this time when the dystopia is here. But Samatar's short story "Honey Bear" offers a model for how to live in a dystopia in a way that tries to build a better society out of the rubble, one action at a time. The story takes place after a planet-changing event that reads like a metaphor for climate change because most "animals" and "many plant species" have gone extinct and the human birth rate has plummeted.[27] Samatar writes about her dread of the climate change apocalypse in a 2021 essay, "Standing at the Ruins," that acknowledges the pandemic is but the beginning of our troubles. She feels "a sense of planetary mourning" when thinking about climate change and turns to literature to help her comprehend these feelings because she "need[s] everything to face the future . . . all the facets of [her] experience."[28] Literature is an essential part of her survival kit because it teaches her how to deal with apocalypse. The essay's reading of pieces such as Imru al-Qays's *Muallaqa*, the Old English poem "The Wanderer," and *Frankenstein* is therefore theapoetic. The essay offers directions for how to deal with the emotions our apocalyptic reality causes by showing us how literature can provide succor and begs us to change our ways so that this reality does not continue to get worse. If the pandemic is not a sign that the planet is trying to rid itself of humanity because we continue to act as a virus upon it, then I don't know what is. If we do not take immediate action to heal our relationship with Earth so that we can continue to coexist with it, catastrophes even worse than the pandemic will be the result.

In "Honey Bear," the "Fair Folk" invade Earth and create a situation that has many similarities to pandemic life, especially its early days.[29] For instance, there is no air travel anymore (63), and the Fair Folk's waste is poisonous in ways that are not fully understood (58), so there is always a fear of contact with them, and humans who live with them are social outcasts whom government agents must interact with while wearing masks and hazmat suits (57, 65–66). Like *The Body in Four Parts*, "Honey Bear" investigates human hybridity with other species. The Fair Folk invade because "they don't seem able to raise their own children" and thus need other species to do so (67). For most of the story Honey Bear appears to be a human child, but readers find out she is not when she nurses by biting her human mother's armpit "with her teeth [while] . . . her longer, hollow teeth come down and sink in" like a vampire's (67). Honey Bear's mother makes a free choice to parent a Fair Folk child despite this painful feeding process and the "decrease in life expectancy" that it entails (62). Her mothering is a disability, but she accepts this change in her body to save Honey Bear, rejecting ableism's deification of long life and becoming a futuristic Mennonite martyr.[30] Like the mothers in *Summer of My Amazing Luck*, Honey Bear's mother uses her decision and her consistently positive outlook to teach an ethic of care for the Other. The full societal effects of the pandemic remain unknown and may cause some kind of societal collapse. But "Honey Bear" reminds us that our treatment of others still makes a difference.

Samatar's 2017 essay "The Scope of This Project" is an essential theapoetic companion to her queer speculative ethics because it shows how Mennonite literary studies can make these ethics decolonial as well. It is an example of Mennonite literary thinking that has relevance for the broader Mennonite community. "The Scope of This Project" develops the concept of "postcolonial Mennonite literature," which

> means work by Mennonite writers of the postcolony. It means work by writers from Asia, Africa, and Latin America. It means the literary production of those regions where the Mennonite church is largest. It means the writing of the majority. It also means the work of minority writers in North America, of black, Latinx, and [I]ndigenous Mennonites, whom I include in the postcolony, not only because they are marginalized members of settler states but because, historically, they came to the Mennonite community through a process of missionary outreach. Only a constellation of all of these writers would allow us to speak of global Mennonite literature.[31]

In her memoir, Samatar speculates about archiving this literature, imagining herself editing anthologies "in which Mennonites of color are not referred to in parentheses, in which the global majority is not a special issue.... Reading th[ese] book[s], you will not wonder whether all the Mennonites of color have disappeared from the face of the earth" like it is often possible to do within the field.[32]

"The Scope of This Project" is ripe for exploration by theologians and literary critics alike. Its emphasis on the global Mennonite community rather than North America is one that North American Mennonites should take heed of because learning to think decolonially would help eradicate Mennonites' racism. Theologians can especially learn from the above passage because it works just as well with the words "theologians" and "theology" substituted for "writers" and "literature." Theapoetics reminds us that theologians are themselves writers because theology is a kind of writing,[33] so Samatar's essay asserts itself into Mennonite theological discourse. It does so explicitly by naming "hymns" (by which Samatar means songs sung in church, not more narrowly the genre found in books such as *The Mennonite Hymnal*) as a starting point for the study of postcolonial Mennonite literature because all Mennonite communities use them.[34] Hymns epitomize theapoetics because of their literature-music hybridity. "The Scope of This Project" exemplifies successful queer decolonial thinking because it offers a clear path for making Mennonite studies and the Mennonite community as a whole more inclusive. We just need to take it.

On the surface, another of Samatar's stories, "Fallow" is a piece of stereotypical science fiction in that it takes place in space in a dystopian future. The story takes its name from the Mennonite community that it portrays, which its residents establish on a planet located hundreds of years of flying time away from Earth (213). The community's ancestors leave Earth because of increasingly apocalyptic times that no longer allow them to practice their pacifism. This is the traditional Mennonite displacement narrative, which the story illustrates by recalling how "the hills of Pennsylvania replaced the lost hills of Germany and the wheat fields of Saskatchewan those of Russia" for Mennonite migrants of the past (260). Writer Armin Wiebe remarks that "Mennonites spent 450 years trying to escape from the world, but now there is no place left to escape to."[35] Similarly, in one of the more famous passages in Mennonite fiction, a character in Rudy Wiebe's *The Blue Mountains of China* says with much accuracy "'You know the trouble with Mennonites? They've always wanted to be Jews. To have land God had given them for their very own, to which they were called.... They are still trying to find it, and it isn't anywhere on earth.'"³⁶ "Fallow" offers a possibility that neither Wiebe considers. Like "Request for an Extension on the *Clarity*," it plays with the question of what Mennonitism might look like if we no longer had to be "in the world but not of it" and could actually be out of the world instead. Fallow's members hope their descendants can return to Earth someday, but they will only be able to return after it is no longer the "world" in the theological sense: they will go back once their supercomputer that monitors Earth tells them the planet has been free of humans for "five hundred years" (214). They will become the chosen people by default as the only people left.

"Fallow" does not actually include the word "Mennonite," however. Instead, it contains a number of details that reveal itself as Mennonite to Mennonite readers or to readers who take the time to do some research. Several of these details are historical facts. Aside from the migrations mentioned above, the narrator names Jan van Leyden and Claas Epp as "misguided prophets" from her community's past (235). As I explain elsewhere, "van Leyden was the leader of the Anabaptist Münsterite uprising in 1534–35, and Epp led Mennonites who believed Jesus's return was imminent on the 'Great Trek' from Russia to Turkmenistan in 1880."³⁷ Other terms and activities are also Mennonite markers if one is familiar with Mennonite history and thought. For instance, the words "ARBEITE UND HOFFE" (German for "work and hope") are written over a schoolyard gate (207, Samatar's capitalization). This is the phrase made famous as the caption of the etching of a man digging on the cover page of the *Martyrs Mirror*.³⁸ The narrator says that her teacher, Miss Snowfall, practices "*yieldedness*" (226, Samatar's emphasis), which is the English translation of "gelassenheit," the Mennonite practice of erasing oneself in favor of the community. An act that outsiders frequently associate with Mennonites, "shunn[ing]," occurs in Fallow (229), but, in contrast to Mennonite history, "schisms" do not (231). The story's Mennonite references give an extra message to insiders. I focus on its Mennonite aspects because I am examining the story as theological writing. I agree with Robert Zacharias that "Fallow" is ultimately a hopeful story that shows "a willingness to fight for a broader Mennonite future."³⁹ Although it is an excellent work aesthetically that non-Mennonite readers can enjoy, its Mennonite elements are what make me want to write about it.

Abigail Carl-Klassen observes that "the strong collective impulse of Mennonite theology and culture is reflected in its literature."⁴⁰ This is the case in

"Fallow," which interrogates the Mennonite community's policing of its borders and advocates for it to make space for artists, people of color, queers, and other outsiders. As I write in *Queering Mennonite Literature*, one of Fallow's improvements over present-day institutional Mennonitism is that it accepts sexually queer members. Similarly, Zacharias explains Fallow's inclusion of ancestries from all over Earth.[41] This welcoming is one way the story offers proactive steps for improvement rather than warning readers away from possible dystopian outcomes if our ways do not change.

Unfortunately, Fallow's openness to different ethnicities and multiple sexualities is its only redeeming characteristic because it otherwise fits all the negative stereotypes of strict Mennonite communities that punish those who do not conform. "Fallow" depicts four rebellious characters and how the community silences them as a metaphor for the hypocritical violence Mennonite institutions (especially Mennonite Church USA and Mennonite Church Canada, but other institutions—colleges, mission organizations, and so on—share culpability) inflict on those who are not straight white men because of these institutions' focus on perpetuating their power rather than on adhering to nonviolent principles. Samatar names each of the story's three sections for one of these characters, and they are told by the fourth, Agar.

The first section tells stories about Agar's favorite teacher, Miss Snowfall. Agar loves Miss Snowfall because her "one goal seemed to be to whip [students'] imaginations into a frenzy" (207). In a 2022 personal essay, Samatar uses a similar tone to describe one of her Goshen professors, the poet Nick Lindsay. She describes his unconventional poetry workshops and writes that "part of the joy of studying with Nick, for me, was the easing of a certain pressure, a sense of being out of place so constant it became unremarkable, like the cold in winter."[42] In contrast to the racist anthropology professor in "Request for an Extension on the *Clarity*," who makes the narrator feel even more like an outsider, Samatar describes Lindsay as someone who helped her learn how to find community with other outsiders. This is what Miss Snowfall does for Agar. Therefore, Miss Snowfall might be considered another of the Mennonite elements in "Fallow." Instead of following the prescribed curriculum, she teaches her students to think for themselves and develop their gifts. She tells Agar, "'You can be a writer'" and that "'writing is a noble pursuit'"—another Lindsay echo—which is a phrase that Agar says "sounded awkward, as words do when they have never been said before" (220). The story names the traditional Mennonite view of art as sinful and of writers as "liars and rascals" and then works against it through Agar's act of writing.

Predictably, the settlement's leaders strip Miss Snowfall of her teaching post. She chooses to hang herself rather than acquiesce to Fallow's authority over her life, refusing to agree with its ways just because it is bigger than her. Agar makes a Mennonite move by celebrating Miss Snowfall's martyrdom, offering her as an example of how to help others by recognizing them as unique persons rather than as faceless congregants.

The second section in "Fallow" is about Brother Lookout, who used to be the settlement's archivist. He sins against the community by being part of the "Young Evangelists," a group who wanted to return to Earth to proselytize to the humans that remained rather than keeping the truth locked up in Fallow. Their viewpoint illustrates the "trouble" that Rudy Wiebe names and that the settlement's leaders embrace. Believing one group is "chosen" by God implies that God rejects everyone else. The Young Evangelists refuse this view, arguing that Mennonite beliefs should be available to anyone who chooses them. They agree with the early Anabaptists and present-day Mennonites that church membership should be voluntary, but Fallow loses sight of this principle and functions as a state church instead. Agar must undertake her own archiving effort to piece together Brother Lookout's story because Fallow censors it. She preserves it "as a kind of rescue" because she believes there should be room for everyone in the community like the Young Evangelists (242).

The third section is about Agar's sister Temar, who, like her Biblical almost-namesake Tamar in 2 Samuel 13, suffers violence in the home. Temar's father beats her because she questions community standards and because she values formal education, and he is a stereotypical Mennonite farmer who does not see its worth (230–31). Temar calls out her father's hypocrisy, which is a microcosm of Fallow's, when she asks him one evening "'How can a man call himself a pacifist while he beats a girl with a hose?'" (244). There is a long history of writers asking this question about Mennonite domestic violence, most notably in the early work of Di Brandt and Patrick Friesen.[43] Instead of trying to reconcile herself with the community that has produced such a man, Temar leaves Fallow with an Earthling whose spaceship has accidentally landed there. The section's epigraph, "*This world is not my home*" (248, Samatar's emphasis), repeats the traditional Mennonite sentiment that "Fallow" investigates throughout, except that there is a twist because the world that Temar leaves is a Mennonite one. As a theocracy, Fallow has become the "world" theologically. Temar answers the story's question of what Mennonitism would look like if it no longer had to be in the world with the argument that it would remain flawed. "Fallow" therefore makes the argument that we should interact with the world to make it a better place instead of shunning it. This interaction creates a theapoetic space in which we may encounter the Divine.

"Temar" also means "to be obsessed with" in Spanish. Agar's obsession with writing the history of her fellow rebels even though Fallow discourages such activity is an act of resistance. She knows her work will probably be destroyed because of its unorthodoxy instead of being accepted into the archives (261). The community views writing as wasteful because it doesn't seem to do anything; it is unclear what it adds to Fallow's society. But, with Weinstone, Agar knows it has value. She writes as an act of love for those she documents and for the community itself. "Fallow" celebrates Agar's attempt to change the community from within by writing about its outsiders as just as valid as Miss Snowfall's and Temar's decisions to leave. A combination of these strategies is necessary for change.

CASEY PLETT'S TRANS THEAPOETICS

Among the many Mennonite speculative fiction writers, Casey Plett joins Samatar as the most prominent.[44] In light of Samatar's definition of speculative fiction as queer, it is no surprise that Mennonite speculative fiction overlaps with sexually queer Mennonite literature. Indeed, four of the nine texts I examine in *Queering Mennonite Literature* are speculative because the two traditions entwine with each other in an embrace as the vanguard of current Mennonite literature.[45] One of these texts is Plett's 2014 short story collection *A Safe Girl to Love*. Many of the book's stories investigate trans characters' queer relationships with other humans.[46] "Portland, Oregon" also examines a queer relationship, albeit not a sexual one: that between the human Adrienne and the talking cat, Glen, who makes the story speculative fiction. Like several of *A Safe Girl to Love*'s other stories, "Portland, Oregon" examines sex work via Adrienne's job driving sex workers to their outcalls. I situate the story within the collection because this context gives the story its defamiliarizing force. Although it shares similarities with other stories in the book and with Plett's 2018 novel *Little Fish*, it is the collection's only speculative narrative, which causes it to stand out and entice readers to pay extra attention to it.[47] For instance, when I teach the book, "Portland, Oregon" gets the most enthusiastic response, and lots of students think that Glen deserves his own novel.

The story's epigraph immediately hints at its speculative nature by referencing dreaming, a speculative endeavor. It is a quotation from the last chapter of Toews's hit novel *A Complicated Kindness*: "Life being what it is, one dreams not of revenge. One just dreams."[48] This sentiment gives readers a sense of optimism as we begin "Portland, Oregon" because of the potential for new things that daydreaming entails. Its hopefulness is especially apparent for readers who have read *A Complicated Kindness* because the quotation is a revision of Paul Gauguin's statement "LIFE BEING WHAT IT IS, ONE DREAMS OF REVENGE," which the novel's narrator, Nomi, says is her "favourite quote" earlier in the book.[49] Nomi's willingness to exchange revenge for hope by the end of her story even though her life has not gotten better is an ethical choice. *A Complicated Kindness* is heartbreaking, just as "Portland, Oregon" is heartbreaking, but they both end with the possibility that life will get better for their characters. The epigraph's extra layer of meaning, one that many Mennonite readers are able to notice, makes the story an explicitly Mennonite one just like "Fallow" and Toews's *Women Talking*, even though none of its characters are Mennonite. Its Mennonite character reminds us to read it theologically as well as aesthetically.

"Portland, Oregon" contains little action. Adrienne gets home from her unnamed day job exhausted, gratefully goes on driving assignments at night because she is desperate for the pay, neglects Glen because of her lack of sleep; rinse, repeat. The story derives its impact from Glen's thoughts about his relationship with Adrienne, which is difficult, although it is much better than that with his previous owners, from whom he escaped.

Aside from being a way to get us to think about Adrienne's plight from different angles, which I discuss below, Glen's status as a cat places "Portland, Oregon" in the field of animal studies alongside *The Body in Four Parts*. It therefore causes us to think about our relationship with nature. The question of how humans relate to the natural world is now more important than ever in a time of impending climate change apocalypse. Jack Halberstam observes that "transgenderism has long been situated as a site of futurity and utopian/dystopian potential."[50] Glen and Adrienne's relationship offers an example of how it might get closer to utopian if we take Glen's actions into account and work on adapting ourselves to nature rather than forcing it to conform to our destructive desires. The housemates are both genuinely interested in each other and care about their community of two. This interspecies dialogue acts as a metaphor for concern for the Other, and it challenges the distorted relationships that have led to present crises.

Adrienne also tries to build connections with the women she chauffeurs. Another story in the collection, "Not Bleak," includes a trans woman, Lish,[51] describing "reuniting with some girl who drove for her when she escorted in the nineties" and the "driver-girl's old cat" to that story's narrator (174). *A Safe Girl to Love* thereby reveals that the escort service's employees are trans. Adrienne is also trans. It is unclear whether she knew any of the women before she began driving—perhaps she acquired the job through a connection with one—but they become a community for her once she is driving, and she "worr[ies]" about them (113). Although the job is tiring and dangerous, the solidarity Adrienne feels with the other women is one way the story argues for the ethical importance of welcoming communities.

"Portland, Oregon" is also a story about addiction and abuse. Adrienne drinks frequently when she is home, and when she forgets to feed Glen, her most important function as his owner, she falls into the common abuser cycle of promising it will never happen again and then relapsing quickly into her abusive behavior (e.g., 103, 107). However, the story differs from other narratives that depict such situations because of the twist that Glen provides as a cat rather than as another human. Society abuses Adrienne with its transphobia, putting her in an economically precarious position, and she passes this abuse onto Glen because of her lack of sleep due to working two jobs, at least one of which is high stress because of society's persecution of sex work. Therefore, in contrast to other narratives where the abuser is clearly the villain, in "Portland, Oregon" Adrienne is less so because her transphobic, misogynist, sex-negative context imprisons her. As a parent of three cats, I am horrified by how she fails to feed Glen sometimes and do not mean to justify her neglect at all. She retains agency over, and thus responsibility for, her actions. But the story's use of a cat in the position of the abused rather than another person is another example of how its speculative elements defamiliarize its narrative, which urges readers to focus more on the causes of Adrienne's troubles rather than viewing the situation binaristically. Plett's oeuvre includes sympathetic portrayals of sex work throughout *Little Fish*, in other stories from *A Safe Girl to Love*, such as "How Old Are You Anyway?" and "How to Stay Friends," in her 2021 collection *A Dream of a Woman*, and in nonfiction that documents her own history of sex work.[52] Within this context, Adrienne is a sympathetic character because of the societal violences that force her into her untenable situation. *A Safe Girl to Love*'s title comes from its epigraph, a passage from Michelle Tea's memoir *The Chelsea Whistle*.[53] Tea writes about her own experiences as a sex worker throughout her nonfiction,[54] so the title of Plett's book is one way it places itself into sex work's literary lineage. The epigraph, which is unpaginated and appears two pages after the Contents page, is about how

Tea grew up deprived of beauty and is angry about this lack. (She was raised in a working-class home barely more well-off than Adrienne is in the story.)[55] Adrienne suffers from the same kind of downtrodden existence because of the systemic violences she experiences. Therefore, from a theological perspective, readers' responses to her should keep in mind Jesus's concern for "the least of these" in Matthew 25:45.

As the story progresses, Glen tries to understand Adrienne as a full being rather than just as the entity that feeds him. Instead of letting his curiosity about human experience lead to a fetishization of that experience, he learns to acknowledge that Adrienne's life often simply involves "pain" rather than being "tragically glamorous" (118). His emotional growth helps him—and, by extension, readers—see her as a person, not as a fantasy. Glen's cat lineage tells him that humans are only good for giving him food and that if they stop feeding him, he should "leave" (97). At the end of the story, his refusal to accept this teaching unquestioningly and his attempt to sympathize with Adrienne (119) is an example for readers because it teaches us to question what our various heritages have taught us. This questioning is a Mennonite theme, as "Fallow" and *Women Talking* show.

"Portland, Oregon's" title also functions as an indicator of hope. The story does not mention Portland until the second-to-last page when Adrienne tells Glen that her friend Tracy has "moved" there (120). Tracy's choice to take steps to change her life by moving somewhere less bleak is itself an act of hope. It is unclear where Adrienne lives, but considering the descriptions of the frigid weather throughout the story and the broader context of Plett's fiction it is probably Winnipeg. Tracy's choice to move to Portland is especially significant considering the city's frequent depiction during the 2010s as a 1990s utopia. For instance, the television series *Portlandia*'s first episode includes a sketch, "Dream of the '90s," that celebrates the city for being a place where the decade never ended, as though "Portland is almost like an alternative universe. It's like Gore won; the Bush administration never happened." Chelsey Johnson's novel *Stray City* portrays Portland specifically as a queer utopia in the 1990s because of the tight-knit community that became a home for refugees from queerphobic locales such as Nebraska.[56] In these narratives, Portland becomes a speculative landscape that nurtures queer hope, allowing such optimism to flourish.

"Portland, Oregon" draws on *Portlandia*'s positive portrayal of the city to significant rhetorical effect, but it is important to note that some critique the show's depiction. For instance, in a 2016 interview, Portland artist N. O. Bonzo asserts that

> for folks working here, that show is disruptive as hell, hated, maligned, and novelty-washes this city. Portland is not a good place for many folks. We have some of the most extraordinary white supremacist history (and present), we are the third most polluted city in the country, and we have extraordinary violence daily to our most vulnerable people. That show is helping keep PDX contrived as hell and helping to ensure that when folks talk about this city, they aren't talkin [sic] about our openly Nazi police captain (Mark Kruger "The Claw") or the huge cancer clusters around Warren Buffett's military developer making drones (Precision CastParts).[57]

Plett lived in Portland for a number of years, so I read her depiction of the city as a hopeful space as an intentional, informed one rather than one that is oblivious to the problems Bonzo names, especially in light of Plett's willingness to interrogate some of Portland's flaws in her novella "Obsolution" from her 2021 collection, *A Dream of a Woman*.[58] The violence perpetrated against peaceful protestors in Portland by the 2017–2021 White House occupant's minions in the summer of 2020 also lends the city a different meaning than that found in Plett's story. But the intention of its title remains. Plett's story uses Portland's utopian associations to highlight the possibility that Adrienne's life (and, presumably, Glen's) might get better if she also finds a way to get to a healthier place, whether geographically or emotionally. "Not Bleak" rewards this hope because we learn from Lish's statement that Adrienne is still alive in the 2010s, which is a doubtful proposition at the end of "Portland, Oregon." The speculative potential for change that "Portland, Oregon" offers us comes to fruition in Adrienne's life, showing us that such potential is worth pursuing.

Plett's speculative work is also present in the 2017 short story anthology *Meanwhile, Elsewhere: Science Fiction and Fantasy from Transgender Writers*, which she coedited with Cat Fitzpatrick, and which was a finalist in the 2018 Lambda Literary Awards anthology category and won the 2018 American Library Association Stonewall Prize for Literature. This success shows that the literary community immediately recognized the book as an important queer text. Like Becca J. R. Lachman's *A Ritual to Read Together*,

Meanwhile, Elsewhere is an excellent example of a Mennonite writer interacting with the broader world by utilizing Mennonite principles such as concern for the community and the importance of archiving communal experiences, which are also queer values.[59] Fitzpatrick and Plett hope that the anthology "redefin[es] what saving the world looks like" through its portrayals of "small pockets of knowledge, strength, and survival" that show "the heroic everydayness of real trans people's lives" rather than engaging in traditional speculative fiction narratives about winning a war or saving the galaxy.[60] Like "Honey Bear," *Meanwhile, Elsewhere* propagates a theapoetic ethic based in day-to-day actions to show that radical change can start from the ground up.

The anthology's title also highlights the intersection of queer and Mennonite thinking that Mennonitism must pay more attention to. The emphasis on place and displacement in the phrase "meanwhile, elsewhere" names the other-worldly speculative locales of some of the stories and indicates a sense of being on the margins and not fitting in with the world. In its trans context the title is meant as a queer one, and Plett's involvement makes it a Mennonite one as well. It brings to mind stories of displacement that are individual and communal at the same time, such as the immigrations of Russian Mennonites that Plett's ancestors undertook or the immigrations of Swiss Mennonites that Samatar's ancestors undertook. *Meanwhile, Elsewhere* shows that it is possible for Mennonites to interact with the world and experience "worldly" success without abandoning our values.

WOMEN TALKING'S SPECULATIVE CRITIQUE OF MENNONITE MISOGYNY

Like "Fallow," Toews's 2018 novel *Women Talking* examines the Mennonite trope of leaving an oppressive situation that *Queering Mennonite Literature* shows is a common one in recent Mennonite literature and that literary critics should add to Ervin Beck's list of archetypes that help Mennonite literature cohere as a distinctive tradition.[61] The novel also raises the question explored in "Fallow" about how one can claim to be a pacifist when one is violent in the home. Like *I Hear the Reaper's Song*, *Women Talking* retells a significant event from the Mennonite community's past, albeit much more recent. The novel consists of two days of conversations between women in a South American Mennonite colony based on the one in Bolivia where, as Toews recounts in a 2016 essay, between 2005 and 2009, . . . 130 women and girls between the ages of three and sixty were raped by what many in the community believed to be ghosts, or Satan, as punishment for their sins. . . . These mysterious attacks went on for years. If the women complained they weren't believed and their stories were chalked up to "wild female imagination."

Finally, it was revealed that the women had been telling the truth. Two men from the community were caught in the middle of the night as they were climbing into a neighbor's bedroom window. . . . They and seven other locals would spray an animal anaesthetic created by a local veterinarian through the screen windows of a house, knocking unconscious all occupants. They would climb in, rape the victims, and get out.[62]

She adds further in Women Talking's "A Note on the Novel" that "in 2011, these men were convicted in a Bolivian court and received lengthy prison sentences. In 2013, while the convicted men were still in jail, it was reported that similar assaults and other sexual abuses were continuing to take place in the colony."[63] These horrific crimes boggle the mind, and the women the men attacked deserve to have their full story told, which is why I choose to quote Toews's accounts at length and why I choose to write about Women Talking. As its title highlights, the novel gives the women a voice.

The women meet to talk about what to do in response to the attacks. They can "1. Do Nothing. 2. Stay and Fight. 3. Leave" (6). The endpapers of the novel's hardcover printing include three pictures that correspond to these choices: clouds hanging over a field, a Mennonite woman and man having a knife fight, and a horse's ass. These visual elements relate to the novel's first speculative element. The women cannot read or write, so they ask a man, August Epp, to take minutes of their conversations, and he is the book's narrator. The book's visuals symbolize the kinds of figures that the women can read. Mennonite women in Bolivia attend classes through the end of elementary school at a minimum, so the novel's portrayal of the women's illiteracy is factually inaccurate. But it works in the novel as a metaphor for how the Mennonite community has silenced women throughout the centuries, and it allows the book to imagine the possibility of a healed community by bringing it away from a purely realist space to a speculative one.

The first and third choices represent typical Mennonite responses. Mennonites often choose to avoid conflict by refusing to talk about it or refusing to act against those who have wronged them. As "Fallow" shows, Mennonites also sometimes choose to avoid conflict by leaving the site of it. But the second choice, especially in its version that includes physical violence as represented by the picture's knives, is a striking one for the women to contemplate. The violence that the men have committed is so bad that the women realize normal Mennonite passivity is inadequate and that they must take steps to protect themselves and their loved ones, especially their children. August says that the women show that "faith is action" (214). The novel argues that fighting injustice requires an active ethical response, not just words of faith that things are in God's hands, a purely theological one.

Along with its endpaper pictures, the first (i.e., the Canadian) edition of the book has "LOVE" in large letters stamped on its front cover and "ANGER" stamped on its back cover.[64] The front of the dust jacket spells out "love," with the "l" in "Talking," the "ov" in "Novel," and the "e" in "Toews" in color and the rest of the letters in gray. The back of the jacket does the same with "anger," with the "a" and "ng" in "Talking," the "e" in "Novel," and the "r" in "Miriam" in color. Although the Mennonite community often tries to claim that anger is never a legitimate emotion, like Di Brandt's poetry and *I Hear the Reaper's Song*, *Women Talking* asserts that "love" and "anger" can coexist and that sometimes anger is the proper ethical response to oppression. Sometimes love requires anger as a goad in order to confront a loved one about their hurtful behavior.

The book's emphasis on talking things out within the faith community epitomizes the Mennonite ideal of communal discernment that often fails to materialize because of our Mennonite reticence to talk about difficult subjects. Toews examines numerous examples of this reluctance in her essay. For instance, she tells the story of her alcoholic paternal grandmother who would steal bottles of vanilla from the grocery store in their small Mennonite town. Instead of confronting her, the grocer would have her son pay for them.[65] If someone had talked with her about this behavior, it may have been possible for her to get treatment for her addiction and therapy for what may have caused her to begin drinking in the first place. It is important that *Women Talking* does not reject Mennonite ideals despite its anger with the Mennonite community. It rejects Mennonite hypocrisy that causes a failure to live up to those ideals.

It might seem paradoxical for a book called *Women Talking* to have a male narrator, but this choice helps to make the book's argument. Although the women leave, the novel does not argue for a form of feminist separatism because, as Toews says, "we [i.e., women] need men in our struggle."[66] Instead, the book argues for a coalition of the oppressed to fight systemic violence through direct action by portraying August as another outsider. The men of the community construct August as not-male, as what is derogatorily called a "sissy," "because he is single, because he is bad at farming, and because his parents were shunned when he was a child so he has just recently been allowed to return to the colony."[67] Although some of the women also initially dislike August, they ultimately recognize this construction, which is why they trust him to record their story faithfully and not reveal their plans to the other men. August is not sexually queer, but he is a queer character politically. Therefore, the women see him as a "sissy" in the original meaning of the word according to the *OED*: "a sister. Often as a term of endearment."[68] Mennonites traditionally refer to one another as "Sister" or "Brother." The women's view of August epitomizes the affectionate ideal that these terms represent. Their alliance with him is a healthy, chosen community akin to that of the early Anabaptists, as opposed to the ethnic, theocratic community the women are born into.

One way the novel affirms Mennonite ideals is in the women's decision to be nonviolent and leave instead of fighting. The women decide to love themselves and choose physical safety over their salvation, which the men claim they will lose if they do not forgive the rapists, a claim that the women take seriously even though readers clearly are supposed to view this belief as another example of the community's violence. Instead of choosing destruction through violence, the women focus on building something new. Their choice to do so makes *Women Talking* "an invitation to restore lived practices of nonviolence," as Grace Kehler asserts.[69] The women imagine a community where "men and women will make all decisions for the colony collectively. Women will be allowed to think. Girls will be taught to read and write. The schoolhouse must display a map of the world so that we can begin to understand our place in it. A new religion, extrapolated from the old but focused on love, will be created" (56). This speculative vision exemplifies queer theory's emphasis on building a radical new society. It also acknowledges along with "Fallow" that it is impossible to be in the world and not be of it to some extent. The women choose to embrace their place in the world so that they can figure out how relate to it in a healthy way.

One might argue that the women's choice to leave is also speculative in the sense that it is unrealistic for a group of plain Mennonite women to mount a concentrated protest, let alone leave their community en masse.[70] But it is possible. Redekop writes that, in choosing to leave, "the women are in touch with an Anabaptist vision that always insists on beginning again and again."[71] The optimism of this vision is the positive side of Mennonite migration. There is a speculative hope here that *Women Talking* advocates for as a way to heal the Mennonite community. We see this desire in "Fallow" in Agar's choice to tell her story, and we also get this new beginning for Adrienne in *A Safe Girl to Love* between "Portland, Oregon" and "Not Bleak," even though we do not receive the details of it.

The women are unable to read the minutes, but they want August to take them so they can be "an artifact for others to discover" (51). Like Agar and the narrator of "Request for an Extension on the *Clarity*" writing their stories, the women's insistence on a written record that probably will have no practical use is a speculative act that affirms the importance of ethical actions even when no one will know about them or history will forget them. Toews writes in her essay that "dissenting Mennonites" have often kept their feelings "secret."[72] The writers in these narratives refuse this option, doing everything they can to give their voice a permanent home on paper even if their gesture may end up being a futile one. In Samatar's and Toews's narratives, writing is forbidden by the Mennonite community to various extents. In "Portland, Oregon," Adrienne censors herself despite her desire to be a writer because she is afraid of the stories she has to tell (114–15). But the three pieces use writing as an act of resistance themselves. In doing so, they serve as examples of theapoetics.

Although this chapter is at an end, it is important to remember that the speculative fiction examined in this chapter and the next is not about endings. It is about integrating queer hope for new futures into everyday life. It offers us possibilities for how to live in the world and be of it in ethical ways.

CHAPTER 6

Samuel R. Delany's Surrealist Anabaptist Ethics

While studying for my PhD exams, I stumbled across an intriguing headnote in *The Norton Anthology of African American Literature* for an author I had never heard of, Samuel R. Delany. I decided to investigate his work further because of the headnote's description of one of his books, *The Tides of Lust*, as a "'pornographic' novel."[1] I admit that mere titillation is what first drew me to Delany. In retrospect, it is odd that the anthology mentions *The Tides of Lust* at all because it is one of Delany's most obscure works due to its troubled publication history.[2] After buying a used copy online, I read the novel and liked it enough that I decided to read more of Delany's work. As I did so, I was happily surprised to learn that he is queer.

I quickly grew obsessed with Delany's corpus and decided I needed to read through his entire oeuvre. As I hunted online for his books, I found that his work is plagued with publication difficulties because of its unique vision, which makes it less appealing to mainstream publishers, and that copies of a significant number of his books are difficult to find. This knowledge fueled my acquisitive desires. I began haunting the science fiction and fantasy sections of bookstores, looking for old Delany paperbacks, wanting to own every volume—that is, not just every work, every edition of every work—of his. I feverishly compiled my collection of Delanyiana over a matter of months in 2009, adding them to my queer killjoy survival kit as I studied for my exams and started writing my dissertation. I continue to add to my collection as Delany releases new books. I describe my Delany archive because, as Sara Ahmed writes, "It matters, how we assemble things, how we put things together. Our archives are assembled out of encounters, taking form as a memory trace of where we have been."[3] It is a spiritual experience whenever I encounter Delany's ideas in one of his new books. The shelves I devote to his work in my home library and the file cabinet drawer of continuously accumulating articles about him are altars where I pay homage to his influence on my life.

One manifestation of my Delany obsession is that I chose to write a chapter on *The Tides of Lust* as part of my dissertation on violence against whites in African American novels from the 1970s.[4] Although I did not want to admit it, my pacifist Mennonite background affected my choice of topic because of my desire to understand motivations behind violence better. My thinking about violence in the project helped prepare a path for my turn toward Mennonite studies a few years later. Similarly, even though I did not focus on *The Tides of Lust*'s queer elements, my research on Delany paved the way for my queer scholarship and for my decolonial scholarship because of how he investigates the intersection between queerness and ethnicity in the novel and many of his other works.

Immersing myself in Delany's corpus while researching for my dissertation changed how I view the world. Jordy Rosenberg argues that because of the sprawling profusion of Delany's writing "we can never be [Delany] experts. We can only be enthusiasts. We cannot hope to describe his oeuvre, only our encounter with his oeuvre, and how this encounter has transformed us."[5] I do so here. Like many queers, I have had to search for queer community. Literature is often this community for me, most prominently in Delany's work. Ernesto Javier Martínez argues that literature can give us "the knowledge we need" from queer minority experience as opposed to "the knowledge that we often get" from a queerphobic, racist society that tries to erase such experience.[6] I found and continue to find such knowledge in all of Delany's writing, not just his fiction.

Delany's work illustrates how to be queer sexually and politically. Dorothy Allison contends that Delany's "ability to treat queer sexuality is still unsurpassed."[7] He exhibits this ability in all his books since *The Tides of Lust*. His depictions of BDSM in the Return to Nevèrÿon series are the first I found outside of erotica, and they helped me to see myself as a sexual being in a way I had searched for since realizing that I am queer.[8] His frank and jubilant accounts of his sex life in his memoirs always fill me with awe.[9] For example, I will never forget his audacious choice to discuss his penis size, which he describes thusly: "On a scale of small, medium, and large I fall directly on the border line between the latter two."[10] It might be tempting to regard this claim as either unreliable or as bragging, but within the context of Delany's work's emphasis on the necessity of honesty about sexuality I read it simply as reportage. Similarly, in a 1984 letter he claims to have had "ten to fifteen thousand sexual encounters" since he was "seventeen," and in a 2007 documentary about him, he ups the number to fifty thousand.[11] This seems like an incredible number, but it averages out to just under three encounters a day between when Delany began having sex at seventeen and the time of the interview when he was sixty-five. That number of acts is possible in a big city if one knows where to look and one is a cock-sucking devotee as Delany repeatedly reports he is throughout his nonfiction. Note that he claims fifty thousand encounters, not fifty thousand of his own orgasms, and that it would be possible to service three men within the span of an hour or less, so having this many partners would not even take that much time on a daily basis.

Delany's openness is a model for me in everyday interactions and in my writing as I work to unlearn the Mennonite silencing of sex that lasted through my college years. The descriptions of Delany's promiscuity and the promiscuity of his fictional characters teach an ethic of relationality that emphasizes interactions across lines of class, race, gender, sexuality, and ability and that breaks down the boundary between platonic and erotic interactions. By doing so, it insists on the importance of creating collectives that show concern for all their members even if these communities only consist of two people or only last the span of a sexual encounter. Although I enjoy Delany's work for its aesthetic elements, learning its relational ethic is the element of my reading experience that changed my life. All of Delany's work had the defamiliarizing effect on me that Sami Schalk attributes to speculative fiction. The more I contemplated it as I first devoured his work, the more I realized that I needed to begin living my life differently, finding different relationship forms and practices.

Ultimately, this necessity convinced me to end my marriage. There were many smaller issues making the relationship difficult, but reading Delany was the catalyst that sparked me to question whether I could still participate in the institution of marriage in light of its heterosexist, sex-negative nature. I realized that I needed space to explore my queer sexuality, and I realized that I could no longer be a part of the violence marriage perpetuates as the cornerstone of capitalist society, that I needed to find ways to work toward the transformed society that queer theory calls for instead.[12] It was a struggle to accept the idea that I needed a change because I was unaware of any model for ending a marriage for the reason I wanted to do so. I had not yet encountered thinking such as Kathryn Bond Stockton's assertion that "divorce . . . can be heroic" because of its queer emphasis on pleasure rather than security.[13] How could I tell my wife, someone I still loved, that I was breaking up with her because I read some books? How could I explain it to our mutual friends or my parents? Even though I could not find a way to articulate it successfully, my unhappiness began to show, and after several years of discussion about whether our relationship was salvageable, I asked for a divorce.

Reading Delany also influences my writing because he is the first author I read who showed me how to intertwine memoir and scholarship. He refers to his own experiences in his scholarship frequently enough that it is tempting to name books such as *Shorter Views* memoir even though they are not designated as such. Indeed, Delany calls for the dissolution of the boundaries between "creative writing" and "academic writing," advocating for more of the kind of memoir-infused scholarship he does, much of which is autotheoretical.[14] In an interview with Annie Mok, Delany explains that he began writing memoir because of "[Jean] Cocteau's advice: 'What your friends criticize, cultivate.' And one of the things people criticized me for was, whenever I wrote criticism, I was what a friend would call 'promiscuously autobiographical.' So I thought, well, I better cultivate it."[15] Delany's work epitomizes the queer, theapoetic ideal that theory must come from embodied experience, but unlike much queer theory, it is written in a manner that is accessible to nonspecialists, and its memoirish passages are a key ingredient in this accessibility.

DELANY'S ANABAPTIST AFFINITIES

I have such a strong affinity with the values in Delany's work because I find them akin to some elements of Mennonite thinking. After finding Delany on my own, while getting involved in the field of Mennonite literature I found that numerous Mennonite writers also admire his work. Sofia Samatar and I discussed our mutual love of him during our first conversation. Jeff Gundy documents his appreciation for Delany as a speculative fiction writer who influences mainstream literary discourse. The award-winning Canadian Mennonite science fiction writer Karl Schroeder calls Delany one of his "writing models."[16] Jesus says in Matthew 18:20 that "where two or three are gathered together in my name, there am I in the midst of them." Delany is present in the Mennonite literary scene in this way. Therefore, to illustrate the inclusiveness of theapoetics I want to claim Delany as a secular Anabaptist in the spirit of Gundy's "Manifesto of Anabaptist Surrealism," which claims many non-Mennonite thinkers as inspirations for Mennonite scholars to draw from in our work.[17] Delany, who names himself a surrealist via his definition of speculative fiction "as epistemologically ordered, informed, and redeemed surrealism"—yet another genre to go along with those in Schalk's list—is also an Anabaptist in spirit and in deed even if not in word.[18] He is an atheist, but I claim him as a valid theological source because I answer "no" to the first and "yes" to the second of queer theorist Elizabeth Freeman's questions "Must queer theology always involve ... God? Is affect—that intensity felt when an experience passes from one body to another, transforming one or both—divine in and of itself, rather than merely evidence of the divine?"[19] I experience Delany as a spiritual teacher because of the affective weight reading his work carries for me.

Indeed, Delany's atheism is Anabaptist-friendly because of its roots in ethical principles. He feels that it is impossible to truly believe in a "complex," omniscient "god" when many humans "are incapable of believing that other people are human" if they have different beliefs. Instead, Delany prefers to put his "spiritual energy ... into believing in the humanity of all of [his] fellow folk on the planet and the importance of [his] very distant cousins, such as grass, oaks, mushrooms, not to mention fish, bats, dogs, and birds."[20] This belief is so Whitmanic that it does not even seem like atheism to me.[21] Delany has a clear sense of a "spiritual" life even if he happens not to believe in a specific higher power. Biblical literary analysis is among the numerous genres Delany writes in, so he is interested in the history of thinking about the Divine even though he does not believe in it.[22] Delany has also been a lifelong "pacifist," another way his ethics coincide with Anabaptism's.[23]

I first thought about Delany's work as Anabaptist when I read his novel *The Mad Man*. It was first published in 1994 as a response to the apocalyptic forces of AIDS and houselessness in 1980s New York City.[24] A revised edition appeared in 2002. I initially responded to Delany's writing, and it remains important for me, because it is the first secular and first queer work I encountered that showed me how my Mennonite beliefs in social justice could translate into a nonreligious framework. I do a brief surrealist Anabaptist reading of *The Mad Man* here as an example of such translation, which is a necessary aspect of theapoetics, to show how we can apply a theapoetic framework to texts from whatever literary tradition we happen to be part of. Recall Schalk's hybrid definition of speculative fiction. Queer theologian Mark D.

Jordan agrees with the spirit of her inclusive list, making the theapoetic statement that "the distinction between fact and fiction is too crude for theology." In this light, it makes perfect sense to read speculative fiction such as Delany's through the lens of a spiritual tradition, something that Jordan does with Delany's *Trouble on Triton*.[25] Schalk asserts that we need more scholarship on Black speculative fiction that engages religion and spirituality, and she names Delany as an author whose work is appropriate for such an endeavor.[26] Marjorie Sandor echoes Schalk's idea, proposing envisioning the "close-reading" of literary texts as akin to a spiritual endeavor, "midrash," the practice of commenting on the Torah. She writes that when approaching a text, "each of us will notice gaps or cracks in different places," and it is the exploration of these spaces that makes literary criticism rewarding.[27] I see an opening for productive conversation between Anabaptism and Delany's work, a place where both of my ethnicities and my queerness intersect. Alongside Sandor and Schalk, Ytasha L. Womack compares Afrofuturism's "recontextualizing [of] the past" as a strategy for transforming "the present and the future" to writing "midrash."[28] This idea is relevant for my explorations of Delany's writing, as I find reading it to be a spiritual experience. This concept is especially appropriate for my interpretation of *The Mad Man*.

The Mad Man is an example of Delany's long, rich, profuse books that exemplify Rosenberg's assertion that "we can never be experts" on Delany's work because there is so much going on in the novel's five hundred pages. Nevertheless, here are some of my thoughts about what has stuck with me to make it one of my favorite books. When I first read *The Mad Man*, I was struck by its ethics.[29] At the time, Gundy's manifesto was one of my favorite pieces of theory (it remains so) because of how profuse and shaggy and, ultimately, politically queer it is. It is worth quoting at length. It "proclaims the fusion of dream and reality, chaos and order, faith and doubt, past and future," asserting that "all human beings, and all interested animals, plants and other creatures, are immediately declared both members in good standing of the Union of Anabaptist Surrealists and perpetually and simultaneously under its ban." It urges its followers to "give up your goods if anybody wants them" and names as some of its "forerunners" writers such as "the great poet, soldier, and casualty of war Guillaume Apollinaire for his invention of the term surrealism and his praise of the beauty of the shells bursting over the trenches like flowers, like breasts. . . . , William Blake, . . . Mary Oliver, . . . Leonard Cohen, Leonard Nimoy, Leonard Gross [a prominent Mennonite historian . . .], Boy George, George Harrison [the name of a Beatle and also the name of a character in Delany's novel *Dhalgren* . . . , and] Frantz Fanon."[30] It does not take itself too seriously, enjoying its lists of Leonards and Georges. At the same time, it is a profound statement of inclusivity, especially in its willingness to include figures associated with violence, such as Apollinaire and Fanon despite Anabaptism's pacifism. The manifesto uses its Whitmanic list to posit that to live a righteous life you must be open to encountering the Divine anywhere.[31] This inclusivity is why surrealist Anabaptism has room for Delany. *The Mad Man* likewise advocates for an inclusive ethic of wonder and kindness throughout its entirety. Most importantly, the "Manifesto of Anabaptist Surrealism" proclaims that "Anabaptist Surrealism" is "helpless before all manifestations of beauty."[32] Part of why *The Mad Man* is so powerful is because its protagonist, John Marr, finds beauty in an unconventional place, the bodies of the unhoused, and always responds to it.

The Mad Man's ethics pop out at me because one of its first scenes describes John approaching an unhoused man for sex because this is something the subject of John's dissertation, Timothy Hasler, used to do, and John wonders what it is like. The unhoused in the novel are the first developed unhoused characters I encountered in literature.[33] At first, I was surprised that they play such a prominent role, and then I realized that I condemned myself via this attitude because of its anti-unhoused bias. Instead, as a reader I should expect more writers to work to make the unhoused visible to highlight the need for housing for all. Thereby, reading the novel has helped me grow as a person, a theapoetic occurrence. John's first encounter with the man, who calls himself "Piece of Shit," is sixteen pages long and includes a detailed conversation between them as John sucks Piece of Shit's cock, eats his dick cheese, and swallows his urine.[34] Through its high level of detail, the length of the passage helps to establish two of the novel's central subjects: its portrayal of the unhoused as full human beings and its frank, celebratory portrayal of taboo sexual practices. *The Mad Man*'s lengthy, at times pornographic sex scenes are important for its ethics. In an essay on Delany's sex books, Ray Davis notes that pornography is a kind of "fantasy."[35] Thus is it important to acknowledge that *The Mad Man* is speculative fiction even though it is otherwise realistic aside from a monster that makes several brief appearances and the size of some of its characters' genitals. Alongside its sex scenes, the novel includes numerous discussions about sexual consent, especially within the realm of BDSM (e.g., 351–54), reaffirming alongside texts such as *Summer of My Amazing Luck* and *The Body in Four Parts* that any acts between consenting adults are acceptable. These discussions are another way *The Mad Man* relates to Anabaptist thought in light of the tradition's emphasis on adult consent when joining the faith community.[36]

Along with its pornographic elements, *The Mad Man*'s vision of a queered society also makes it speculative. John continues to interact with unhoused men throughout the novel. He has numerous sexual encounters with them (e.g., 194, 300, 377), which are important because queer sex is always revolutionary in a queerphobic society and because he engages in some of the most intimate acts possible with those whom society claims have no value. Jeffrey Allen Tucker observes that the book causes readers to ask, "Do the [unhoused] really need blow jobs as much as they need food, shelter, or employment?"[37] Its answer is a resounding yes, that like the women in *Summer of My Amazing Luck* and the rest of us the unhoused need regular physical affection, including that which enters the sexual realm. These sexual encounters are just as much about making human connections as they are about sexual pleasure itself. Even in the most fleeting of the encounters, John shows concern for the men's overall well-being by sharing his meagre graduate student resources with them, thereby living up to Surrealist Anabaptism's ideals. His actions epitomize Jesus's concern for "the poor and the oppressed" that Anabaptism urges its adherents to live out. For instance, he buys food for the men several times (e.g., 167, 221–22), and he invites them to his house (e.g., 195, 342), ultimately asking one of them, Leaky, to move in with him (436). John's communion with them, whether sexual or social, is an attempt to create community. The novel offers a model of queer community through its same-sex physical encounters and its radical rejection of societal class phobias in favor of a new transformed society where everyone has value.

If we think of Delany as a secular Anabaptist writer, then *The Mad Man* also relates to Samatar's concept of postcolonial Mennonite writing, which shares an affinity with Surrealist Anabaptism, because almost all the novel's characters are people of color. The book's depiction of revolutionary community among John and the unhoused is set against the city's war on the unhoused begun by a white mayor, Ed Koch, in the 1980s. Readers of the 2002 edition would also have the intensification of this war by another white mayor, Rudy Giuliani, in mind. Unlike these authority figures, John, like Hasler before him, views the unhoused as humans deserving of love rather than as a problem to be hidden away for tourism's sake. Although Delany asserts in the novel's "Disclaimer" that "*The Mad Man* is not a book about the" unhoused because it does not include "scenes of winter" or other deprivations (x), the novel's ethical force arrives via John's interactions with them. Gundy argues that "Anabaptist Surrealism seeks to perform itself by creating through poetic, artistic, mystical, transcendental, concrete practices."[38] *The Mad Man* is therefore a queer surrealist Anabaptist performance because of how it embodies these ethics within its narrative.

The Mad Man is famous for its graphic scenes of literally dirty sex, which often include piss drinking and shit eating (e.g., 100–104, 371–72). These scenes are hard to encounter for most readers, including myself, and this difficulty forces us to read slowly and thus contemplate what we have read, learning from it. Reading it therefore becomes an act of queer meditation, a spiritual practice. The celebration of all aspects of bodies, however maligned (e.g., foreskins, 30–33), and their excretions (shit, piss, cum, dick cheese) is reminiscent of how Whitman's "Song of Myself" sings all of the body and its products as good, especially in section 24: "Through me forbidden voices, / Voices of sexes and lusts. . . . voices veiled, and I remove the veil, / Voices indecent by me clarified and transfigured. . . . Divine am I inside and out, and I make holy whatever I touch or am touched from; / The scent of these arm-pits is aroma finer than prayer."[39] *The Mad Man* unveils the voices of the unhoused and shows that they and their sexual desires are holy despite their dirt. Reed Woodhouse contends that "knowing his story *will* shock, [Delany] writes in plain belief that it ought not to."[40] Delany argues that we should write and speak about sex openly, including kinky sex. While these sexual acts are rarely mentioned in discourse and thus may be uncommon, Michael Bucher and Simon Dickel argue that "the point of the novel is precisely to think of such encounters as part of regular life. [As in theapoetics, t]he focus is on the everyday, and on building lasting relationships."[41] It may be that few readers find the novel erotic, but the important thing is that its characters do find their practices erotic and are honest about it. The novel calls for all of us to find this kind of joyfulness in exploring our bodies. It reminds us that the theapoetic experiences that reveal the Divine to us are sometimes sexual. It also reminds us that we can encounter these experiences via texts that make no claim to a spiritual tradition.

EPILOGUE

THEAPOETICS AND OTHER TRADITIONS

Ann Hostetler observes that the Mennonite literary "community celebrates multiple perspectives and perceptions."[1] In its writing, it now encompasses the service to the faith community that John Ruth calls for in *Mennonite Identity and Literary Art* and the emphasis on artistic freedom that Al Reimer calls for in *Mennonite Literary Voices*. This celebration of openness has been of much help to me as Mennonite literature has played a major role in my relationship to spirituality over the past twenty years. Although I am no longer a theological Mennonite, I still believe in the power of community and its potential to affect society in revolutionary ways. Since 2013, I have published regularly in Mennonite journals due to my interest in Mennonite literature as part of a far-flung scholarly community, but I do miss being in physical community with Mennonites. If I lived near a Mennonite church, I would attend sometimes for the hymn singing and just ignore the theological bits, tuning out during the sermons. I find succor for this distance via the theapoetic aspects of my current spiritual practice, which encompasses haiku and tarot, two traditions that exemplify ordinary theology and research-creation,[2] and that possess strong relationships to literature that make them perfect for theapoetic consideration. I discuss these traditions as a reminder that the theapoetic idea of encountering the Divine (which, again, will be a secular presence for some) through literary language that describes lived experience is transferable alongside the secular ethics it teaches. I take Jeff Gundy's personal essay "The Fields Have Edges, but the Roads Keep Going" as a model for using texts that are extra-canonical to the Christian tradition theapoetically. Gundy's essay traces the influence of various non-Mennonite poets on him as a young man as he began to learn about the vastness of the non-Mennonite world. He ends the essay with an image from the Gospel of Thomas to remind us that "the spark of God is somehow present" everywhere, not just in the faith "tradition" that is his and mine.[3] He uses his everyday experiences rather than formal theology as the basis for this assertion.

Eric Amann documents that many writers consider haiku a Zen Buddhist practice, and Bruce Ross highlights the importance of Shintoism for the genre's development. Lee Gurga observes that the genre became popular "in the West in the 1950s and '60s" because of these "spiritual" elements.[4]

However, as literature based in religious practice, haiku does not fall into the trap of didacticism because it is the act of writing itself that connects the writer to the Divine rather than the writing's message. Gabriel Rosenstock also considers haiku a spiritual practice, explaining that "haiku is your prayer, your meditation," and that writing it fits within all theologies, including "atheis[m]." He also makes the theapoetic argument that haiku must respond to actual human experiences for its "ethical" message to succeed.[5] A poem by Suzanne Richardson reveals that these experiences include queer ones:

> tattooed girlfriend
> still decorated
> when naked[6]

Haiku is also theapoetic because its ethical stance is political. For instance, Terry Ann Carter describes how some writers see haiku as a liberating practice because of its origins outside of colonial geographies, which gives it a decolonial outlook.[7] The genre fits within the work of all theapoetic literature that I explain in the introduction. Stephen Addiss shows that the genre's theapoetic elements date back to its origins, writing that *"the purpose of haiku was to use the mundane while exceeding the mundane."*[8] For instance, even disturbing daily moments can transform into something beautiful through haiku's pinpointed gaze, as in this poem by Elizabeth Threadgill:

> at the back of the throat
> a hawk's talons
> pin a little pink rabbit[9]

Theapoetics teaches that the way to encounter the Divine is to be open to it in all activities, even the most ordinary. Haiku emphasizes such encounters through the shortness of its form, which only allows writers space to describe a single moment of life.[10]

Writing haiku has helped me survive the mental anguish of the pandemic because my writing helps me focus on these moments. The practice of composing a haiku every morning as a way to center myself helps me appreciate the beauty of everyday life despite the restrictions the pandemic places on how we can safely live our lives. Anita Hooley Yoder speculates, "Maybe as a Mennonite writer I need to feel some sense of duty, so it helps to think that beauty demands something of me, that I have some kind of responsibility to fulfill—and writing can be my way to take responsibility for the beauty that is present to me."[11] I write haiku as one way of meeting this responsibility. My morning ritual reminds me to be mindful and to appreciate the time I have even though my life is different than what it was before. I notice little things about my body that I might not see otherwise:

> pandemic
> no tan lines
> where I wear my watch[12]

I also pay more attention to the seasons and to how the pandemic affects some of their usual markers:

> summer solstice
> the empty
> Little League field[13]

My haiku writing makes me more open to encountering the Divine, whether in my writing and reading or elsewhere.

The Christian roots of theapoetics and the Buddhist roots of haiku find a place to mingle in the tarot. Tarot teacher Rachel Pollack notes that "tarot comes out of a Christian background" and is highly ecumenical because numerous faith traditions influence it.[14] Theologians Chic Cicero and Sandra Tabatha Cicero offer an example of tarot's ecumenism from the Qabalistic tarot tradition, which itself comes out of Jewish mysticism. They write that this tradition views "Christ" and "Buddha" as two manifestations of "the Reconciler or Redeemer."[15] This is another example of how theapoetics is useful for whatever spiritual tradition one might come from. Spiritual practice attempts to make sense of existence and the question of whether something larger than us exists. Dawn G. Robinson addresses this question by arguing that tarot "bridg[es] the gap between rationality and belief."[16] Her implication that belief is not "rational" queers mainstream prejudices that view tarot as either illegitimate and "woo-woo" or dangerously esoteric (or paradoxically somehow both) because it asserts that tarot and other spiritual practices inhabit a position closer to rationality than most people give them credit for. Tarot reminds us that sometimes it is rational to be irrational according to the world's standards. This transgressiveness is a Mennonite and a literary ideal.

Pollack also explains that the tarot reminds us that "our small lives, which so often can seem random, or meaningless, are actually an organic part of the cosmos."[17] Her statement concurs with the theapoetic belief in the importance of personal experience as a way to encounter the Divine. Similarly, in her book about queering the tarot, Cassandra Snow remarks that "the whole point of deconstructing tarot is to bring it into our everyday, modern lives."[18] This is a theapoetic gesture because theapoetics is a way to bring the Divine into our daily lives by nontraditional means: viewing literature as a place where lots of minor sacred texts reside so that we do not have to confine ourselves to the major ones—the Bible, the Bhagavad Gita, and so on.

Like haiku, tarot offers one of the many paths to get to the ethical destinations that Mennonite literature urges us toward. Cicero and Cicero document the importance of ethics in the Qabalistic tarot tradition, declaring that ethics are what create "Beauty" as a Divine force.[19] We can create beauty through all our actions, not just our artistic ones. Gundy agrees, declaring that "we cannot pursue truth without beauty" and that beauty is "something as essential as food."[20] We are created to encounter and consume beauty as another kind of fuel to keep us alive. Tarot helps me do so because it reminds me to create beauty every day by living ethically, just as studying any other traditional sacred text would.

I first got into the tarot because of a gift that quickly became part of my killjoy survival kit. My friend Suzanne Richardson gave me a black T-shirt designed by Marie Sena that depicts the tarot's Devil card in gold as a Christmas gift in 2018. Unbeknownst to Suzanne, I had been thinking about exploring tarot for around a decade after encountering a reproduction of the Hanged Man card in Samuel R. Delany's *Return to Nevèrÿon*.[21] According to Pollack, "writers" are "often drawn to this card" because of "its hints of great truths in a simple design" and its fame due to its inclusion in T. S. Eliot's "The Wasteland."[22] Therefore, it is no wonder that the card stuck with me, waiting for me to pick it up along with the rest of the deck. When Suzanne gave me the shirt, I took it as a sign that it was time for me to begin my explorations. Since then, I have been reading queer interpretations of the tarot and pulling a card for my day each morning just before I write my daily haiku, reminiscent of the morning Bible devotionals I practiced in high school and college. The cards help to highlight the various elements of what is going on in my life at the time and offer advice for how to approach them. For instance, when the upheaval of the pandemic caused me to seek a new direction for my life, I kept getting cards such as the Page of Wands, which signifies apprenticeship in creative pursuits; the Two of Wands, which signifies the need to make a change that often involves travel; and the Page of Pentacles, which signifies success in major life changes. These cards affirmed my sense that I should quit my job and return to graduate school to pursue an MFA.

A few months after Suzanne gave me the shirt, I read Snow's *Queering the Tarot*. Snow writes that "queering" the Devil card means seeing its "positive" aspects and that these aspects are often related to the "sex-positive," "liberat[ing]" aspects of BDSM because "so much of queering the tarot comes down to breaking down our own misconceptions and biases on what relationships should and shouldn't be, or do and do not look like."[23] Recognizing the Devil card's empowering association with BDSM is a way of releasing myself from Christianity's negative attitudes toward the body in general and toward sexuality specifically.[24] The shirt now symbolizes my journey toward doing so. In the traditional Rider-Waite-Smith deck, the Devil card depicts the Devil as an angry satyr with bat wings sitting on a pillar that has a woman and man chained to it. The design on the shirt is similar, but it is quintessentially queer because the Devil is intersex, with a male head and woman's breasts. They hold a whip in their left hand, an explicit nod to the card's kinky nature. In Sena's design, the Devil thereby represents the celebration of queer bodies that Snow attributes to the card. Thus, the shirt represents my kinky queerness and my spirituality, two parts of myself that felt incompatible for many years.

I end *Ethics for Apocalyptic Times* by asking us how we can pay homage to beauty as one way of acting ethically in these apocalyptic times. The world seems like a terrible place these days, and I often feel despondent as a result. But I believe that we can make it a little better every day with our actions. Theapoetic literature helps show us how.

NOTES

INTRODUCTION

1. Axelson, "Coronavirus Timeline in NY."
2. Lauren Friesen, email message to author, 6 December 2019; Maxwell Kennel, email message to author, 10 December 2019. Mennonites are descended from the sixteenth-century Anabaptist wing of the Protestant Reformation.
3. Mookerjea, "Intermedia Research-Creation and Hydropolitics," 137. Mookerjea's description is inspired by Natasha Myers's adanceaday [sic] project, which Myers describes in "Anthropologist as Transducer."
4. For instance, see Cruz, "Writing Back, Moving Forward."
5. See Wiebe, *Temptations of Big Bear*, and Wiebe, *Scorched-Wood People*. Ervin Beck notes that some critics see Wiebe as one of the first writers to make Canadian literature "'consciously postcolonial'" in "Postcolonial Literary Detection," 195. Except for Samatar, who writes about outer space and other fantastical contexts, the writers I name above all focus on settings in the Americas. However, it is worth noting that Beck documents a long tradition of Mennonites writing fiction about "postcolonial" contexts outside of the Americas, usually from the perspective of white characters serving as mission workers (196). Samatar examines how Mohamud Siad Togane's poetry responds to this epistemologically violent mission work in "Scope of This Project" and *White Mosque*, 133–39.
6. Richard K. MacMaster describes how two of my ancestors, Hans Herr and Martin Kendig, acted as land agents for William Penn in Lancaster in *Land, Piety, Peoplehood*, 81, 85, 89–90. For two recent attempts by Mennonite writers to confront the legacy of Mennonite settler colonialism, see Kasdorf, "God and Land," and Ruth, *This Very Ground*. For a theological attempt, see Wiebe, "Reassessing Mennonite Environmentalism Through Settler-Colonialism." For another discussion of the in-between space that half–Puerto Rican, half–Swiss Mennonite folx inhabit, see Falcón, "Hexadecaroon."
7. Piepzna-Samarasinha, *Future Is Disabled*, 41.
8. Kasdorf, "Sunday Morning Confession," 7. On the major texts used to tell the field's narrative of transgression, including Kasdorf's *Sleeping Preacher*, see Beck, "Mennonite Transgressive Literature."
9. For papers from the After Identity symposium, see Zacharias, *After Identity*. For work from the LGBT Fiction panel, see Harnish, "LGBT Mennonite Fiction"; Harnish, "Excerpt from *Plain Love*"; Braun, "Complicated Becoming"; Cruz, "Reading My Life in the Text"; Plett, "Natural Links of Queer and Mennonite Literature." See also Zacharias, "'Garden of Spears'"; Zacharias, *Reading Mennonite Writing*; Gundy, "Mennonite/s Writing"; Samatar, "Scope of This Project"; Samatar, "In Search of Women's Histories"; Cruz, *Queering Mennonite Literature*.
10. Kasdorf, "Sunday Morning Confession," 7–8n, and Zacharias, *Reading Mennonite Writing*, 1–3, 32, 34, his emphasis.
11. I have used this term for myself since I came out in November 2002 because I didn't know the term "pansexual" at the time. As most bisexuals will tell you (the ones who disagree are generally transphobic, and they can go to hell), the terms are synonymous, indicating possible attraction to all genders, not just men and women.
12. Redekop, *Making Believe*, xiv–xv. Redekop notes that her age influences her view

because, as she states, "When I began my studies, there was not even a Canadian literature, let alone a Mennonite literature," and that she realizes that critics of my generation have a different view of minoritarian literatures (xxiii). This generation gap may be evident in a glowing review of *Making Believe* by Lauren Friesen, who is Redekop's contemporary (Friesen was born in 1943 and Redekop in 1944), in *Mennonite Quarterly Review* in 2020. Whether one agrees or disagrees with *Making Believe*'s arguments, it is to its credit that it is thought-provoking enough to elicit strong reactions in either direction.

13. Aside from Redekop, Maurice Mierau and John D. Roth are the other notable voices that question the field's validity. See, for instance, Mierau, "Voice Is Coming," and Roth, "In This Issue."
14. Ruth, *Mennonite Identity and Literary Art*, 10–19. Regarding this lack of storytelling, Ruth says elsewhere that "I feel abused by my [i.e., Swiss] Mennonites [because] . . . they don't know their own story nor did they tell it to me." Quoted in Gray and Hostetler, "Mennonite Creators' Discussion Group." Ruth's career has attempted to correct this lack of knowledge for others via his writing.
15. Ruth, *Mennonite Identity*, 21.
16. Ruth, *Mennonite Identity*, 70.
17. However, Ruth constructs this "identity" as white because he conflates Mennonite theology and Mennonite ethnicity via a misguided comparison of Blackness and Mennonite plainness, as Sofia Samatar shows in *White Mosque*, 132–33; see also Ruth, *Mennonite Identity*, 58. Samatar documents throughout *White Mosque* that these well-meaning Mennonite racisms occur with alarming frequency when we Mennonites of color interact with white Mennonites. I struggle to know how to respond to this violence—as I say above, it is difficult to exist as a queer Latinx Mennonite when the Mennonite community frequently tries to silence the first two of those identities—but I am writing this book with a spirit of hope, so I don't spend much time here considering such responses. I am, however, writing a memoir that takes my attempts to do so as its central theme.
18. Ruth, *Mennonite Identity*, 64.
19. Ruth, *Mennonite Identity*, 2.
20. Ruth, "Genius and the Verbal Dance," 283.
21. Ruth, *Mennonite Identity*, 33–42.
22. Ruth, "Genius and the Verbal Dance," 289, and Gundy, "Mennonite/s Writing."
23. Reimer, *Mennonite Literary Voices*, 1. By the time of *Mennonite Literary Voices*'s publication, there was a small but noticeable body of critical essays on Mennonite literature, including a book of collected essays from the first Mennonite/s Writing conference, Hildi Froese Tiessen and Peter Hinchcliffe's *Acts of Concealment*. Jeff Gundy's "Humility in Mennonite Literature" is an early attempt to summarize literature in the field and includes a few paragraphs about Ruth's book (8–10). But Reimer's book is the first extended engagement with the ideas offered in *Mennonite Identity and Literary Art*.
24. Ruth, *Mennonite Identity*, 24, 57.
25. See Wiebe, *Peace Shall Destroy Many*; Wiebe, *Blue Mountains of China*; Kliewer, *Violators*; Wiebe, *Skyblue the Badass*; Good, *Happy as the Grass Was Green*. The monotony of men in this list is an imbalance that is now corrected in the field, as this book shows.
26. Kasdorf, "Dreams of the Written Character," 32, and Reimer, *Mennonite Literary Voices*, 19.
27. Reimer, *Mennonite Literary Voices*, 60–63.
28. Ruth, "Genius and the Verbal Dance," 281.
29. Reimer, *Mennonite Literary Voices*, 20, 23, 55.
30. Reimer, *Mennonite Literary Voices*, 64.
31. Ruth, "Genius and the Verbal Dance," 273. For details of Ruth's life, see Ruth, *Branch*.
32. Reimer, *Mennonite Literary Voices*, 69. *My Harp Is Turned to Mourning* is Reimer's novel.
33. Beck, "Mennonite Transgressive Literature," especially 61–66. In a statement in her foreword to Kirsten Eve Beachy's anthology *Tongue Screws and Testimonies* that does not defend Ruth's book but acknowledges its continued relevance, Julia Spicher Kasdorf argues that the anthology is "the fulfillment of 'Mennonite Identity and Literary Art' [sic]"

because Beachy's contributors wrestle with the faith tradition via literature (12).

34. Kasdorf, "Dreams of the Written Character," 32, and Janzen, Ruth, and Wiebe, "Literature, Place, Language, and Faith," 90. Russian Mennonites and Swiss Mennonites (what I am) are the two major Mennonite ethnicities in North America. The important difference between them for understanding Janzen and Ruth's exchange is that Swiss Mennonites are stereotypically more conservative and less engaged with the world culturally and politically, which is why most early Mennonite literature is by Russian Mennonites. As Craig Haas and Steve Nolt put it in a list comparing the two ethnicities in their humor classic *The Mennonite Starter Kit*, "Russian Mennonites write vivid disturbing poetry" and "Swiss Mennonites don't" (11). However, this stereotype was no longer true in the Mennonite literary community when Janzen and Ruth spoke, and that continues to be the case. I describe these ethnicities further in Cruz, *Queering Mennonite Literature*, 7–8. Ervin Beck provides a convincing argument that Mennonites are an ethnic group in *MennoFolk*, 36–37.

35. For example, Suderman, "Mennonites"; Tiessen, "Beyond the Binary," 13–15; Loewen, "Mennonite Literature," 566–70; Gundy, *Walker in the Fog*, 102–4; Gundy, "Mennonite/s Writing"; Zacharias, "Introduction," 9–10; Beck, "Mennonite Transgressive Literature," 63–65.

36. Ruth, "Revolution and Reverence," 186–87, 179–80. I came across this sermon while perusing Paul Erb's book *From the Mennonite Pulpit*, which Ervin Beck, one of the earliest scholars of US Mennonite literature, gave me in May 2019 during a visit to his home when he was culling his personal library. I am unaware of other authors who examine the sermon, and I am grateful to Ervin for the gift.

37. Ruth, "Revolution and Reverence," 182–83, 186–87.

38. Piet Visser's "Bible and the Literary Arts" argues that the global non-Anglophone Mennonite literary tradition dates from seventeenth-century poetry in the Netherlands. Samatar's "Scope of This Project," which I examine further in chapter 5, discusses contemporary aspects of global Mennonite literature.

39. See Dunham, *Trail of the Conestoga*; Dunham, *Toward Sodom*; Friesen, *Flamethrowers*; Bender, "Literature, Mennonites in," 372. My thanks to Robert Zacharias for bringing *Trail of the Conestoga* to my attention. He writes about its position in the field in *Reading Mennonite Writing*, 16–18. By 1986 Ruth was aware of Dunham's work and briefly discusses it in "Knowing the Place for the First Time," 256.

40. Ruth, "Revolution and Reverence," 179. One might add Paul Hiebert's *Sarah Binks* (1947) to this list. Redekop offers a lengthy discussion of why this novel has often not been considered a Mennonite one along with an argument for it to be in *Making Believe*, 130–53. Kasdorf suggests Elaine Sommers Rich's young adult novel *Hannah Elizabeth* as another early text in "Sunday Morning Confession," 8–10. However, like Kliewer's, it came out in 1964, so it is unlikely that Ruth had a chance to read it before his sermon.

41. Ruth, "Revolution and Reverence," 181, 183, 184–85. Note that the latter two items in Ruth's list of reading recommendations contain queer elements!

42. Aside from the writers I cite in the following discussion, see, for instance, Holland, "Theopoetics Is the Rage"; Janzen, "Nine Streams Towards the River of Theopoetics"; Hooley Yoder, "Know Your Place." Examples of essays that are theopoetic without explicitly using the term include Kroeker, "Scandalous Displacements"; and Kennel, "Violence and the Romance of Community." For an introduction to theopoetics, see Keefe-Perry, *Way to Water*. Note that there is a long tradition of conservative critics reading allegorical literature, such as C. S. Lewis's *The Chronicles of Narnia* series, theologically. It should be clear throughout this book that this is not a tradition that I am conversing with, especially in my discussions of theapoetics' queer feminist decolonial nature.

43. Bergen, "Ecumenical Vocation of Anabaptist Theology," 118n43.

44. Gundy, *Songs from an Empty Cage*, 18.
45. Hooley Yoder, "I've Read Too Much Poetry for That," 454.
46. Kennel, "Secular Mennonite Critique," 58.
47. Gundy, *Songs from an Empty Cage*, 38, and Braun, "Selection," 86–87.
48. Reimer, *Mennonite Literary Voices*, 63.
49. Remer, *Earthprayer*, 8. I read Remer's choice to self-publish her book despite having academic credentials that might have allowed her to find a traditional publisher for it (she has a doctorate and is a college instructor) as a theapoetic move focused on making her work quickly and cheaply available to as many readers as possible because it is meant for everyday use. She emphasizes writing as a tool for enriching daily life rather than as a tool for professional advancement. This humility feels very Mennonite to me even though Remer is not a Mennonite to my knowledge.
50. Tea, *Modern Tarot*, 263.
51. See, for instance, Loughlin, *Queer Theology*.
52. Redekop, *Making Believe*, 6.
53. Kennel, "Secular Mennonites." Kennel further develops his definition of secular Mennonitism in "Secular Mennonite Social Critique."
54. Zacharias, *Reading Mennonite Writing*, 214–15, and Hostetler, "Dancing on the Bridge," 238–39.
55. On the 1990, 1997, 2002, 2006, 2009, 2012, and 2015 conferences, see Cruz, "Bibliography and Subject Index." Papers from the 2017 conference are in the *Journal of Mennonite Studies* 36 (2018). For a report on the 2022 conference, see Zuercher, "Writers' Conference at Age 32." As of *Ethics for Apocalyptic Times*'s copyediting phase in February 2023, papers from the 2022 conference are scheduled to appear later in 2023 in the *Journal of Mennonite Writing* 15, no. 1, and *Mennonite Quarterly Review* 97, no. 2.
56. "Mennonite Lit. Writers," Facebook, 30 July 2020–present, https://www.facebook.com/groups/879145212575864.
57. For instance, Kirsten Eve Beachy mentions Becca J. R. Lachman, Julia Spicher Kasdorf, and Anita Hooley Yoder in her poem "Wives Like Us."
58. Reimer and Caple, "CanLit Hierarchy vs. the Rhizome," 130.
59. Bennett, *Influx and Efflux*, 86.
60. Remer, *Earthprayer*, 13, her emphasis, and Hooley Yoder, "I've Read Too Much Poetry for That," 462.
61. Remer, *Earthprayer*, 82.
62. Doty, *What Is the Grass*, 31.
63. Gundy, *Songs from an Empty Cage*, 32.
64. Kampen, "On the Need," 98–99, 101.
65. Acevedo, *Poet X*, 356.
66. Gundy, "Toward a Poetics of Identity," 170.
67. Redekop, *Making Believe*, 316.
68. Redekop, *Making Believe*, 327, her emphasis.
69. Lerner, *Hatred of Poetry*, 5, 54; Reimer, DOWNVERSE, n.p. For a classic example of the debate Lerner names that illustrates how it keeps reoccurring, see Gioia, *Can Poetry Matter?*
70. Reimer, DOWNVERSE, 61, quotation marks and lack of punctuation in the original.
71. Baraka, *SOS*, 545. Baraka expresses this idea more directly in his famous poem "Black Art," which argues that "Poems are bullshit" unless they act like assassins to "Clean out the world for virtue and love" (149–50). Jamila Woods offers a feminist revision of Baraka's statement in her poem "Blk Girl Art," which begins "Poems are bullshit unless they are eyeglasses, honey / tea with lemon, hot water bottles on tummies" (261). Poems should provide some kind of comfort, which is a radical act in the face of capitalism's violence. For a queer discussion of the concept of usefulness, see Ahmed, *What's the Use?*
72. Williams, "Asphodel, That Greeny Flower," 200.
73. Zapruder, *Why Poetry*, 98, 216.
74. Whitman, "Backward Glance O'er Travel'd Roads," 481, his emphasis.
75. Perdomo, "Breakbeat, Remezcla," 2.
76. Graham et al., "I'm Writing to You," 58. Numerous other writers of color are making similar arguments about writing as resistance. For instance, a recent issue of *The Writer's Chronicle* includes three different pieces that express this idea. Helena María Viramontes insists that

"commitment to your writing is a commitment to dismantling these systems [such as capitalism and racism] one word at a time," so it is necessary to "make all the words in your sentences muscular and ready to work" in "My Insurgent Heart," 26. Camille T. Dungy posits that "it is incumbent upon writers to tell stories of refusal and resistance and connection," noting that community building is a necessary revolutionary activity, in "Catastrophe and Survival," 34. Sahar Khalifeh observes that "when you have a cause, your writing includes fighting" in "'Nothing Will Stop Me,'" 50.

77. Chee, *How to Write an Autobiographical Novel*, 275. I intend my choice to highlight writers' ethnicities in this paragraph, and my frequent naming of other writers as "Mennonite" or "queer," as a way of calling my people in, a way of gathering an intersectional literary community that gives me strength as a queer Latinx Mennonite. It is a way of building a citational community, as I describe later in this chapter. But I also think about Matthew Salesses's correct observation in *Craft in the Real World* that naming some characters' ethnicities in fiction and not others reinforces the assumption that all characters are white unless named otherwise (xiii–xiv, 46). I think that this dynamic works somewhat differently in nonfiction, when authors are paired with their ideas rather than being a plot element, and I hope that my own positionality and my discussions of theapoetics' queer, decolonial nature show that I reject whiteness as the default. Note also that I do not always name authors who are Mennonite, queer, or people of color; I do so when it feels relevant to my argument. This admittedly may be a contradictory practice, so I'll cite Whitman here: "Do I contradict myself? / Very well then.... I contradict myself; / I am large.... I contain multitudes." Whitman, *Leaves of Grass*, 85, ellipses in the original.

78. Stenson, *Showing Up*, 35.
79. Gundy, *Songs from an Empty Cage*, 163n12; Back, *What Use Is Poetry*, 9; Lindenberg, "Brief History of the Future Apocalypse," 100–104, 203–4. James Henry Knippen asks a provoking question regarding poetry and peace in his poem "Morning" from *Would We Still Be*: "What if poetry / has no place in a peaceful / world?" (9). Poetry's job is activist, so what if the world became peaceful enough that we no longer needed its activism?

80. On this genre, see Martha Himmelfarb's *The Apocalypse*. Himmelfarb discusses important elements of the genre such as "ascent to heaven" (15); "the fate of souls after death" (75); "heaven as a temple" (83); and "tours of paradise and hell" (97). My use of the term does not concern itself with the afterlife, instead focusing on the earthly ramifications of our current apocalypses and how to respond to them. Samatar gives a history of would-be prophets, including some Mennonites, who have predicted eschatological apocalypses in *White Mosque*, 152–55.

81. Redekop, *Making Believe*, 332.
82. Nye, "You Are Your Own State Department," 133–34, 208–9.
83. Redekop, *Making Believe*, 169.
84. Gundy, *Songs from an Empty Cage*, 50. Gundy enumerates this variety throughout "Mennonite/s Writing."
85. Redekop, *Making Believe*, 10; Tiessen, "Homelands," 21–22. Maurice Mierau's claim regarding Patrick Friesen in *How Mind and Body Move* that although Friesen is not a theological Mennonite, his encounters with language in his Mennonite upbringing influences "the level of craft [within] ... Friesen's artistic practice" is one recent example of a literary critic identifying such traces (11).
86. Cruz, "Reading My Life in the Text," 283. I discuss how Mennonite thinking is politically queer in *Queering Mennonite Literature*, 11–13. One example of literary criticism that examines Mennonite thinking in literature without Mennonite characters is Jeff Gundy's "'There Is No Knife,'" especially 70–71, 80–81, 83–84.
87. Koop, "Contours and Possibilities," 23.
88. In "Knowing the Place for the First Time," Ruth recalls that "in my own boyhood the Mennonite Publishing House [which

became Herald Press] at Scottdale, Pennsylvania was issuing more fiction, in our Sunday School magazines, *The Christian Monitor* and various novels, than I could keep up with" (256). I assume that these reading experiences influenced *Mennonite Identity and Literary Art* to some extent. However, Ruth acknowledges the legitimacy of the kind of admittedly elitist gatekeeping I engage in above in "Genius and the Verbal Dance," 274. Elsewhere in the interview, he differentiates writing for writing's sake and writing propaganda as using "a meditative voice rather than a badgering one" (279). Robert Zacharias wonders what the field of Mennonite literature would look like if scholars questioned its "assumptions of high *literariness*" in *Reading Mennonite Writing*, 23, his emphasis. I am sympathetic to such questioning, which feels very queer to me, but choose not to participate in it here as part of my choice to take the field as a given and examine how theapoetics plays a role in it instead.

89. Burns, "Queering Anabaptist Theology," 84–85, 78. My academic training includes a BA in Bible and Religion (so I have a little theological training), an MA and PhD in English, and, as of May 2023, an MFA in Creative Nonfiction.

90. Mennonite Church USA's Delegate Assembly recently acknowledged one of these issues that directly relates to me. In a resolution passed on 29 May 2022, they admit that "LGBTQIA Mennonite people of color are virtually erased" by the church. See "Resolution for Repentance and Transformation." This is a step in the right direction, but until acts of restitution follow it up it is just lip service.

91. Quoted in Gray and Hostetler, "Mennonite Creators' Discussion Group."

92. Janzen, Ruth, and Wiebe, "Literature, Place, Language, and Faith," 88.

93. Friesen, *Outlasting the Weather*, 216.

94. For instance, Gallop, *Anecdotal Theory*; Loveless, *How to Make Art*; Fournier, *Autotheory*.

95. Loveless, *How to Make Art*, 57; Brostoff and Fournier, "Introduction," 490–91; Fournier, *Autotheory*, 8; see also Moraga and Anzaldúa, *This Bridge Called My Back*; Lorde, *Zami*; and Anzaldúa, *Borderlands/La Frontera*. On academia's prejudice against the genre, see Nadir, "More Life After Ruins," 548–49.

96. Fournier, *Autotheory*, 15, and Pope, Lowry, and Knowles, "'Dear Simon...,'" 294–96. See also Buller, "Learning from Our Ancestors." Like Buller, I taught as a professor after getting my PhD and then returned to school for an MFA. *Ethics for Apocalyptic Times*'s form reflects this trajectory of recognizing the need for something more than traditional academic discourse in these horrific times.

97. Loveless, *How to Make Art*, 16, 105, 100.

98. Fournier, *Autotheory*, 2–3.

99. Loveless, *How to Make Art*, 12–13, 70, her emphasis.

100. Fournier, *Autotheory*, 93.

101. Brostoff and Fournier, "Introduction," 494, and Fournier, *Autotheory*, 174.

102. Brostoff and Fournier, "Introduction," 490.

103. Ruiz, *Ricanness*, 191n21.

104. Ahmed, *What's the Use?*, 167–68.

105. Cooppan, "Skin, Kin, Kind," 601; Fournier, *Autotheory*, 191–204. Note that the genre includes critiques of traditional citation styles because these practices only work for citing traditional media such as books and journal articles. For instance, see Cambre, "Crisis of Literacies." Although I use a standard citation style here because I happen to cite source types that this style covers, I am generally sympathetic to these critiques and like Cambre's suggestion "to have citation processes not regulated, described by authors on a case-by-case basis, as an individual practice responding to needs of paper or performance" (88). The act of citation is more important than the form it takes.

106. Ahmed, *Living a Feminist Life*, 15–16.

107. brown, *Pleasure Activism*, 21.

108. Fournier, *Autotheory*, 135.

109. Lisowski, "The Girl, the Well, the Ring," 49n1.

110. This insight is inspired by the story of finding Lorene Cary's memoir *Black Ice* via a citation in Patricia Hill Collins's *Black Feminist Thought* that Sara Ahmed tells in *Complaint!*, 2. Likewise, I read *Complaint!*

on the recommendation of one of *Ethics for Apocalyptic Times*'s anonymous peer reviewers.
111. Quoted in Fournier, *Autotheory*, 195.
112. See, for instance, Cruz, "Brief History and Bibliography," and Cruz, *Queering Mennonite Literature*.
113. Samatar, "Sofia Samatar on Kafka," and Samatar, "Conversation with Sofia Samatar."
114. Nussbaum, "Narrative Emotions," 218–19.
115. Thieleman J. van Braght's *The Bloody Theater or Martyrs Mirror of the Defenseless Christians Who Baptized Only Upon Confession of Faith, and Who Suffered and Died for the Testimony of Jesus, Their Saviour, From the Time of Christ to the Year A.D. 1660* is an 1,100-page collection of martyr narratives that traditionally has been the second most important book for Mennonites after the Bible. This statement about the book's importance is found at least as far back as Mabel Dunham's novel *Toward Sodom*, in which the narrator notes that the *Martyrs Mirror*'s "reputation was above reproach by reason of the fact that it had a place beside the Bible and the hymn-book in every Mennonite home" (16). Julia Spicher Kasdorf offers a nonfiction example in "Mightier Than the Sword," 44, 65. But this importance varies. For instance, Magdalene Redekop writes, "I have often been told that the *Martyrs Mirror* (Van Braght 1660) is a book that has a status next to that of the Bible in many Mennonite homes. Where are these homes? I never saw that book in my home or in anyone else's home while growing up. Indeed, I did not know it existed until I was in graduate school" in *Making Believe*, 27. I must admit that I also grew up without it in my home until my parents gave me a copy for Christmas when I was sixteen after I asked for it as a joke because I somehow already knew the stereotype that most Mennonites had one and thought it was weird that our family did not. For the *Martyrs Mirror*'s history, see Luthy, *History of the Printings*; and Weaver-Zercher, "Martyrs Mirror."

Other examples of such sacrificial stories include the common practice of having returning missionaries as guest speakers in church to share about their work in the field, or Elizabeth Hersberger Bauman's *Coals of Fire*, a children's book published by Herald Press that has been in print for over sixty years and combines the retelling of stories from the *Martyrs Mirror* with stories from twentieth-century Mennonites (mostly missionaries) who were imprisoned or killed for their faith.
116. Not only are there all the tomes of Mennonite history published by Herald Press, but there are also independent Mennonite presses such as Cascadia Publishing House, Pandora Press, and Masthof Press adding to the stream of writing, as well as at least four Mennonite academic journals.
117. Sabrina Reed's *Lives Lived, Lives Imagined: Landscapes of Resilience in the Works of Miriam Toews* was published as *Ethics for Apocalyptic Times* was going to press, so I have not been able to incorporate Reed's work into my discussions of *Summer of My Amazing Luck* and *Women Talking*. Reed's examinations of these novels appear in chapters 2 and 3 of *Lives Lived, Lives Imagined*.

CHAPTER 1

1. Samatar, *Tender*, 23. I give further citations of this collection in the text. Samatar, "Hi."
2. Samatar, "Hi."
3. In addition to Samatar's archiving of herself, other writers archive encounters with her frequently enough that it is a notable trend. For instance, she appears throughout Kate Zambreno's hybrid memoir *To Write as If Already Dead* and Zambreno's autofictional novel *Drifts*; throughout Diana R. Zimmerman's memoir *Marry a Mennonite Boy and Make Pie* under the pseudonym "Beth"; and in an email exchange from Ashon T. Crawley's queer theological hybrid memoir *The Lonely Letters*, 103–4. Amina Cain references Samatar's story "Olimpia's Ghost" (in Samatar's *Tender*, 32–44) as an example of how Cain wants her own writing to "create ... the *sense* of another actuality, a glimpse of a shadow world" in *Horse at Night*, 20–21, her emphasis.

4. However, it might only be obvious as Goshen to other Goshen alums. The clue that reveals it as Goshen for me is the narrator's interaction with a dead squirrel (183), an animal that is ubiquitous on campus.
5. For instance, Lisa Schirch documents how some Mennonites have played an important role in the North American white supremacy movement in "Anabaptist-Mennonite Relations with Jews."
6. Incidentally, Samatar says in "Hi" that the three books she would bring to a deserted island are "the Bible, *A Thousand and One Nights*, and *In Search of Lost Time*," all of which fit this criterion.
7. Womack, *Afrofuturism*, 59. Samatar discusses Afrofuturism in "Toward a Planetary History of Afrofuturism."
8. The queer tradition also includes a precursor. Eve Kosofsky Sedgwick asserts that queers of her generation's "childhood . . . [finding of] a few cultural objects, objects of high or popular culture or both, objects whose meaning seemed mysterious, excessive, or oblique in relation to the codes most readily available to us [i.e., queer objects], became a prime resource for survival" in *Tendencies*, 3.
9. Ahmed, *Living a Feminist Life*, 240. The full list of the kit's items is on pages 240–49. Although Ahmed's discussion of objects' emotional effects and affects does not cite Ann Cvetkovich's germinal 2003 book about the affects of queer objects, *An Archive of Feelings*, and although Ahmed does not use the language of "archiving" when describing her kit, I see a relationship between the two writers' ideas. Ahmed's thinking extends Cvetkovich's because Ahmed focuses on the process of claiming any object as queer if it is in one's survival kit, whereas Cvetkovich focuses on the preservation of explicitly queer (i.e., synonymous with LGBTQ2IA+) objects that nonqueers do not value. Ahmed's concept would not affect me nearly as much as it does if I had not read Cvetkovich first. Ahmed turns to the language of archiving in a later book, *What's the Use?*, e.g., 14, 20, 81, 219.
10. Ahmed, *Living a Feminist Life*, 74–75, 6.
11. Ahmed, *Living a Feminist Life*, 5.
12. Ahmed, *Living a Feminist Life*, 240.
13. Ahmed, *What's the Use?*, 82.
14. I think here of "Song of Myself's" description of "letters from God dropped in the street" that "will punctually come forever and ever." Whitman, *Leaves of Grass*, 83.
15. Zoltan, *Praying with "Jane Eyre,"* 5, 18.
16. Ruti, *Ethics of Opting Out*, 103–4.
17. Snow, *Queering the Tarot*, 115, their emphasis. Snow's language here reminds me of Matthew 10:22, "And ye shall be hated of all men for my [i.e., Jesus's] name's sake," a verse that Mennonites have often used to comfort themselves in the face of persecution.
18. Koestenbaum, *Queen's Throat*, 62.
19. Smith and Watson, *Reading Autobiography*, 262.
20. Fournier, *Autotheory*, 138, and Samatar, "Sofia Samatar on Kafka." Samatar "advise[s]" readers "not to try carrying [the *Martyrs Mirror*] in your backpack" in *White Mosque*, 175, which implies that she might be writing from experience.
21. Snaza, *Animate Literacies*, 121–22. I feel obligated to note that Snaza argues that such pleasurable interactions with books necessitate "forms of discipline that are always violent" because of books' economic inaccessibility to many people and because of the negative environmental impact of print books and ebooks (141, 97). Although I recognize the truth of his argument, I hope that the positive effects of publishing *Ethics for Apocalyptic Times* will outweigh its negative ones, much as I assume Snaza hopes publishing *Animate Literacies* will.
22. Ahmed discusses her "love" of used books in *What's the Use?*, 14, 35–37, 78.
23. Samatar, "Sofia Samatar on Kafka."
24. Gatchalian, *Double Melancholy*, 11.
25. Solís, "mestizXXX," 513.
26. Samatar, *White Mosque*, 74.
27. Valente, *Palimpsest*, 314.
28. Sanchez, *Queer Faith*, 21.
29. I argue for this relevance throughout *Queering Mennonite Literature*, e.g., 13–14.
30. Lachman, "Creative (M)othering," 192.
31. Weinstone, "Science Fiction," 43, her emphasis.

32. Williams, "Asphodel, That Greeny Flower," 200.
33. For the record, in contrast to "Request," the course's limitations came from its institutional Mennonite context, not from the professor. My professor was supportive of my extracurricular investigations.
34. For a discussion of how this heading is oppressive because it silences the experiences of women and queers, see Adler, *Cruising the Library*.
35. Waugh, "Men's Pornography," 309, and Blake, "Tom of Finland," 348–49.
36. The narrator of another story in *Tender*, "Ogres of East Africa," literally writes on the "margins" of his white British employer's documents, claiming space for the narrator's stories of resistance alongside the official one of colonization (10, 15).

CHAPTER 2

1. Beck discusses this course in "Mennonite Literature at Goshen College." According to the syllabus, which I still have, we read more than twenty authors, eleven of them poets. See Ervin Beck, "ENGL 207/307: Interdisciplinary Literature: Mennonite Literature" (syllabus, January 2001). Incidentally, the second page of the syllabus, titled "Perspectives," contains quotations about Mennonites and our relationship to writing and the world. There is one each from John Ruth's *Mennonite Identity and Literary Art* and Al Reimer's *Mennonite Literary Voices*, with Ruth's being last on the list. Both books were already out of print, so Beck gave us chapter 4 of Reimer's book as a handout, and the entirety of Ruth's book, with four of its pages squished onto both sides of each 8.5 × 11 sheet of the handout.
2. See Di Brandt's "missionary position" poems in *questions i asked my mother*, 28–33, and Julia Spicher Kasdorf's "The Sun Lover" in *Eve's Striptease*, 7–8.
3. Jeff Gundy describes a similar poetry-motivated pilgrimage to Goshen's library in "Fields Have Edges," 78.
4. Perdomo, "Breakbeat, Remezcla," 1, his emphasis.
5. Cruz, *Queering Mennonite Literature*, 141n82. Other hybrid poetry genres include documentary poetry, such as Julia Spicher Kasdorf and Steven Rubin's *Shale Play*, which I examine later in this chapter, and visual poetry, such as Shira Dentz's *Sisyphusina*.
6. Many of Brandt's essays in *Dancing Naked* and *So this is the world & here I am in it* are authotheoretical because they use her own experiences to offer a feminist vision for the writing and Mennonite communities, among others. Gundy frequently uses a research-creational blend of academic essay and his own poems. This is especially the case in *Songs from an Empty Cage* but is also present in *Walker in the Fog* and more recent essays such as "The Fields Have Edges."
7. Gundy, *Walker in the Fog*, 133. Chapter 6 of *Walker in the Fog* is a revised version of the essay that I first encountered as Gundy, "In Praise of the Lurkers (Who Come Out to Speak)."
8. See Tiessen, *Liars and Rascals*, which argues against such attitudes. Mennonite literature has documented this view of writers since the field's earliest days. Mabel Dunham calls fiction "lies" in her 1924 novel *Trail of the Conestoga*, 15. She repeats this metafictional move in the 1927 sequel, *Toward Sodom*, 16.
9. Gundy, *Walker in the Fog*, 136.
10. Gundy, *Walker in the Fog*, 138.
11. Gundy, *Walker in the Fog*, 140.
12. Gundy, "Fields Have Edges," 87.
13. Gundy, *Songs from an Empty Cage*, 36.
14. Kasdorf and Reed, "Field Language."
15. Gundy, "Bad Mennonites," 423.
16. Gundy, *Inquiries*, 15–16.
17. Whitman, *Leaves of Grass*, 83.
18. Gundy, *Flatlands*, 9.
19. Gundy, *Flatlands*, 17.
20. Gundy, *Flatlands*, 58–59.
21. Gundy, "Fields Have Edges," 87.
22. Wright, "Community, Theology, and Mennonite Poetics," 155.
23. Gundy, *Rhapsody with Dark Matter*, 7.
24. Gundy, *Rhapsody with Dark Matter*, 17–18.
25. Gundy, *Rhapsody with Dark Matter*, 17.
26. Gundy, *Rhapsody with Dark Matter*, 29, 31.
27. Gundy, *Rhapsody with Dark Matter*, 29–31.

28. Gundy, *Rhapsody with Dark Matter*, 48.
29. Gundy, *Rhapsody with Dark Matter*, 56. On Dirk Willems, see Luthy, *Dirk Willems*.
30. Gundy, *Rhapsody with Dark Matter*, 76–77.
31. Gundy, *Rhapsody with Dark Matter*, 53.
32. Gundy, *Without a Plea*; Elliott, "Just as I Am," 235.
33. Gundy, *Without a Plea*, 27.
34. Gundy, *Without a Plea*, 31.
35. Gundy, *Without a Plea*, 32.
36. Dueck, *sing me no more*.
37. At the time of writing my essay, I missed that while I was still in my self-imposed Mennonite exile the 2009 issue of the *Journal of Mennonite Studies* included two reviews of queer Mennonite literature. See Milne, "Review of *Somewhere Else*," and Klassen, "Review of *The Widows of Hamilton House*." I also did not discover until after finishing my essay that an essay about *Somewhere Else* appeared in Europe as I was writing. See Kuester, "Between European Past and Canadian Present."
38. See Cruz, "Queer Mennonite Literature."
39. Brandt acknowledges the influence of feminism on her work in *Dancing Naked*, 35.
40. Redekop, *Making Believe*, 265.
41. Brandt, *Dancing Naked*, 14.
42. Hostetler, "After Ethnicity," 88.
43. See Leonard Neufeldt's poem "The Tree with a Hole in Our Front Yard," which is "*For Di Brandt, and to those who were angry*," and paternalistically dismisses this anger in favor of healing, in *Yarrow*, 35, his emphasis.
44. Brandt, "Paradigms of Re:placement, Re:location, and Re:vision," 154–55, 157. The persecuted wanderers myth is especially present in the Russian Mennonite community from which Brandt comes because Russian Mennonites had to flee more recently (in the 1870s and 1920s) than Swiss Mennonites, who have been living in North America reasonably undisturbed for the last three hundred years. Robert Zacharias's *Rewriting the Break Event* examines some of the fictional retellings of this wandering.
45. Brandt, "Paradigms of Re:placement," 158.
46. Brandt, "Paradigms of Re:placement," 158, 164.
47. Brandt, "Paradigms of Re:placement," 167.
48. Brandt, *So this is the world*, 1–2.
49. Brandt, *So this is the world*, 6–7.
50. Brandt, *So this is the world*, 4–5.
51. Brandt, *So this is the world*, 10, her emphasis.
52. Brandt, *Dancing Naked*, 12.
53. Brandt, *questions i asked my mother*, 17.
54. Brandt, *questions i asked my mother*, 5–6.
55. Brandt, *questions i asked my mother*, 36.
56. Brandt, *Agnes in the sky*, 42.
57. Brandt, *Dancing Naked*, 144.
58. Brandt, *Dancing Naked*, 145.
59. Brandt, *questions i asked my mother*, n.p., her emphasis.
60. Brandt relays an instance of this continued oppression when she describes how she came to the final realization that she could not remain a theological Mennonite after hearing a preacher say "firmly, loudly, as if he were God himself: 'One thing is clear. The Bible says, Woman was made for the Man,'" in *Dancing Naked*, 51.
61. Brandt, *mother, not mother*, 30.
62. Brandt, *mother, not mother*, 30.
63. Brandt, *Jerusalem, beloved*, back cover.
64. Brandt, *Jerusalem, beloved*, 6.
65. Brandt, *Jerusalem, beloved*, 10.
66. Brandt, *Walking to Mojácar*, 154.
67. Brandt, *Jerusalem, beloved*, 13.
68. Brandt, *Jerusalem, beloved*, 13.
69. Brandt, *Jerusalem, beloved*, 15.
70. Brandt, *Dancing Naked*, 152.
71. Brandt, *Jerusalem, beloved*, 6.
72. Brandt, *Walking to Mojácar*, 136.
73. Brandt, *Walking to Mojácar*, 176–78.
74. For more on Brandt's ecofeminism in *Now You Care* and *So this is the world & here I am in it*, see Hostetler, "Valediction Forbidding Excommunication."
75. Brandt, *Agnes in the sky*, 16.
76. Brandt, "Going Global," 112.
77. Brandt, *Now You Care*, 13.
78. Brandt, *Now You Care*, 15–16.
79. Hostetler, "After Ethnicity," 97.
80. Brandt, *Glitter and Fall*, xviii.
81. Brandt, *Glitter and Fall*, xix, and Brandt, "Going Global," 111.
82. Brandt, *Glitter and Fall*, xv.
83. Brandt, *Glitter and Fall*, 4.
84. Brandt, *Glitter and Fall*, 9.
85. Brandt, *Glitter and Fall*, 38.
86. Remer, *Earthprayer*, 13.

87. Hooley Yoder, "I've Read Too Much Poetry for That," 454.
88. On the distinction between the first and second generations of Mennonite writers, see Cruz, *Queering Mennonite Literature*, 141n83.
89. See Lachman, *Apple Speaks*, Lachman, *Other Acreage*, and Lachman and Kaemmerling, *What I say to this house*.
90. Lachman, *Ritual to Read Together*.
91. I use the literary canon to represent "the world" here because what is more worldly than the mainstream success that the canon represents? As I have said, Mennonites prefer the margins. Even Mennonite writers whom scholars might include in the canon of Canadian literature, such as Rudy Wiebe and Miriam Toews, write from the perspective of the marginalized.
92. Carl-Klassen, *Shelter Management*, n.p. *Shelter Management* is unpaginated, therefore I will not give any further citations of it other than poem titles. It includes twenty poems, so it is easily navigable.
93. See section 15 of "Song of Myself," in Whitman, *Leaves of Grass*, 37–40.
94. Carl-Klassen, *Ain't Country Like You*, 11, 13.
95. Carl-Klassen, *Ain't Country Like You*, 16.
96. Carl-Klassen, *Ain't Country Like You*, 46.
97. Kauffman, *Eco-Dementia*, 34.
98. Kauffman, *Eco-Dementia*, 39.
99. Kauffman, *Eco-Dementia*, 20.
100. Kasdorf and Rubin, *Shale Play*, xxiii.
101. Kasdorf, "Introduction."
102. Kasdorf and Rubin, *Shale Play*, 39, 41.
103. Kasdorf and Rubin, *Shale Play*, 40, 39.
104. Kasdorf and Rubin, *Shale Play*, 9, 10, Kasdorf's emphasis. I have felt this kind of suicidal wish many times since the pandemic began, but writing and reading have helped me survive.
105. Kasdorf, "Mightier Than the Sword," 51–54, 57–59, 65–66.
106. Kasdorf, "Introduction."
107. Johnson, *Orchard Light*, 34–38. Johnson was Kasdorf's student at Penn State, and this relationship is another example of the first generation of Mennonite writers' influence on the second generation that I discuss in Cruz, *Queering Mennonite Literature*, 12, 20. Like Lachman, Johnson has also done anthologizing work. Although I do not read *Beyond Earth's Edge: The Poetry of Spaceflight*, which Johnson coedited with Christopher Cokinos, as theapoetic, the speculative nature of its subject matter makes it akin to Sofia Samatar's space stories because, as Johnson and Cokinos write, this subject matter "form[s] an archive of possibility" (x).
108. Johnson, *Orchard Light*, 1.
109. Johnson, *Orchard Light*, 16–18.

CHAPTER 3

1. Reimer, *Mennonite Literary Voices*, 59, 63.
2. Good, "Tribute to Sara Stambaugh," 78.
3. See Stambaugh, "How Lena Got Set Back" and "Old Eby." Warren Kliewer is the other writer originally from the United States in the anthology. Katie Funk Wiebe was living in the United States at the time, though she was born in Saskatchewan.
4. Johnson, *Orchard Light*, 16, 35. Miller, *Shadows*; *Loyalties*, which includes Kline's story; and *Passages*.
5. Reed, *Both My Sons*, 99, 369–71, 375. Reed's most famous novel, *Mennonite Soldier*, also has a historical setting, World War I.
6. Incidentally, one of the real-life characters from *Trail of the Conestoga*, Benjamin Eby, was Stambaugh's great-great-great-great uncle. See the family tree in Stambaugh, *Yon Far Country*, 9.
7. The novel's adaptation, *Hazel's People* (Charles Davis, director) played in New York City and other locales and starred Hollywood actors Pat Hingle and Geraldine Page. There are plans to make Rachel Yoder's 2021 novel *Nightbitch* into a film. See Fleming, "Amy Adams."
8. Lapp, "Embodied Voices, Imprisoned Bodies." The only other scholarship to examine Lancaster-related texts since then is work on the poet Jane Rohrer. See Hostetler, "Coming into Voice"; Kasdorf, "Coming Back"; Kasdorf, Reed, and Robinson, *Field Language*.
9. Good, "Tribute to Sara Stambaugh," 79.
10. Friesen, *Interim*, 17, 22.
11. I write more about hearing these stories in *Queering Mennonite Literature*, 53–54, 145n21.

12. Good, "Tribute to Sara Stambaugh," 78.
13. Kasdorf and Reed, "Field Language." Kasdorf says later in the interview that she "dislike[s] (and can't resist) making broad generalizations about groups." She is correct, though, about Mennonite artists needing to look outside of Mennonitism's boundaries because the Mennonite community has been and often still is anti-art, so artists have had to go out into the world and then return, as Jeff Gundy's lurkers, creating a vibrant Mennonite literary community in the process.
14. Juhnke, *Vision, Doctrine, War*, 106.
15. Stambaugh, *I Hear the Reaper's Song*, 129–30. Further references to this novel are given in the text except when paired with references to historians' texts.
16. Ruth, *Earth Is the Lord's*, 726.
17. See Aldrich, *Death Rode the Rails*.
18. Ruth, *Earth Is the Lord's*, 727, and Stambaugh, *I Hear the Reaper's Song*, 185.
19. Juhnke, *Vision, Doctrine, War*, 106, and Stambaugh, *I Hear the Reaper's Song*, 158–59.
20. Ruth, *Earth Is the Lord's*, 727.
21. Ruth, *Earth Is the Lord's*, 741.
22. Stambaugh, *Yon Far Country*, 55, 75.
23. John S. Coffman was another of these evangelists according to Ruth, *Earth Is the Lord's*, 728–32. Ruth speaks favorably of Coffman's revivals, comparing Coffman's unlicensed preaching to the necessary "irreverent" work of writers, in his sermon "Revolution and Reverence," 184.
24. Stambaugh, *Yon Far Country*, 81.
25. Stambaugh, *Yon Far Country*, 60. According to family stories that Stambaugh retells in her memoir, Barbie and Martha's mother Barbara joined the plain revival because Barbie did not want to go to the gathering the night of her death, but Barbara cajoled her into going and felt guilty about it for the rest of her life (75–76, 78).
26. Ruth, *Earth Is the Lord's*, 737, 743.
27. Ruth, *Earth Is the Lord's*, 1077.
28. Silas, Stambaugh's grandfather, is an appropriate choice to narrate the novel because she writes that he "and Martha talked about it all their lives" in *Yon Far Country*, 75.
29. Indeed, Peter Hershey never adopted plain dress according to Stambaugh, *Yon Far Country*, 85.
30. Sofia Samatar names how the railroad remains a place where the sectarian elements of Mennonitism and the world meet in her description of "Amish and Old Order people['s]" frequent use of Amtrak (because of these groups' rejection of automobile ownership) alongside "a large, random selection of the American public" in "On Dwelling," 270.
31. Mennonites from Lancaster still engage in this long-distance farming, as Marie Mutsuki Mockett describes throughout *American Harvest*.

CHAPTER 4

1. Toews, "'It gets under the skin,'" 119–20, her emphasis.
2. Toews, *Swing Low*, 8, e.g., 47, 158.
3. Toews, "'A place you can't go home to,'" 56.
4. Toews acknowledges this continuing rejection in "'A place you can't go home to,'" 57; in "'It gets under the skin,'" 108, 122; and in "Novelist Miriam Toews."
5. Toews uses "secular Mennonite" in "Novelist"; "'It gets under the skin,'" 122; and "Complicated Kind of Author." Toews affirms that Mennonite ethnicity exists apart from theological Mennonitism in a similar manner as Jewish ethnicity is separate from Judaism in "'It gets under the skin,'" 122, and "'A place you can't go home to,'" 56.
6. See, for instance, the 1990s–early 2000s zine *Mennonot*, whose tagline was "For Mennos on the Margins," or Jeff Gundy's concepts of "lurkers" and "Bad Mennonites" discussed in chapter 2.
7. Tiessen, "Homelands," 21–22.
8. Toews, "'A place you can't go home to,'" 60.
9. Toews, *Summer of My Amazing Luck*, 173, 74. Further references to this novel are given in the text except when paired with references to Toews's nonfiction. Although there is nothing exclusively Mennonite about Dutch Blitz, many Mennonites play it avidly, especially at large Mennonite gatherings, so it serves as a kind of Mennonite shibboleth. Similarly, Toews's second novel, *A Boy of Good Breeding*,

has no Mennonite markers except that its protagonist's last name is "Funk," which is a common Mennonite last name. Therefore, the novel is a Mennonite one in its subject matter even as it pretends not to be. My speculation, which is informed by my own attempts to leave Mennonitism behind and Mennonite literature's insistence on pulling me back in, is that these begrudging Mennonite traces in Toews's first two novels are her trying to separate herself from the tradition and failing. She embraces this failure by writing openly about Mennonites in most of her subsequent books.

10. Van Braght, *Bloody Theater or Martyrs Mirror*, 741. Portrayals of intra-Mennonite strife (many of which are autobiographical) are legion in Mennonite literature. Prominent examples include Toews's *A Complicated Kindness* and *Irma Voth*.

11. Toews, *Swing Low*, 201, *Summer*, 3; *Swing Low*, 57–58, *Summer*, 175; *Swing Low*, 139, *Summer*, 49, respectively.

12. Kirch, "Road Tripping with Miriam Toews," 22.

13. Toews, "'A place you can't go home to,'" 54–55. Toews worked for the CBC at the time.

14. Kirch, "Road Tripping," 22.

CHAPTER 5

1. Schalk, *Bodyminds Reimagined*, 17, her emphasis. Schalk's inclusion of "hybrid genres" in this list highlights how speculative fiction is often research-creation.

2. Weinstone, "Science Fiction," 43.

3. Note that Schalk's definition implicitly rewrites the history of African American speculative fiction because it makes space for a text such as Toni Morrison's 1973 novel *Sula* (Schalk names Morrison's 1987 novel *Beloved* in relation to her definition [*Bodyminds* 21, 67, 69] but does not apply it back to *Sula*), which is a magical realist and a religious text because of its "plague of robins" (89), its fortune-telling dreams (74), and its eponymous Christ figure character who has an ever-changing birthmark that is sometimes the mark of evil and sometimes the mark of peace (114, 156). Therefore, Schalk's definition complicates even further the already problematic oft-repeated narrative that this history begins with Samuel R. Delany's and his student Octavia Butler's work. Delany himself questions this narrative in "Racism and Science Fiction," in *"Atheist in the Attic" Plus . . .* , 73–74. I thank Suzanne Richardson for a Facebook conversation on 21 October 2019 that helped me to articulate this idea.

4. Samatar, "Writing Queerly."

5. Quoted in Sanchez, *Queer Faith*, 16–17, their emphasis.

6. Indeed, the subtitle of Klaassen's *Anabaptism: Neither Catholic nor Protestant* is so prominent that people often forget it is not the book's main title.

7. Sanchez, *Queer Faith*, 4.

8. "Theory, n."

9. Redekop, *Making Believe*, 153.

10. Schalk, *Bodyminds Reimagined*, 114, 134.

11. Gundy, *Songs from an Empty Cage*, 215.

12. Zacharias, *Reading Mennonite Writing*, 76.

13. Mennonite examples include Davis, "Laboring Through *The Weather Book*," and Lapp, "Embodied Voices, Imprisoned Bodies." Non-Mennonite examples include Dwyer, "Janet Kauffman's 'Patriotic'"; Hinnefeld, "For the Collaborators"; Hollywood, "On the Materiality of Air."

14. Zacharias, *Reading Mennonite Writing*, 224n1.

15. Kauffman, *Body in Four Parts*, 110. Further references to this novel are given in the text.

16. For an introduction to mermaid studies, see Bacchilega and Brown, *Penguin Book of Mermaids*.

17. Donovan O. Schaefer's *Religious Affects* is one work that does this from a religious perspective.

18. Hollywood discusses the elements' role in the novel in "On the Materiality of Air," 509–10.

19. *My Lovely Enemy* did so poorly that it was not reprinted in paperback until 2009 despite Wiebe's prominent position in the field of Canadian literature at the time. It is now back out of print.

20. Bechtel, "Interview with Greg Bechtel."

21. See Dorsey, "Being One's Own Pornographer."
22. Bechtel, *Boundary Problems*, 52–53. Further references to this collection are given in the text.
23. Bechtel, "Interview with Greg Bechtel," his emphasis.
24. Another way that the Smutsters are like Anabaptists is that their name was given to them by outsiders as a term of derision (169n.).
25. Fred Kniss's *Disquiet in the Land* offers a history of numerous official Mennonite schisms.
26. Ruth, *Mennonite Identity and Literary Art*, 19–20.
27. Samatar, *Tender*, 67. Further references to this collection are given in the text.
28. Samatar, "Standing at the Ruins," 169, 179. Samatar also writes about the intersection of the pandemic and climate change in a 2022 essay, "On Dwelling," 265–66. This essay appeared in July 2022 despite its official 2021 publication date because *Conrad Grebel Review*'s publication schedule has suffered from pandemic-related delays. The essay, which partially uses a diaristic format, begins on "January 2, 2022," and Samatar notes that she gave the lecture the essay "is based on ... in March 2022" (265, 277n21).
29. The story describes the Fair Folk as "fifteen, twenty feet tall" with wings and says that "they came here" from some unnamed place. Samatar, *Tender*, 62, 67. Therefore, although the story does not explicitly say that they are aliens it is fair to assume that they are something different than the "fair folk" of various fairytales: fairies, sprites, pixies, and the like. I thank Geraldine Long for a comment in a class discussion on 10 December 2019 that helped me to articulate this distinction.
30. On disability in Mennonite literature, see Cruz, *Queering Mennonite Literature*, 65–71, 89–90, 94–95.
31. Samatar, "Scope of This Project." Some scholars differentiate between the terms "postcolonial," which names the state of affairs after the end of political colonization, and the more recent "decolonial," which puts more emphasis on undoing the effects of colonization rather than rising above them. I view Samatar's use of "postcolonial" as basically synonymous with "decolonial," which was barely in use at her time of writing. Therefore, I treat them as such in my discussion of her essay.
32. Samatar, *White Mosque*, 138.
33. My phrasing is inspired by the title of another Mennonite of color, Peter Dula's, essay, "Theology Is a Kind of Reading."
34. Samatar, "Scope of This Project." Although neither cites Samatar, Melanie Kampen calls for the decolonization of Mennonite theology in "On the Need," and Karl Koop names hymns as shared ground for discussing theology historically and globally in "Contours and Possibilities," 22, 25.
35. Quoted in Redekop, *Making Believe*, 113.
36. Wiebe, *Blue Mountains of China*, 271–72.
37. Cruz, *Queering Mennonite Literature*, 154n30. Samatar writes about the Great Trek throughout *White Mosque*.
38. For a history of this etching that includes reproductions of the different versions used in various editions of the *Martyrs Mirror*, see chapter 7 of Kasdorf, *The Body and the Book*.
39. Zacharias, *Reading Mennonite Writing*, 187. Zacharias further explores the story's "theologically informed critique" (204) throughout his discussion of it, especially 204–5, 211–12.
40. Carl-Klassen, "Review of *The Farm Wife's Almanac*," 259.
41. Cruz, *Queering Mennonite Literature*, 136, and Zacharias, *Reading Mennonite Writing*, 206–7.
42. Samatar, "Centaur's Recipe," 322. Other writers who attended Goshen during Lindsay's long tenure there have likewise written about his influence. See Gundy, "Tribute to Nicholas C. Lindsay, Sr."; Kasdorf, "Essential Stranger"; and Beck, "Tribute to Nick Lindsay." Lindsay was still at Goshen during my first year there, though I did not care about poetry yet and thus did not sign up for his workshop, which I now regret. But I remember flyers he posted around campus for a poetry contest that asked for entries using a line something like "I am sitting by the fountain, dying of thirst" (an appropriate

subject considering the centrality of fountains on Goshen's campus), and that the prize was $25.00, and that the way the flyer announced this prize money was striking enough that I thought to myself, "Wow, this guy is weird." I definitely got the vibe that Samatar's father names when she tells him in "The Centaur's Recipe" that she is taking a course with Lindsay and her father "delight[edly]" replies "Nick Lindsay! That crazy guy is still there?" (317).

43. See Brandt, *questions i asked my mother*, and Friesen, *Unearthly Horses*, 15–26.

44. Plett's first two books, *Safe Girl to Love* and *Little Fish*, each won the Lambda Literary Award for Transgender Fiction (in 2015 and 2019, respectively), and *Little Fish* also won the 2019 Amazon.ca First Novel Award, which came with a $60,000 prize. There is a profusion of Mennonite speculative fiction that far outstrips the writing I examine in this chapter. For a helpful introduction to the field, see Gundy, "Speculative Fiction."

45. See chapters 3, 5, the second half of chapter 6, and the epilogue in Cruz, *Queering Mennonite Literature*.

46. See Cruz, *Queering Mennonite Literature*, 105–16, 118–19, for commentary on five of these stories.

47. See Plett, *Little Fish*. Sex work is one of *Little Fish*'s major themes, and it shares two characters with *Safe Girl to Love*, Sophie from "Other Women" and Carla from "Not Bleak." These two stories are the collection's only two explicitly Mennonite ones, so it makes sense that they are the ones referenced in the novel, which is also explicitly Mennonite.

48. Plett, *Safe Girl to Love*, 93, and Toews, *Complicated Kindness*, 244, emphasis in Plett, not Toews. Further citations of *Safe Girl to Love* are given in parentheses in the text.

49. Toews, *Complicated Kindness*, 73, her capitalization.

50. Halberstam, *Trans**, 21.

51. Lish's name is a reference to Toews's *Summer of My Amazing Luck*, as I say in *Queering Mennonite Literature*, 105.

52. See Plett, *Dream of a Woman*, and "Coke." Julia Serano documents the commonality of trans sex work due to economic hardship in *Whipping Girl*, 261.

53. Plett, *Safe Girl to Love*, n.p., second page after the table of contents; Tea, *Chelsea Whistle*, 55.

54. For instance, Tea, *How to Grow Up*, viii.

55. Tea, *How to Grow Up*, 57–59, 245–47.

56. The sketch, which first aired in 2011, and which includes singing by a gay men's choir, is available as "Dream of the '90s | Portlandia | IFC"; see also Johnson, *Stray City*. Incidentally, there is a blurb by one of *Portlandia*'s costars, Carrie Brownstein, on the back cover of *Stray City*'s dustjacket, and the front cover has a picture of a cat. Although it does not focus solely on Portland, Brownstein's memoir, *Hunger Makes Me a Modern Girl*, is a nonfiction example of this kind of laudatory Portland portrayal.

57. Bonzo, "Spray Paint and Patriarchy."

58. Plett, *Dream of a Woman*, e.g., 46.

59. Cruz, *Queering Mennonite Literature*, 18–19, 25, 142n3. In 2021, Plett and Fitzpatrick began another endeavor that also archives queer stories, LittlePuss Press. See https://www.littlepuss.net/.

60. Fitzpatrick and Plett, afterword to *Meanwhile, Elsewhere*, 440.

61. Cruz, *Queering Mennonite Literature*, e.g., 37, 53–54, 110, and Beck, "Signifying Menno." Beck's ten archetypes are Trickster as Deceiver, Trickster as Subverter, Self-Sacrifice, The Martyr, "Work and Hope," Noble Savage, Good Community, Bad Community, Coy Sexuality, and Community on the Move. The inclusion of all but the first two in "Fallow" is more evidence of the story's Mennonite character.

62. Toews, "How Pacifism Can Lead to Violence."

63. Toews, *Women Talking*, n.p., third page after the copyright page. Further citations of this novel are given in parentheses in the text.

64. My thanks to Ruth Yoder Wenger for confirming in a Facebook comment on 30 May 2020 that the first US edition, which was published in 2019, has a different dust jacket and does not have stamped covers.

65. Toews, "How Pacifism Can Lead to Violence."

66. Quoted in Kennel, "Secular Mennonites." Margaret Steffler argues that the novel "convers[es] with early French feminist theory" in "Breaking Patriarchy."
67. Cruz, "Review of *Women Talking*," 429.
68. "Sissy, n. and adj."
69. Kehler, "Becoming Divine Women: Miriam Toews's *Women Talking* as Parable." As her subtitle suggests, Kehler also reads the novel theologically, albeit through the lens of a different genre.
70. I thank Ervin Beck for a conversation on 29 May 2019 that helped me to articulate this idea. More recently, Kehler makes a more unequivocal statement, claiming that the women's leaving "is implausible by any rational standards," in "Becoming Divine Women."
71. Redekop, *Making Believe*, 210.
72. Toews, "How Pacifism Can Lead to Violence."

CHAPTER 6

1. "Samuel R. Delany," 2393.
2. In 1968, Delany wrote the book, originally titled *Equinox*, hoping that Essex House, a publisher of literary erotica, would accept it. However, Essex House went out of business shortly after Delany completed the manuscript, so he put it aside. After Essex House's demise, Delany's agent sent the novel to several publishers before coming to an agreement with Lancer Books in 1972. They published it in 1973 and then folded "a week" later. The book remained out of print in the 1970s despite Delany's ascension into the realm of commercially stable publishing. Delany explains that even though Bantam bought the American rights to all his books in 1977, they refused to reprint *The Tides of Lust* because of its sexual explicitness (Delany, *Shorter Views*, 299–303). Savoy Books published a British edition taken from the original Lancer plates in 1980, but it failed to raise the novel's profile. This edition is almost as rare as the first because the police "impounded and burned" the unsold copies of the book shortly after it was printed according to Seth McEvoy's *Samuel R. Delany*, 117. Rhinoceros (their emphasis) reprinted the novel in 1994 before also going out of business. This edition restored Delany's original title and added one hundred years to each character's age to avoid child pornography charges. Delany, *Equinox*, 6. Lancer had renamed the book *The Tides of Lust* for marketing purposes. For a survey of the publication difficulties suffered by all of Delany's "pornographic" works, see Hemmingson, "Trouble with Samuel R. Delany's Pornography," 376–78. A recent example of how Delany's writing continues to have publication difficulties occurred in 2022 when the *Georgia Review*, which had planned to serialize Delany's novel-in-progress *This Short Day of Frost and Sun*, stopped this serialization after its first installment because the journal's editor "decided that *The Georgia Review* is not the right venue for the publication of the entire novel" despite the book's "sophistication of thought and artistry befitting one of the most accomplished and continually daring writers alive." Maa, "To Our Readers," 366; see also Delany, "*This Short Day of Frost and Sun*."
3. Ahmed, *Promise of Happiness*, 19. On a related note, Delany's bibliophilia also involves large amounts of book buying. See, for instance, his 2005 statement, "I spend as much on reading matter weekly as I do on food . . . for a family of two. That includes a fair amount of eating out" in *About Writing*, 36–37.
4. See chapter 3 of Cruz, "Third Way to Change."
5. Rosenberg, "In Praise of Samuel R. Delany."
6. Martínez, *On Making Sense*, 3.
7. Allison, *Skin*, 100.
8. See especially the scenes about Gorgik's sex life in Delany, *Tales of Nevèrÿon*, 152–54, 238.
9. *The Motion of Light in Water*, *Heavenly Breakfast*, *Times Square Red*, *Bread and Wine*, and *1984* are the ones I read at the time, in that approximate order. They have now been joined by the first volume of Delany's journals, *In Search of Silence*, and another volume of his letters, *Letters from Amherst*.
10. Delany, *Times Square Red*, 44.

11. Delany, *1984*, 213, and Taylor, *Polymath*.
12. For a summary of queer theory's critique of marriage's relationship to capitalism, see Ruti, *Ethics of Opting Out*, 23–25. Speaking of actions we sometimes must take to survive the violence of capitalism, despite my continuing reservations about the institution of marriage I got married for a second time in April 2022 so that I could get on my partner's medical insurance.
13. Stockton, *Avidly Reads Making Out*, 114. Stockton does note that divorce requires economic "privilege" (115). That I asked for a divorce after acquiring a tenure-track job is not a complete coincidence.
14. Delany, *Shorter Views*, x–xi.
15. Delany, "Samuel R. Delany on His Legacy." Mok is a link between Delany and Mennonite literature because she illustrated a chapbook by Casey Plett, *Lizzy and Annie*.
16. Gundy, "Introduction," and Schroeder, "Mennonite in the Solar System," 277. The conversation with Samatar took place at the 2015 Mennonite/s Writing conference at Fresno Pacific University in Fresno, California. I believe we talked on 14 March, but it may have been the day before.
17. Gundy, *Walker in the Fog*, 264–68. Gundy's titular choice of "Anabaptist" rather than "Mennonite" follows current usage of the terms within theological Mennonite discourse, with the former connoting an ideal expression of Mennonitism in line with its radical Anabaptist roots and the latter connoting institutionalized (and thus impure) Mennonitism. I appreciate Gundy's usage here because in some ways "Anabaptist" is a more open term, which is the point of his essay and my application of it to Delany, although I also acknowledge that the term's recent overuse among Mennonites has led to a vacuity of meaning. As Mennonite historian Theron Schlabach observes wryly, "Whate'er we construe, to be good and true, we name the word Anabaptist." Quoted in Kraybill, *Eastern Mennonite University*, 326. Lavelle Porter does a similar reading of the "spiritual themes" in Delany's 2012 novel *Through the Valley of the Nest of Spiders* in "The Strange Career of Samuel R. Delany."

18. Delany, *American Shore*, 36–37.
19. Freeman, "Afterword," 318.
20. Delany, *Of Solids and Surds*, 61–62.
21. Incidentally, in another example of his sexual openness, Delany can trace the lineage of his sexual partners back to Whitman. Delany had sex with Chuck Bergman, who had sex with Allen Ginsberg, who had sex with Neal Cassady, who had sex with Gavin Arthur, who had sex with Edward Carpenter, who had sex with Whitman. Delany, *Occasional Views*, 225.
22. See Delany, "Eden, Eden, Eden: Genesis 2:4–22," in *Occasional Views*, 68–83. This essay is also relevant to my discussion of *The Mad Man* below because Delany begins it by describing a local park where he converses with the unhoused people who live there before he transitions to his discussion of the interaction between Eve, Adam, and God in the Garden of Eden (68–69).
23. Delany, *Of Solids and Surds*, 28.
24. Delany, *Of Solids and Surds*, 32.
25. Jordan, "In Search of Queer Theology Lost," 304, 299.
26. Schalk, *Bodyminds Reimagined*, 142.
27. Sandor, "Ram in the Thicket," 29, 32.
28. Womack, *Afrofuturism*, 158. Similarly, Robert Zacharias reads Sofia Samatar's "Fallow" as a work of theologically informed Afrofuturism in *Reading Mennonite Writing*, 205–9.
29. Mary Catherine Foltz also reads the novel as ethics in "Excremental Ethics of Samuel R. Delany," focusing on its ecological themes.
30. Gundy, *Walker in the Fog*, 266–67.
31. For an instance of Whitman's lists, see the catalog of professions in section 15 of "Song of Myself" in *Leaves of Grass*, 37–40.
32. Gundy, *Walker in the Fog*, 268.
33. Other pieces of Delany's work also include depictions of the unhoused. In his 2007 novel *Dark Reflections*, which I first read sometime after reading *The Mad Man*, the protagonist marries an unhoused woman. Delany's partner, Dennis, whom he has been with for over thirty years, was unhoused when they met, as Delany documents in *Bread and Wine*. As in *The Mad Man*, Delany includes a portrayal

of the relationship between the AIDS crisis and houselessness in New York City during the late 1980s and early 1990s in the first chapter of *This Short Day of Frost and Sun*, 380, 384.
34. Delany, *Mad Man*, 22–38. Further citations of this novel are given in parentheses in the text.
35. Davis, "Delany's Dirt," 166.
36. I thank one of *Ethics for Apocalyptic Times*'s anonymous peer reviewers for this idea.
37. Tucker, *Sense of Wonder*, 244.
38. Gundy, *Walker in the Fog*, 268.
39. Whitman, *Leaves of Grass*, 48–49. The first ellipsis in this quotation is Whitman's and the second one is mine.
40. Woodhouse, *Unlimited Embrace*, 213, his emphasis.
41. Bucher and Dickel, "Affinity for the Lumpen," 302.

EPILOGUE

1. Hostetler, "Dancing on the Bridge," 233.
2. On this aspect of haiku, see Spikes, "Subjective Criticism and Haiku," 127.
3. Gundy, "Fields Have Edges," 87.
4. Amann is quoted in Carter, *Haiku in Canada*, 55–56; Ross, "General Introduction," vi–vii; Gurga, *Haiku*, 11, and see 126–28 for further description of the Zen principles that haiku contains. In *The Weather in Proust*, Eve Kosofsky Sedgwick explains how her study of Buddhism helps her to appreciate "a mysticism that . . . is made up of dailiness; a mysticism that doesn't depend on so-called mystical experiences; that doesn't rely on the esoteric or occult, but rather on simple, material metamorphoses as they are emulsified with language and meaning" in literature (113), so Buddhism also has relevance for theapoetics in other genres besides haiku.
5. Rosenstock, *Haiku Enlightenment*, 17, 24–25, 40.
6. Richardson, "tattooed girlfriend."
7. Carter, *Haiku in Canada*, 154–55.
8. Quoted in Carter, *Haiku in Canada*, 13, Carter's emphasis.
9. Threadgill, *Tangled in the Light*, 7.
10. Lee Gurga explains that haiku are traditionally only seventeen Japanese "sound" units long, which usually equals "nine to twelve" English syllables, not the five-seven-five seventeen syllable structure often mistakenly taught North American students in elementary school, in *Haiku*, 15–16. Michael Dylan Welch further explores this issue and gives the range of ten to fourteen English syllables in "Heft of Haiku," 111. For more on the impact of haiku's short form, see Stepenoff, "Personal and the Universal in Haiku."
11. Hooley Yoder, "Know Your Place."
12. Cruz, "pandemic," 15.
13. Cruz, "summer solstice."
14. Pollack, *Rachel Pollack's Tarot Wisdom*, xiii, xx, 5.
15. Cicero and Cicero, *Golden Dawn Ritual Tarot*, 8. Lisa Schirch documents that some early Anabaptists were also Qabalists in "Anabaptist-Mennonite Relations with Jews."
16. Robinson, *Pamela Colman Smith*, 12.
17. Pollack, *Rachel Pollack's Tarot Wisdom*, 34.
18. Snow, *Queering the Tarot*, 198.
19. Cicero and Cicero, *Golden Dawn Ritual Tarot*, 16.
20. Gundy, *Songs from an Empty Cage*, 19, 204. Charlene Gingerich makes a similar assertion in "Beauty Happens."
21. Delany, *Return to Nevèrÿon*, 281. The card is from Russell FitzGerald's 1969 deck, Delany's copy of which is now archived with Delany's papers at Yale. See https://collections.library.yale.edu/catalog/16792278. Dodie Bellamy discusses the deck in *Bee Reaved*, 240. I mention Bellamy here because her queer feminist writing exemplifies theapoetics. In addition to frequently writing about her explorations of the tarot, she has also published a book of secular sutras, *The TV Sutras*, and regularly writes about her favorite objects in her nonfiction in the manner of Sara Ahmed's killjoy survival kits (e.g., her fountain pen in *The Buddhist*, 133), as she does regarding her copy of FitzGerald's deck. I only recently encountered Bellamy's work, which is why I don't discuss it further here despite

her becoming one of my favorite writers, but this encounter shows how theapoetic encounters happen all the time from different directions like Walt Whitman's "letters from God dropped in the street" (*Leaves of Grass*, 83) when we are open to them.

22. Pollack, *Seventy-Eight Degrees of Wisdom*, 97, 99, and Eliot, *Selected Poems*, 52.
23. Snow, *Queering the Tarot*, 49.
24. Snow emphasizes the necessity of stripping away the tarot's Christian associations for queer readers and readings throughout *Queering the Tarot*, e.g., 14, 21, 54.

BIBLIOGRAPHY

Acevedo, Elizabeth. *The Poet X*. New York: HarperTeen, 2018.

Adler, Melissa. *Cruising the Library: Perversities in the Organization of Knowledge*. New York: Fordham University Press, 2017.

Ahmed, Sara. *Complaint!* Durham, NC: Duke University Press, 2021.

———. *Living a Feminist Life*. Durham, NC: Duke University Press, 2017.

———. *The Promise of Happiness*. Durham, NC: Duke University Press, 2010.

———. *What's the Use? On the Uses of Use*. Durham, NC: Duke University Press, 2019.

Aldrich, Mark. *Death Rode the Rails: American Railroad Accidents and Safety, 1828–1965*. Baltimore: Johns Hopkins University Press, 2006.

Allison, Dorothy. *Skin: Talking About Sex, Class and Literature*. Ithaca, NY: Firebrand Books, 1994.

Anzaldúa, Gloria E. *Borderlands/La Frontera: The New Mestiza*. 4th ed. 25th anniversary ed. San Francisco: Aunt Lute Books, 2012.

Axelson, Ben. "Coronavirus Timeline in NY: Here's How Gov. Cuomo Has Responded to COVID-19 Pandemic Since January." Syracuse.com, 15 April 2020, https://www.syracuse.com/coronavirus/2020/04/coronavirus-timeline-in-ny-heres-how-gov-cuomo-has-responded-to-covid-19-pandemic-since-january.html.

Bacchilega, Cristina, and Marie Alohalani Brown, eds. *The Penguin Book of Mermaids*. New York: Penguin Books, 2019.

Back, Rachel Tzvia. *What Use Is Poetry, the Poet Is Asking*. Bristol, UK: Shearsman Books, 2019.

Baraka, Amiri. *SOS: Poems 1961–2013*. Edited by Paul Vangelisti. New York: Grove Press, 2015.

Bauman, Elizabeth Hershberger. *Coals of Fire*. Scottdale, PA: Herald Press, 1954.

Beachy, Kirsten Eve. "Wives Like Us." *Journal of Mennonite Writing* 11, no. 2 (2019): https://mennonitewriting.org/journal/11/2/kirsten-beachy-reimagined-scripture/.

Bechtel, Greg. *Boundary Problems: Stories*. Calgary: Freehand Books, 2014.

———. "Interview with Greg Bechtel." By Sofia Samatar. *Journal of Mennonite Writing* 7, no. 3 (2015): https://mennonitewriting.org/journal/7/3/interview-greg-bechtel/#all.

Beck, Ervin. *MennoFolk: Mennonite and Amish Folk Traditions*. Scottdale, PA: Herald Press, 2004.

———. "Mennonite Literature at Goshen College." *Journal of Mennonite Writing* 8, no. 1 (2016): http://www.mennonitewriting.org/journal/8/1/mennonite-literature-goshen-college/#all.

———. "Mennonite Transgressive Literature." In Zacharias, *After Identity*, 52–69.

———. "Postcolonial Literary Detection in *Fear of Landing*." *Journal of Mennonite Studies* 39 (2021): 193–207.

———. "The Signifying Menno: Archetypes for Authors and Critics." In Roth and Beck, *Migrant Muses*, 49–67.

———, ed. "Tribute to Nick Lindsay." Special issue, *Journal of Mennonite Writing* 12, no. 2 (2020): https://mennonitewriting.org/journal/12/2/.

Bellamy, Dodie. *Bee Reaved*. South Pasadena, CA: Semiotext(e), 2021.

———. *The Buddhist*. Portland, OR: Allone Co. Editions, 2011.

———. *The TV Sutras*. Brooklyn: Ugly Duckling Presse, 2014.

Bender, Elizabeth Horsch. "Literature, Mennonites in: United States and Canada." In *The Mennonite Encyclopedia*, vol. 3, edited by

Harold S. Bender, 372–74. Scottdale, PA: Mennonite Publishing House, 1957.
Bennett, Jane. *Influx and Efflux: Writing Up with Walt Whitman*. Durham, NC: Duke University Press, 2020.
Beowulf. Translated by R. M. Liuzza. Peterborough, ON: Broadview Press, 2000.
Bergen, Jeremy M. "The Ecumenical Vocation of Anabaptist Theology." In Schmidt Roberts, Martens, and Penner, *Recovering from the Anabaptist Vision*, 103–26.
Blake, Nayland. "Tom of Finland: An Appreciation." In Creekmur and Doty, *Out in Culture*, 343–53.
Bonzo, N. O. "Spray Paint and Patriarchy: An Interview with N. O. Bonzo." By *It's Going Down*, *It's Going Down*, 31 August 2016, https://itsgoingdown.org/spray-paint-patriarchy-interview-n-o-bonzo/.
Braght, Thieleman J. van. *The Bloody Theater or Martyrs Mirror of the Defenseless Christians Who Baptized Only Upon Confession of Faith, and Who Suffered and Died for the Testimony of Jesus, Their Saviour, From the Time of Christ to the Year A.D. 1660.* 1660. Translated by Joseph F. Sohm. Scottdale, PA: Herald Press, 1950.
Brandt, Di. *Agnes in the sky*. Winnipeg: Turnstone Press, 1990.
———. *Dancing Naked: Narrative Strategies for Writing Across Centuries*. Stratford, ON: Mercury Press, 1996.
———. *Glitter and Fall: Laozi's "Dao De Jing" Transinhalations*. Winnipeg: Turnstone Press, 2018.
———. "Going Global." *Essays on Canadian Writing* 71 (2000): 106–13.
———. *Jerusalem, beloved*. Winnipeg: Turnstone Press, 1995.
———. *mother, not mother*. Stratford, ON: Mercury Press, 1992.
———. *Now You Care*. Toronto: Coach House Books, 2003.
———. "Paradigms of Re:placement, Re:location, and Re:vision: The Creative Challenge of the New Mennonite Writing of Manitoba (and the World)." *Journal of Mennonite Studies* 36 (2018): 153–69.
———. *questions i asked my mother*. Winnipeg: Turnstone Press, 1987.
———. *So this is the world and here I am in it*. Edmonton: NeWest Press, 2007.
———. *Walking to Mojácar*. Winnipeg: Turnstone Press, 2010.
Braun, Connie T. "A Selection from *An Inheritance of Words, Unspoken*." In Buller and Fast, *Mothering Mennonite*, 85–102.
Braun, Jan Guenther. "A Complicated Becoming." *Journal of Mennonite Studies* 34 (2016): 291–97.
Brintnall, Kent L., Joseph A. Marchal, and Stephen D. Moore, eds. *Sexual Disorientations: Queer Temporalities, Affects, Theologies*. New York: Fordham University Press, 2018.
Brostoff, Alex, and Lauren Fournier. "Introduction: Autotheory ASAP! Academia, Decoloniality, and 'I.'" *ASAP Journal* 6, no. 3 (2021): 489–502.
brown, adrienne maree. *Pleasure Activism: The Politics of Feeling Good*. Chico, CA: AK Press, 2019.
Brownstein, Carrie. *Hunger Makes Me a Modern Girl: A Memoir*. New York: Riverhead Books, 2015.
Bucher, Michael, and Simon Dickel. "An Affinity for the Lumpen: Depictions of Homelessness in Delany's *Bread and Wine* and *The Mad Man*." *African American Review* 48, no. 3 (2015): 289–304.
Buller, Rachel Epp. "Learning from Our Ancestors: Listening to the Patterns in Our Hands." In Friesen and Koehn, *Anabaptist ReMix*, 325–33.
Buller, Rachel Epp, and Kerry Fast, eds. *Mothering Mennonite*. Bradford, ON: Demeter Press, 2013.
Burns, Stephanie Chandler. "Queering Anabaptist Theology: An Endeavor in Breaking Binaries as Hermeneutical Community." In Schmidt Roberts, Martens, and Penner, *Recovering from the Anabaptist Vision*, 77–91.
Cain, Amina. *A Horse at Night: On Writing*. St. Louis: Dorothy, a Publishing Project, 2022.
Cambre, Carolina. "Crisis of Literacies: How Does the Orchid Cite the Bee?" In Loveless, *Knowings and Knots*, 75–94.
Carl-Klassen, Abigail. *Ain't Country Like You*. Maywood, NJ: Digging Press, 2020.

———. "Review of *The Farm Wife's Almanac*," by Shari Wagner. *Mennonite Quarterly Review* 94, no. 2 (2020): 258–60.

———. *Shelter Management*. Chicago: Dancing Girl Press, 2017.

Carter, Angela. *Nights at the Circus*. 1984. New York: Penguin Books, 1993.

Carter, Terry Ann. *Haiku in Canada: History, Poetry, Memoir*. Victoria, BC: Ekstasis Editions, 2020.

Cavendish, Margaret. *"The Blazing World" and Other Writings*. Edited by Kate Lilley. London: Penguin Books, 2004.

Chee, Alexander. *How to Write an Autobiographical Novel: Essays*. Boston: Mariner Books, 2018.

Cicero, Chic, and Sandra Tabatha Cicero. *Golden Dawn Ritual Tarot: Keys to the Rituals, Symbolism, Magic and Divination*. Woodbury, MN: Llewellyn Publications, 1994.

Cooppan, Vilashini. "Skin, Kin, Kind, I/You/We: Authotheory's Compositional Grammar." *ASAP Journal* 6, no. 3 (2021): 583–605.

Crawley, Ashon T. *The Lonely Letters*. Durham, NC: Duke University Press, 2020.

Creekmur, Corey K., and Alexander Doty, eds. *Out in Culture: Gay, Lesbian, and Queer Essays on Popular Culture*. Durham, NC: Duke University Press, 1995.

Cruz, Daniel Shank. "A Bibliography and Subject Index of Published Work from the Mennonite/s Writing Conferences." *Mennonite Quarterly Review* 91, no. 1 (2017): 93–130.

———. "A Brief History and Bibliography of Queer Mennonite Literature." *Journal of Mennonite Writing* 10, no. 3 (2018): https://mennonitewriting.org/journal/10/3/brief-history-and-bibliography-queer-mennonite-lit/#all.

———. "pandemic." *Frogpond* 44, no. 1 (2021): 15.

———, ed. "Queer Mennonite Literature." Special issue, *Journal of Mennonite Writing* 10, no. 3 (2018): http://www.mennonitewriting.org/journal/10/3/.

———. *Queering Mennonite Literature: Archives, Activism, and the Search for Community*. University Park: Pennsylvania State University Press, 2019.

———. "Reading My Life in the Text: Adventures of a Queer Mennonite Critic." *Journal of Mennonite Studies* 34 (2016): 280–86.

———. Review of *Women Talking*, by Miriam Toews. *Mennonite Quarterly Review* 93, no. 3 (2019): 428–31.

———. "summer solstice." *Stardust Haiku*, August 2020, 5, https://drive.google.com/file/d/1uoJ9x4G8Mdq5vZhgAHCCpvqfqWNwehqr/view.

———. "A Third Way to Change: Violence Against Whites in African American Novels from the 1970s." PhD diss., Northern Illinois University, 2011.

———. "Writing Back, Moving Forward: *Falling Man* and DeLillo's Previous Works." *Italian Americana* 29, no. 2 (2011): 138–52.

Cvetkovich, Ann. *An Archive of Feelings: Trauma, Sexuality, and Lesbian Public Cultures*. Durham, NC: Duke University Press, 2003.

Davis, Charles, dir. *Hazel's People*. Burt Martin Associates, 1973.

Davis, Ray. "Delany's Dirt." In *Ash of Stars: On the Writing of Samuel R. Delany*, edited by James Sallis, 162–88. Jackson: University Press of Mississippi, 1996.

Davis, Todd. "Laboring Through *The Weather Book*: The Value of Work in the Poetry of Janet Kauffman." In Roth and Beck, *Migrant Muses*, 159–68.

Delany, Samuel R. *About Writing: Seven Essays, Four Letters, and Five Interviews*. Middletown, CT: Wesleyan University Press, 2005.

———. *The American Shore: Meditations on a Tale of Science Fiction by Thomas M. Disch—"Angouleme."* Middletown, CT: Wesleyan University Press, 2014.

———. *"The Atheist in the Attic" Plus. . . .* Oakland: PM Press, 2018.

———. *Bread and Wine: An Erotic Tale of New York*. Illustrated by Mia Wolff. New York: Juno Books, 1999.

———. *Dark Reflections*. 2007. Mineola, NY: Dover Publications, 2016.

———. *Equinox*. New York: Rhinoceros, 1994.

———. *Heavenly Breakfast: An Essay on the Winter of Love*. 1979. Whitmore Lake, MI: Bamberger Books, 1997.

———. *In Search of Silence: The Journals of Samuel R. Delany.* Vol. 1, *1957–1969.* Edited by Kenneth R. James. Middletown, CT: Wesleyan University Press, 2017.

———. *Letters from Amherst: Five Narrative Letters.* Middletown, CT: Wesleyan University Press, 2019.

———. *The Mad Man.* Ramsey, NJ: Voyant, 2002.

———. *The Motion of Light in Water: Sex and Science Fiction Writing in the East Village.* 1993. Minneapolis: University of Minnesota Press, 2004.

———. *1984: Selected Letters.* Rutherford, NJ: Voyant, 2000.

———. *Occasional Views.* Vol. 1, *"More About Writing" and Other Essays.* Middletown, CT: Wesleyan University Press, 2021.

———. *Of Solids and Surds: Notes for Noël Sturgeon, Marilyn Hacker, Josh Lukin, Mia Wolff, Bill Stribling, and Bob White.* New Haven, CT: Yale University Press, 2021.

———. *Return to Nevèrÿon.* 1987. Hanover, NH: Wesleyan University Press/University Press of New England, 1994.

———. "Samuel R. Delany on His Legacy, Creativity, and 'Promiscuously Autobiographical' Work." By Annie Mok. *io9*, 2 May 2019, https://io9.gizmodo.com/samuel-r-delany-on-his-legacy-creativity-and-promisc-1833407173.

———. *Shorter Views: Queer Thoughts and the Politics of the Paraliterary.* Hanover, NH: Wesleyan University Press/University Press of New England, 1999.

———. *Tales of Nevèrÿon.* 1979. Hanover, NH: Wesleyan University Press/University Press of New England, 1993.

———. "*This Short Day of Frost and Sun*: To Sleep Before Evening." *Georgia Review* 76, no. 2 (2022): 377–90.

———. *The Tides of Lust.* New York: Lancer Books, 1973.

———. *Times Square Red, Times Square Blue.* 1999. New York: New York University Press, 2001.

Dentz, Shira. *Sisyphusina.* N.p.: PANK Books, 2019.

Dorsey, Candas Jane. "Being One's Own Pornographer." *ParaDoxa* 2, no. 2 (1996): 191–203.

Doty, Mark. *What Is the Grass: Walt Whitman in My Life.* New York: W. W. Norton, 2020.

"Dream of the '90s | Portlandia | IFC." YouTube, 1 December 2017, https://www.youtube.com/watch?v=U4hShMEk1Ew.

Dueck, Lynnette. *sing me no more.* Vancouver: Press Gang, 1992.

Dula, Peter. "Theology Is a Kind of Reading." *Conrad Grebel Review* 31, no. 2 (2013): 113–20.

Dungy, Camille T., et al. "Catastrophe and Survival: Women Ecopoets Navigate Pathways Past Denials: A Conversation with Camille T. Dungy, Allison Adelle Hedge Coke, Brenda Hillman, Sandra Meek, and Aimee Nezhukumatathil." *Writer's Chronicle*, September 2020, 30–41.

Dunham, Mabel. *Toward Sodom.* Toronto: Macmillan, 1927.

———. *The Trail of the Conestoga.* 1924. Cambridge, ON: Aden Eby, 1990.

Dwyer, June. "Janet Kauffman's 'Patriotic': Woman's Work." *Studies in Short Fiction* 28, no. 1 (1991): 55–62.

Eliot, T. S. *Selected Poems.* 1930. San Diego: Harvest, 1936.

Elliott, Charlotte. "Just as I Am, Without One Plea." In *The Mennonite Hymnal*, 235. Scottdale, PA: Herald Press, 1969.

Falcón, Bryan Rafael. "Hexadecaroon." In Friesen and Koehn, *Anabaptist ReMix*, 177–92.

Fitzpatrick, Cat, and Casey Plett, eds. *Meanwhile, Elsewhere: Science Fiction and Fantasy from Transgender Writers.* New York: Topside Press, 2017.

Fleming, Mike. "Amy Adams, Annapurna Pictures Team on Adaptation of Rachel Yoder Novel *Nightbitch*." msn.com, 30 July 2020. https://deadline.com/2020/07/amy-adams-annapurna-pictures-rachel-yoder-novel-nightbitch-1202999813/.

Foltz, Mary Catherine. "The Excremental Ethics of Samuel R. Delany." *SubStance* 37, no. 2 (2008): 41–55.

Fournier, Lauren. *Autotheory as Feminist Practice in Art, Writing, and Criticism.* Cambridge: MIT Press, 2021.

Freeman, Elizabeth. "Afterword." In Brintnall, Marchal, and Moore, *Sexual Disorientations*, 315–19.

Friesen, Gordon. *Flamethrowers*. Caldwell, ID: Caxton Printers, 1936.

Friesen, Lauren. Review of *Making Believe: Questions About Mennonites and Art*, by Magdalene Redekop. *Mennonite Quarterly Review* 94, no. 4 (2020): 561–64.

Friesen, Lauren, and Dennis R. Koehn, eds. *Anabaptist ReMix: Varieties of Cultural Engagement in North America*. New York: Peter Lang, 2022.

Friesen, Patrick. *Interim: Essays and Mediations*. Regina, SK: Hagios Press, 2006.

———. *Outlasting the Weather: Selected and New Poems, 1994–2020*. Vancouver: Anvil Press, 2020.

———. *Unearthly Horses*. Winnipeg: Turnstone Press, 1984.

Gallop, Jane. *Anecdotal Theory*. Durham, NC: Duke University Press, 2002.

Gatchalian, C. E. *Double Melancholy: Art, Beauty, and the Making of a Brown Queer Man*. Vancouver: Arsenal Pulp Press, 2019.

Gingerich, Charlene. "Beauty Happens." In Friesen and Koehn, *Anabaptist ReMix*, 275–86.

Gioia, Dana. *Can Poetry Matter? Essays on Poetry and American Culture*. St. Paul: Graywolf Press, 1992.

Good, Merle. *Happy as the Grass Was Green*. Reprinted as *Hazel's People*. 1971. Scottdale, PA: Herald Press, 1973.

———. "A Tribute to Sara Stambaugh." In *What Mennonites Are Thinking, 2002*, edited by Merle Good and Phyllis Pellman Good, 78–80. Intercourse, PA: Good Books, 2002.

Graham, Melva, et al. "I'm Writing to You: Letters from Writers of the Black Literary Community." *Poets and Writers*, September–October 2020, 57–77.

Gray, Lois Frey, and Ann Hostetler. "Mennonite Creators' Discussion Group, 1993–2000." *Journal of Mennonite Writing* 13, no. 1 (2021): https://mennonitewriting.org/journal/13/1/mennonite-creators-discussion-group-1993-2000/#all.

Gundy, Jeff. "Bad Mennonites, Raspberry Migrations, and Usable Narratives: Grace Jantzen, Julia Kasdorf, and Sofia Samatar." *Mennonite Quarterly Review* 92, no. 3 (2018): 423–37.

———. "The Fields Have Edges, but the Roads Keep Going: 10,000 Things, Assorted Worlds, and Me." *Journal of Mennonite Studies* 36 (2018): 75–88.

———. *Flatlands*. Cleveland: Cleveland State University Poetry Center, 1995.

———. "Humility in Mennonite Literature." *Mennonite Quarterly Review* 63, no. 1 (1989): 5–21.

———. "In Praise of the Lurkers (Who Come Out to Speak)." In Roth and Beck, *Migrant Muses*, 23–30.

———. *Inquiries*. Huron, OH: Bottom Dog Press, 1992.

———. "Introduction: SF Special Issue." *Journal of Mennonite Writing* 11, no. 1 (2019): https://mennonitewriting.org/journal/11/1/introduction-sf-special-issue/#all.

———. "Mennonite/s Writing: Explorations and Exposition." *Mennonite Life* 70 (2016): https://mla.bethelks.edu/ml-archive/2016/mennonites-writing-explorations-and-exposition.php.

———. *Rhapsody with Dark Matter*. Huron, OH: Bottom Dog Press, 2000.

———. *Songs from an Empty Cage: Poetry, Mystery, Anabaptism, and Peace*. Telford, PA: Cascadia, 2013.

———, ed. "Speculative Fiction." Special issue, *Journal of Mennonite Writing* 11, no. 1 (2019): https://mennonitewriting.org/journal/11/1/.

———. "'There Is No Knife, but Only Flesh': Sofia Samatar and the Language of Other Worlds." In *11 Encounters with Mennonite Fiction*, edited by Hildi Froese Tiessen, 69–85. Winnipeg: Mennonite Literary Society, 2017.

———. "Toward a Poetics of Identity." In Zacharias, *After Identity*, 159–74.

———. "Tribute to Nicholas C. Lindsay, Sr." *Conrad Grebel Review* 26, no. 1 (2008): 91–93.

———. *Walker in the Fog: On Mennonite Writing*. Telford, PA: Cascadia, 2005.

———. *Without a Plea*. Huron, OH: Bottom Dog Press, 2019.

Gurga, Lee. *Haiku: A Poet's Guide*. Lincoln, IL: Modern Haiku Press, 2013.

Haas, Craig, and Steve Nolt. *The Mennonite Starter Kit: A Handy Guide for the New Mennonite (Everything They Forgot to Tell You in Church Membership Class!)*. Intercourse, PA: Good Books, 1993.

Halberstam, Jack. *Trans*: A Quick and Quirky Account of Gender Variability*. Oakland: University of California Press, 2018.

Harnish, Andrew. "An Excerpt from *Plain Love*." *Journal of Mennonite Studies* 34 (2016): 297–302.

———. "LGBT Mennonite Fiction: A Panel from Mennonite/s Writing VII: An Introductory Reflection." *Journal of Mennonite Studies* 34 (2016): 279–80.

Hemmingson, Michael. "The Trouble with Samuel R. Delany's Pornography." *Science Fiction Studies* 38, no. 2 (2011): 376–78.

Hiebert, Paul. *Sarah Binks*. 1947. Toronto: McClelland and Stewart, 1971.

Himmelfarb, Martha. *The Apocalypse: A Brief History*. Malden, MA: Wiley-Blackwell, 2010.

Hinnefeld, Joyce. "For the Collaborators (Thoughts on Narrative, on the Works of Janet Kauffman, on I and She, on Autobiography, on Suicide or Not)." *Denver Quarterly* 31, no. 2 (1996): 70–78.

Holland, Scott. "Theopoetics Is the Rage." *Conrad Grebel Review* 31, no. 2 (2013): 121–29.

Hollywood, Amy. "On the Materiality of Air: Janet Kauffman's Bodyfictions." *New Literary History* 27, no. 3 (1996): 503–25.

Hooley Yoder, Anita. "I've Read Too Much Poetry for That: Poetry, Personal Transformation, and Peace." *CrossCurrents* 64, no. 4 (2014): 454–65.

———. "Know Your Place: Writing as Identity." *Journal of Mennonite Writing* 11, no. 2 (2019): https://mennonitewriting.org/journal/11/2/know-your-place-writing-identity/#all.

Hostetler, Ann. "After Ethnicity: Gender, Voice, and an Ethic of Care in the Work of Di Brandt and Julia Spicher Kasdorf." In Zacharias, *After Identity*, 86–105.

———. "Coming into Voice: Three Mennonite Women Poets and the Beginning of Mennonite Poetry in the United States." *Mennonite Quarterly Review* 77, no. 4 (2003): 521–46.

———. "Dancing on the Bridge: Creating Virtual Community Through Mennonite Literature." In Miller and Miller, *Measure of My Days*, 228–39.

———. "A Valediction Forbidding Excommunication: Ecopoetics and the Reparative Journey Home in Recent Work by Di Brandt." *Journal of Mennonite Studies* 28 (2010): 69–86.

Jackson, Major, ed. *The Best American Poetry 2019*. New York: Scribner Poetry, 2019.

Janzen, Jean. "Nine Streams Towards the River of Theopoetics: An Autobiographical Approach." *Conrad Grebel Review* 31, no. 2 (2013): 143–47.

Janzen, Jean, John Ruth, and Rudy Wiebe. "Literature, Place, Language, and Faith: A Conversation Between Jean Janzen, John Ruth, and Rudy Wiebe." By Julia Spicher Kasdorf. *Conrad Grebel Review* 26, no. 1 (2008): 72–90.

Johnson, Chelsey. *Stray City*. New York: Custom House, 2018.

Johnson, Julie Swarstad. *Orchard Light: Poems*. Lewisburg, PA: Seven Kitchens Press, 2020.

Johnson, Julie Swarstad, and Christopher Cokinos, eds. *Beyond Earth's Edge: The Poetry of Spaceflight*. Tucson: University of Arizona Press, 2020.

Jordan, Mark D. "In Search of Queer Theology Lost." In Brintnall, Marchal, and Moore, *Sexual Disorientations*, 296–308.

Juhnke, James C. *Vision, Doctrine, War: Mennonite Identity and Organization in America, 1890–1930*. Scottdale, PA: Herald Press, 1989.

Kampen, Melanie. "On the Need for Critical-Contextual and Trauma-Informed Methods in Mennonite Theology." In Schmidt Roberts, Martens, and Penner, *Recovering from the Anabaptist Vision*, 93–102.

Kasdorf, Julia Spicher. *The Body and the Book: Writing from a Mennonite Life; Essays and Poems*. University Park: Pennsylvania State University Press, 2009.

———. "Coming Back: The Poetry and Life of Jane Rohrer." *Journal of Mennonite Studies* 36 (2018): 43–54.

———. "Dreams of the Written Character." In Miller and Miller, *Measure of My Days*, 29–37.

———. "An Essential Stranger: Nick Lindsay at Goshen College, 1969–2000." *Mennonite Quarterly Review* 82, no. 1 (2008): 85–107.

———. *Eve's Striptease*. Pittsburgh: University of Pittsburgh Press, 1998.

———. Foreword to *Tongue Screws and Testimonies: Poems, Stories, and Essays Inspired by the "Martyrs Mirror,"* edited by Kirsten Eve Beachy, 11–13. Scottdale, PA: Herald Press, 2010.

———. "God and Land: Remembering Dreams of the Commonwealth." *Conrad Grebel Review* 39, no. 1 (2021): 17–32.

———. "Introduction: Documentary Writing and Mennonite/s Writing." *Journal of Mennonite Writing* 10, no. 4 (2018): https://mennonitewriting.org/journal/10/4/introduction-documentary-writing-and-mennonites-wr/#all.

———. "Mightier Than the Sword: *Martyrs Mirror* in the New World." *Conrad Grebel Review* 31, no. 1 (2013): 44–70.

———. *Sleeping Preacher*. Pittsburgh: University of Pittsburgh Press, 1992.

———. "Sunday Morning Confession." *Mennonite Quarterly Review* 87, no. 1 (2013): 7–10.

Kasdorf, Julia Spicher, and Christopher Reed. "Field Language: Poetry and Painting in Conversation." By Melanie Zuercher. *Mennonite Life* 74 (2020): https://ml.bethelks.edu/2020/07/02/field-language-poetry-and-painting-in-conversation/.

Kasdorf, Julia Spicher, Christopher Reed, and Joyce Henri Robinson, eds. *Field Language: The Painting and Poetry of Warren and Jane Rohrer*. University Park, PA: Palmer Museum of Art, 2020.

Kasdorf, Julia Spicher, and Steven Rubin. *Shale Play: Poems and Photographs from the Fracking Fields*. University Park: Pennsylvania State University Press, 2018.

Kauffman, Janet. *The Body in Four Parts*. St. Paul: Graywolf Press, 1993.

———. *Characters on the Loose: Stories*. St. Paul: Graywolf Press, 1997.

———. *Collaborators*. New York: Alfred A. Knopf, 1986.

———. *Eco-Dementia*. Detroit: Wayne State University Press, 2017.

———. *Obscene Gestures for Women: Stories*. New York: Alfred A. Knopf, 1989.

———. *Places in the World a Woman Could Walk: Stories*. New York: Alfred A. Knopf, 1983.

Keefe-Perry, L. Callid. *Way to Water: A Theopoetics Primer*. Eugene, OR: Cascade Books, 2014.

Kehler, Grace. "Becoming Divine Women: Miriam Toews' *Women Talking* as Parable." *Literature and Theology* 34, no. 4 (2020): https://doi.org/10.1093/litthe/fraa020.

Kennel, Maxwell. "Secular Mennonites and the Violence of Pacifism: Miriam Toews at McMaster." *Hamilton Arts and Letters* 13, no. 2 (2020): https://samizdatpress.typepad.com/hal_magazine_thirteen-2/miriam-toews-violence-of-pacifism-by-maxwell-kennel-1.html.

———. "Secular Mennonite Social Critique: Pluralism, Interdisciplinarity, and Mennonite Studies." In Friesen and Koehn, *Anabaptist ReMix*, 49–76.

———. "Violence and the Romance of Community: Darkness and Enlightenment in Patrick Friesen's *The Shunning*." *Literature and Theology* 33, no. 4 (2019): 394–413.

Khalifeh, Sahar. "'Nothing Will Stop Me from Writing What I See': An Interview with Sahar Khalifeh." By Philip Metres. *The Writer's Chronicle*, September 2020, 42–50.

Kirch, Claire. "Road Tripping with Miriam Toews." *Publisher's Weekly*, 1 September 2008, 22.

Klaassen, Walter. *Anabaptism: Neither Catholic nor Protestant*. Waterloo, ON: Conrad Press, 1973.

Klassen, Sarah. "Review of *The Widows of Hamilton House*," by Christina Penner. *Journal of Mennonite Studies* 27 (2009): 262–64.

Kliewer, Warren. *The Violators*. Francestown, NH: Marshall Jones, 1964.

Knippen, James Henry. *Would We Still Be*. Kalamazoo, MI: New Issues Press, 2021.

Kniss, Fred. *Disquiet in the Land: Cultural Conflict in American Mennonite Communities*. New Brunswick, NJ: Rutgers University Press, 1997.

Koestenbaum, Wayne. *The Queen's Throat: Opera, Homosexuality, and the Mystery of Desire*. New York: Poseidon Press, 1993.

Koop, Karl. "Contours and Possibilities for an Anabaptist Theology." In Schmidt Roberts, Martens, and Penner, *Recovering from the Anabaptist Vision*, 17–32.

Kraybill, Donald B. *Eastern Mennonite University: A Century of Countercultural Education*. University Park: Pennsylvania State University Press, 2017.

Kroeker, Travis. "Scandalous Displacements: 'Word' and 'Silent Light' in *Irma Voth*." *Journal of Mennonite Studies* 36 (2018): 89–100.
Kuester, Martin. "Between European Past and Canadian Present: Lesbian Mennonite Writing and Collective Memory." In *Engaging with Literature of Commitment*, vol. 2, *The Worldly Scholar*, edited by Gordon Collier et al., 129–37. Amsterdam: Rodopi, 2012.
Lachman, Becca J. R. *The Apple Speaks*. Telford, PA: DreamSeeker Books, 2012.
———. "Creative (M)othering: An Invitation from a Childless Artist." In Buller and Fast, *Mothering Mennonite*, 180–94.
———. *Other Acreage*. Boston: Gold Wake Press, 2015.
———, ed. *A Ritual to Read Together: Poems in Conversation with William Stafford*. Topeka, KS: Woodley Press, 2013.
Lachman, Becca J. R., and Astrid Kaemmerling. *What I say to this house*. Athens, OH: Becca J. R. Lachman and Astrid Kaemmerling, 2022.
Lapp, Jessica W. "Embodied Voices, Imprisoned Bodies: Women and Words in Janet Kauffman's *Collaborators*." In Roth and Beck, *Migrant Muses*, 135–44.
Lerner, Ben. *The Hatred of Poetry*. New York: Farrar, Straus and Giroux, 2016.
Lindenberg, Rebecca. "A Brief History of the Future Apocalypse." In Jackson, *The Best American Poetry 2019*, 100–104, 203–4.
Lisowski, Zefyr. "The Girl, the Well, the Ring." In *It Came from the Closet: Queer Reflections on Horror*, edited by Joe Vallese, 41–50. New York: Feminist Press, 2022.
Loewen, Harry. "Mennonite Literature in Canadian and American Mennonite Historiography: An Introduction." *Mennonite Quarterly Review* 73, no. 3 (1999): 557–70.
Lorde, Audre. *Zami: A New Spelling of My Name*. Berkeley, CA: Crossing Press, 1982.
Loughlin, Gerard, ed. *Queer Theology: Rethinking the Western Body*. London: Blackwell, 2007.
Loveless, Natalie. *How to Make Art at the End of the World: A Manifesto for Research-Creation*. Durham, NC: Duke University Press, 2019.
———, ed. *Knowings and Knots: Methodologies and Ecologies in Research-Creation*. Edmonton: University of Alberta Press, 2020.
Luthy, David. *Dirk Willems: His Noble Deed Lives On*. Aylmer, ON: Pathway, 2011.
———. *A History of the Printings of the "Martyrs' Mirror": Dutch, German, English 1660–2012*. Aylmer, ON: Pathway, 2013.
Maa, Gerald. "To Our Readers." *Georgia Review* 76, no. 2 (2022): 362–67.
MacMaster, Richard K. *Land, Piety, Peoplehood: The Establishment of Mennonite Communities in America, 1683–1790*. Scottdale, PA: Herald Press, 1985.
Martínez, Ernesto Javier. *On Making Sense: Queer Race Narratives of Intelligibility*. Stanford, CA: Stanford University Press, 2013.
McEvoy, Seth. *Samuel R. Delany*. New York: Frederick Ungar, 1984.
The Mennonite Hymnal. Scottdale, PA: Herald Press, 1969.
"Mennonite Lit. Writers." Facebook.com, 30 July 2020–present, https://www.facebook.com/groups/879145212575864.
Mierau, Maurice. *How Mind and Body Move: The Poetry of Patrick Friesen*. Victoria, BC: Frog Hollow Press, 2018.
———. "The Voice Is Coming (Faintly) from the Grave, and It Says Mennonites Are Dead, and So Is Mennonite Writing...." *Rhubarb*, Summer 2012, 27–29.
Miller, Evie Yoder. *Loyalties: Scruples on the Line, Book II*. Eugene, OR: Resource Publications, 2020.
———. *Passages: Scruples on the Line, Book III*. Eugene, OR: Resource Publications, 2021.
———. *Shadows: Scruples on the Line, Book I*. Eugene, OR: Resource Publications, 2020.
Miller, Reuben Z., and Joseph S. Miller, eds. *The Measure of My Days: Engaging the Life and Thought of John L. Ruth*. Telford, PA: Cascadia, 2004.
Milne, Heather. "Review of *Somewhere Else*," by Jan Guenther Braun. *Journal of Mennonite Studies* 27 (2009): 251–52.
Mockett, Marie Mutsuki. *American Harvest: God, Country, and Farming in the Heartland*. Minneapolis: Graywolf Press, 2020.
Mookerjea, Sourayan. "Intermedia Research-Creation and Hydropolitics: Counterenvironments of the Commons." In Loveless, *Knowings and Knots*, 127–57.
Moraga, Cherríe, and Gloria Anzaldúa, eds. *This Bridge Called My Back: Writings by*

Radical Women of Color. Watertown, MA: Persephone Press, 1981.

Morrison, Toni. *Beloved*. 1987. New York: Vintage International, 2004.

———. *Sula*. 1973. New York: Vintage International, 2004.

Myers, Natasha. "Anthropologist as Transducer in a Field of Affects." In Loveless, *Knowings and Knots*, 97–125.

Nadir, Leila C. "More Life After Ruins: Autotheory, the Politics of Citation, and the Limits of the Scholarly Gaze." *ASAP Journal* 6, no. 3 (2021): 547–50.

Neufeldt, Leonard. *Yarrow: Poems*. Windsor, ON: Black Moss Press, 1993.

Nussbaum, Martha. "Narrative Emotions: Beckett's Genealogy of Love." In *Why Narrative? Readings in Narrative Theology*, edited by Stanley Hauerwas and L. Gregory Jones, 216–48. Eugene, OR: Wipf and Stock, 1997.

Nye, Naomi Shihab. "You Are Your Own State Department." In Jackson, *The Best American Poetry 2019*, 133–34, 208–9.

Perdomo, Willie. "Breakbeat, Remezcla." In *The BreakBeat Poets*, vol. 4, *LatiNext*, edited by Felicia Rose Chavez, José Olivarez, and Willie Perdomo, 1–2. Chicago: Haymarket Books, 2020.

Piepzna-Samarasinha, Leah Lakshmi. *The Future Is Disabled: Prophecies, Love Notes, and Mourning Songs*. Vancouver: Arsenal Pulp Press, 2022.

Plett, Casey. "Coke." *Progress Never Stops for Nostalgic Transsexuals* (blog), 17 February 2017. https://caseyplett.wordpress.com/2017/02/17/coke/.

———. *A Dream of a Woman*. Vancouver: Arsenal Pulp Press, 2021.

———. *Little Fish*. Vancouver: Arsenal Pulp Press, 2018.

———. *Lizzy and Annie*. Illustrated by Annie Mok. N.p.: Casey Plett and Annie Mok, 2013–2014.

———. "Natural Links of Queer and Mennonite Literature." *Journal of Mennonite Studies* 34 (2016): 286–90.

———. *A Safe Girl to Love*. New York: Topside Press, 2014.

Pollack, Rachel. *Rachel Pollack's Tarot Wisdom: Spiritual Teachings and Deeper Meanings*. Woodbury, MN: Llewellyn Publications, 2008.

———. *Seventy-Eight Degrees of Wisdom: A Tarot Journey to Self-Awareness*. Newburyport, MA: Weiser Books, 2019.

Pope, Simon, Glen Lowry, and Rachelle Viader Knowles. "'Dear Simon . . .': Letters Back and Forth, Between Simon Pope, Glen Lowry, and Rachelle Viader Knowles on Creative Practice-Led Research." In Loveless, *Knowings and Knots*, 277–97.

Porter, Lavelle. "The Strange Career of Samuel R. Delany." *Advocate*, 3 October 2013, https://gcadvocate.com/2013/10/03/the-strange-career-of-samuel-r-delany/.

Redekop, Magdalene. *Making Believe: Questions About Mennonites and Art*. Winnipeg: University of Manitoba Press, 2020.

Reed, Ken Yoder. *Both My Sons*. Morgantown, PA: Masthof Press, 2016.

———. *Mennonite Soldier*. Scottdale, PA: Herald Press, 1974.

Reed, Sabrina. *Lives Lived, Lives Imagined: Landscapes of Resilience in the Works of Miriam Toews*. Winnipeg: University of Manitoba Press, 2022.

Reimer, Al. *Mennonite Literary Voices: Past and Present*. North Newton, KS: Bethel College, 1993.

———. *My Harp Is Turned to Mourning*. Winnipeg: Hyperion Press, 1985.

Reimer, Nikki. DOWNVERSE. Vancouver: Talonbooks, 2014.

Reimer, Nikki, and Natalee Caple. "CanLit Hierarchy vs. the Rhizome: A Discussion Between Natalee Caple and Nikki Reimer." In *Refuse: CanLit in Ruins*, edited by Hannah McGregor, Julie Rak, and Erin Wunker, 122–30. Toronto: Book*hug, 2018.

Remer, Molly. *Earthprayer, Birthprayer, Lifeprayer, Womanprayer*. N.p.: CreateSpace, 2015.

"A Resolution for Repentance and Transformation." *Inclusive Mennonite Pastors* (blog), 29 May 2022. https://inclusivepastors.wordpress.com/resolution/.

Rich, Elaine Sommers. *Hannah Elizabeth*. New York: Random House, 1964.

Richardson, Suzanne. "tattooed girlfriend." *#FemkuMag*, 30 July 2021, 15, https://69b046c2-a7e1-4a9a-9a22-1c70986eaa24.filesusr.com/ugd/f4c0ea_6034d374899 7470fbdc18bd0a342445c.pdf.

Robinson, Dawn G. *Pamela Colman Smith, Tarot Artist: The Pious Pixie*. Stroud, UK: Fonthill Media, 2020.

Rosenberg, Jordy. "In Praise of Samuel R. Delany." *New York Times*, 8 August 2019, https://www.nytimes.com/2019/08/08/books/samuel-delany-jordy-rosenberg.html.

Rosenstock, Gabriel. *Haiku Enlightenment*. N.p.: Poetry Chaikhana, 2019.

Ross, Bruce. "General Introduction." In *A Vast Sky: An Anthology of Contemporary World Haiku*, edited by Bruce Ross, Kōko Katō, Dietmar Tauchner, and Patricia Prime, v–xii. Bangor, ME: Tancho Press, 2015.

Roth, John D. "In This Issue." *Mennonite Quarterly Review* 90, no. 1 (2016): 9–10.

Roth, John D., and Ervin Beck, eds. *Migrant Muses: Mennonite/s Writing in the U.S.* Goshen, IN: Mennonite Historical Society, 1998.

Ruiz, Sandra. *Ricanness: Enduring Time in Anticolonial Performance*. New York: New York University Press, 2019.

Ruth, John L. *Branch: A Memoir with Pictures*. Lancaster, PA: TourMagination/Harleysville, PA: Mennonite Historians of Eastern Pennsylvania, 2013.

———. *The Earth is the Lord's: A Narrative History of the Lancaster Mennonite Conference*. Scottdale, PA: Herald Press, 2001.

———. "Genius and the Verbal Dance: A Conversation with John Ruth About Language, Writing, and Community." By Julia Spicher Kasdorf. In Miller and Miller, *Measure of My Days*, 273–89.

———. "Knowing the Place for the First Time: A Response to Hildi Froese Tiessen." In *Mennonite Identity: Historical and Contemporary Perspectives*, edited by Calvin Wall Redekop and Samuel J. Steiner, 253–58. New York: University Press of America, 1988.

———. *Mennonite Identity and Literary Art*. Scottdale, PA: Herald Press, 1978.

———. "Revolution and Reverence." 1964. In *From the Mennonite Pulpit: Twenty-Six Sermons from Mennonite Ministers*, edited by Paul Erb, 179–88. Scottdale, PA: Herald Press, 1965.

———. *This Very Ground, This Crooked Affair: A Mennonite Homestead on Lenape Land*. Telford, PA: Cascadia, 2021.

Ruti, Mari. *The Ethics of Opting Out: Queer Theory's Defiant Subjects*. New York: Columbia University Press, 2017.

Salesses, Matthew. *Craft in the Real World: Rethinking Fiction Writing and Workshopping*. New York: Catapult Books, 2021.

Samatar, Sofia. "The Centaur's Recipe." In Friesen and Koehn, *Anabaptist ReMix*, 317–23.

———. "A Conversation with Sofia Samatar." By Alicia Cole. *Black Fox Literary Magazine*, 22 December 2014, http://www.blackfoxlitmag.com/2014/12/22/a-conversation-with-sofia-samatar/.

———. "Hi, I'm Sofia Samatar, SF and Fantasy Writer. AMA!" Reddit. Accessed 24 May 2018. https://www.reddit.com/r/Fantasy/comments/8lro18/hi_im_sofia_samatar_sf_and_fantasy_writer_ama/.

———. "In Search of Women's Histories: Crossing Space, Crossing Communities, Crossing Time." *Journal of Mennonite Writing* 9, no. 3 (2017): https://mennonitewriting.org/journal/9/3/search-womens-histories-crossing-space-crossing-co/#all.

———. "On Dwelling: Shelters in Place and Time." *Conrad Grebel Review* 39, no. 3 (2021): 265–81.

———. "The Scope of This Project." *Journal of Mennonite Writing* 9, no. 2 (2017), https://mennonitewriting.org/journal/9/2/scope-project/#all.

———. "Sofia Samatar on Kafka, Binge-writing and the Search for Monsters." By Amina Cain. *Literary Hub*, 16 February 2018, https://lithub.com/sofia-samatar-on-kafka-binge-writing-and-the-search-for-monsters/.

———. "Standing at the Ruins." *White Review* 30 (2021): 167–83.

———. *Tender: Stories*. Easthampton, MA: Small Beer Press, 2017.

———. "Toward a Planetary History of Afrofuturism." *Research in African Literatures* 48, no. 4 (2017): 175–91.

———. *The White Mosque: A Memoir*. New York: Catapult Books, 2022.

———. "Writing Queerly: Three Snapshots." *Uncanny: A Magazine of Science Fiction and Fantasy*, 2015, https://uncannymagazine.com/article/writing-queerly-three-snapshots/.

"Samuel R. Delany." In *The Norton Anthology of African American Literature*, 2nd ed., edited by Henry Louis Gates Jr. and Nellie McKay, 2392–93. New York: W. W. Norton, 2004.

Sanchez, Melissa E. *Queer Faith: Reading Promiscuity and Race in the Secular Love Tradition*. New York: New York University Press, 2019.

Sandor, Marjorie. "The Ram in the Thicket: Midrash and the Contemporary Creative Writer." *Writer's Chronicle*, October–November 2018, 29–39.

Schaefer, Donovan O. *Religious Affects: Animality, Evolution, and Power*. Durham, NC: Duke University Press, 2015.

Schalk, Sami. *Bodyminds Reimagined: (Dis)ability, Race, and Gender in Black Women's Speculative Fiction*. Durham, NC: Duke University Press, 2018.

Schirch, Lisa. "Anabaptist-Mennonite Relations with Jews Across Five Centuries." *Mennonite Life* 74 (2020). https://ml.bethelks.edu/2020/07/09/anabaptist-mennonite-relations-with-jews-across-five-centuries/.

Schmidt Roberts, Laura, Paul Martens, and Myron A. Penner, eds. *Recovering from the Anabaptist Vision: New Essays in Anabaptist Identity and Theological Method*. London: T&T Clark, 2020.

Schroeder, Karl. "Mennonite in the Solar System: An Interview with Karl Schroeder." By David Perlmutter and Donovan Giesbrecht. *Journal of Mennonite Studies* 25 (2007): 275–78.

Sedgwick, Eve Kosofsky. *Tendencies*. Durham, NC: Duke University Press, 1993.

———. *The Weather in Proust*. Edited by Jonathan Goldberg. Durham, NC: Duke University Press, 2011.

Serano, Julia. *Whipping Girl: A Transsexual Woman on Sexism and the Scapegoating of Femininity*. 2nd ed. Berkeley, CA: Seal Press, 2016.

Shelley, Mary. *Frankenstein: A Norton Critical Edition*. 1818. Edited by J. Paul Hunter. New York: W. W. Norton, 1996.

"Sissy, n. and adj." *Oxford English Dictionary*, OED Online, June 2018, https://www.oed.com/view/Entry/180429.

Smith, Sidonie, and Julia Watson. *Reading Autobiography: A Guide for Interpreting Life Narratives*. 2nd ed. Minneapolis: University of Minnesota Press, 2010.

Smucker, Barbara. *Henry's Red Sea*. Scottdale, PA: Herald Press, 1955.

Snaza, Nathan. *Animate Literacies: Literature, Affect, and the Politics of Humanism*. Durham, NC: Duke University Press, 2019.

Snow, Cassandra. *Queering the Tarot*. Newburyport, MA: Weiser Books, 2019.

Solís, Migueltzinta C. "mestizXXX: an autotheory." *ASAP Journal* 6, no. 3 (2021): 513–14.

Spikes, Mike. "Subjective Criticism and Haiku." *Frogpond* 45, no. 2 (2022): 121–33.

Stambaugh, Sara. "How Lena Got Set Back." In Tiessen, *Liars and Rascals*, 91–95.

———. *I Hear the Reaper's Song*. Intercourse, PA: Good Books, 1984.

———. "Old Eby." In Tiessen, *Liars and Rascals*, 131–36.

———. *Yon Far Country: A Social and Personal Memoir of Lancaster County, Pennsylvania*. Kitchener, ON: Pandora Press, 2009.

Steffler, Margaret. "Breaking Patriarchy Through Words, Imagination, and Faith: The Hayloft as *Spielraum* in Miriam Toews' *Women Talking*." *Canadian Literature* 243 (2020): 61–78. Gale Academic OneFile. https://canlit.ca/article/breaking-patriarchy-through-words-imagination-and-faith-the-hayloft-as-spielraum-in-miriam-toews-women-talking/. Accessed 6 Dec. 2022.

Stenson, Esther. *Showing Up: Poems*. Georgetown, KY: Finishing Line Press, 2020.

Stepenoff, Bonnie. "The Personal and the Universal in Haiku." *Frogpond* 43, no. 3 (2020): 130–34.

Stockton, Kathryn Bond. *Avidly Reads Making Out*. New York: New York University Press, 2019.

Suderman, Elmer. "Mennonites, the Mennonite Community, and Mennonite Writers." *Mennonite Life* 47, no. 3 (1992): 21–26.

Taylor, Fred Barney, dir. *The Polymath, or The Life and Opinions of Samuel R. Delany, Gentleman*. United States: Maestro Media, 2007. DVD.

Tea, Michelle. *The Chelsea Whistle: A Memoir*. Berkeley, CA: Seal Press, 2008.

———. *How to Grow Up: A Memoir*. New York: Plume, 2015.

———. *Modern Tarot: Connecting with Your Higher Self Through the Wisdom of the Cards*. San Francisco: HarperElixir, 2017.

"Theory, n." *Oxford English Dictionary*, OED Online, June 2015, http://www.oed.com/view/Entry/200431.

Threadgill, Elizabeth. *Tangled in the Light*. Georgetown, KY: Finishing Line Press, 2018.

Tiessen, Hildi Froese. "Beyond the Binary: Re-Inscribing Cultural Identity in the Literature of Mennonites." In Roth and Beck, *Migrant Muses*, 11–21.

———. "Homelands, Identity Politics, and the Trace: What Remains for the Mennonite Reader?" *Mennonite Quarterly Review* 87, no. 1 (2013): 11–22.

———, ed. *Liars and Rascals: Mennonite Short Stories*. Waterloo, ON: University of Waterloo Press, 1989.

Tiessen, Hildi Froese, and Peter Hinchcliffe, eds. *Acts of Concealment: Mennonite/s Writing in Canada*. Waterloo, ON: University of Waterloo Press, 1992.

Toews, Miriam. *A Boy of Good Breeding*. 1998. New York: Counterpoint, 2006.

———. *A Complicated Kindness*. 2004. New York: Counterpoint, 2005.

———. "A Complicated Kind of Author." By Di Brandt. *Herizons*, Summer 2005, http://www.herizons.ca/node/195.

———. "How Pacifism Can Lead to Violence and Conflict." *Literary Hub*, 28 November 2016, https://lithub.com/how-pacifism-can-lead-to-violence-and-conflict/.

———. *Irma Voth*. New York: Harper, 2011.

———. "'It gets under the skin and settles in': A Conversation with Miriam Toews." By Natasha G. Wiebe. *Conrad Grebel Review* 26, no. 1 (2008): 103–23.

———. "Novelist Miriam Toews." By Terry Gross. *Fresh Air*, 5 January 2005. https://freshairarchive.org/segments/novelist-miriam-toews.

———. "'A place you can't go home to': A Conversation with Miriam Toews." By Hildi Froese Tiessen. *Prairie Fire* 21, no. 3 (2000): 54–61.

———. *Summer of My Amazing Luck*. Rev. ed. New York: Counterpoint, 2006.

———. *Swing Low: A Life*. 2000. New York: Harper Perennial, 2011.

———. *Women Talking*. Toronto: Alfred A. Knopf Canada, 2018.

Tucker, Jeffrey Allen. *A Sense of Wonder: Samuel R. Delany, Race, Identity, and Difference*. Middletown, CT: Wesleyan University Press, 2004.

Valente, Catherynne M. *Palimpsest*. New York: Bantam Books, 2009.

Viramontes, Helena María. "My Insurgent Heart: AWP's 2020 Annual Conference and Bookfair Keynote Address." *Writer's Chronicle*, September 2020, 20–27.

Visser, Piet. "The Bible and the Literary Arts Among Dutch Mennonites and Doopsgezinden, 1600–1740." *Journal of Mennonite Studies* 40, no. 2 (2022): 149–87.

Waugh, Thomas. "Men's Pornography: Gay vs. Straight." In Creekmur and Doty, *Out in Culture*, 307–27.

Weaver-Zercher, David L. *"Martyrs Mirror": A Social History*. Baltimore: Johns Hopkins University Press, 2016.

Weinstone, Ann. "Science Fiction as a Young Person's First Queer Theory." *Science Fiction Studies* 26, no. 1 (1999): 41–48.

Welch, Michael Dylan. "The Heft of Haiku." *Frogpond* 44, no. 2 (2021): 109–15.

Whitman, Walt. "A Backward Glance O'er Travel'd Roads." In *"Leaves of Grass" and Other Writings*, edited by Michael Moon, 471–84. New York: W. W. Norton, 2002.

———. *Leaves of Grass*. 1855. New York: Penguin Books, 1976.

Wiebe, Dallas. *Skyblue the Badass*. Garden City, NY: Paris Review–Doubleday, 1969.

Wiebe, Joseph R. "Reassessing Mennonite Environmentalism Through Settler-Colonialism: Political Deficiencies, Historical Omissions, and Indigenous Responses." *Mennonite Quarterly Review* 96, no. 3 (2022): 355–80.

Wiebe, Rudy. *The Blue Mountains of China*. 1970. Toronto: McClelland and Stewart, 1995.

———. *My Lovely Enemy*. Toronto: McClelland and Stewart, 1983.

———. *Peace Shall Destroy Many*. Toronto: McClelland and Stewart, 1962.

———. *The Scorched-Wood People*. Toronto: McClelland and Stewart, 1977.

———. *The Temptations of Big Bear*. Toronto: McClelland and Stewart, 1973.

Williams, William Carlos. "Asphodel, That Greeny Flower." In *Anthology of Modern American Poetry*, edited by Cary Nelson, 194–200. New York: Oxford University Press, 2000.

Womack, Ytasha L. *Afrofuturism: The World of Black Sci-Fi and Fantasy Culture*. Chicago: Lawrence Hill Books, 2013.

Woodhouse, Reed. *Unlimited Embrace: A Canon of Gay Fiction, 1945–1995*. Amherst: University of Massachusetts Press, 1998.

Woods, Jamila. "Blk Girl Art." In *The BreakBeat Poets: New American Poetry in the Age of Hip-Hop*, edited by Kevin Coval, Quraysh Ali Lansana, and Nate Marshall, 261. Chicago: Haymarket Books, 2015.

Wright, David. "Community, Theology, and Mennonite Poetics in the Work of Jeff Gundy." In Roth and Beck, *Migrant Muses*, 145–58.

Yoder, Rachel. *Nightbitch*. New York: Doubleday, 2021.

Zacharias, Robert, ed. *After Identity: Mennonite Writing in North America*. University Park: Pennsylvania State University Press, 2015.

———. "'A Garden of Spears': Reconsidering the Mennonite/s Writing Project." *Mennonite Quarterly Review* 90, no. 1 (2016): 29–50.

———. "Introduction: Mennonite/s Writing in North America." In Zacharias, *After Identity*, 1–18.

———. *Reading Mennonite Writing: A Study in Minor Transnationalism*. University Park: Pennsylvania State University Press, 2022.

———. *Rewriting the Break Event: Mennonites and Migration in Canadian Literature*. Winnipeg: University of Manitoba Press, 2013.

Zambreno, Kate. *Drifts*. New York: Riverhead Books, 2020.

———. *To Write as If Already Dead*. New York: Columbia University Press, 2021.

Zapruder, Matthew. *Why Poetry*. New York: Ecco, 2017.

Zimmerman, Diana R. *Marry a Mennonite Boy and Make Pie*. Newton, KS: Workplay, 2018.

Zoltan, Vanessa. *Praying with "Jane Eyre": Reflections on Reading as a Sacred Practice*. New York: TarcherPerigree, 2021.

Zuercher, Melanie. "Writers' Conference at Age 32 Looks Back, Considers What Comes Next." *Goshen College Bulletin Points*, 14 October 2022, https://www.goshen.edu/news/2022/10/14/writers-conference-at-age-32-looks-back-considers-what-comes-next. Reprinted as "Writers Conference Greets New Wave." *Anabaptist World*, 4 November 2022, 28.

INDEX

Acevedo, Elizabeth, 13
activism. *See* literature: as activist; poetry: activism of; queer: activist worldview of; queer theory: activism of
Addiss, Stephen, 125
Afrofuturism, 28–29, 34, 120, 136n7, 145n28
After Identity symposium, 3, 46–47
Ahmed, Sara, 20, 21, 29–30, 134n110, 136n9, 136n22
  See also killjoy survival kits
AIDS, 119, 145n33
Aldrich, Mark, 66
Allison, Dorothy, 116
al-Qays, Imru, 99
Amann, Eric, 124
Amtrak, 64, 140n30
Anabaptism/Anabaptists, 44, 78, 104, 129n2, 146n15
  history of, 35, 94, 102
  as present-day theological concept, 114, 145n17
  See also Mennonites/Mennonitism; "Surrealist Anabaptist Manifesto"
anecdotal theory. *See* autotheory
animal studies, 93–94, 100, 105–6
anthologies, 61, 109–10, 115
  See also poetry: anthologies
anti-capitalism, 30, 34, 52, 88, 117, 132n71
Anzaldúa, Gloria, 19
apocalypse, 2–3, 9, 11, 13, 87, 101
  literary responses to, 15–17, 25, 60, 128
  and people of color, 2, 64
  politics' role in, 39, 58, 64, 133n80
  See also climate change; pandemic
Apollinaire, Guillaume, 120–21
archives/archiving, 17, 60, 101, 139n107
  See also Cruz, Daniel Shank: archives of; queer: archiving; Samatar, Sofia: and archiving; writing: as archiving
autotheory, 31, 38, 41, 63, 90, 124
  citation in, 20, 134n105
  decolonialism of, 19

prejudice against, 134n95
queerness of, 19, 20, 33

Back, Rachel Tzvia, 16
Baraka, Amiri, 14, 15, 132n71
Barge, Enos, 66–68, 71
baseball, 42, 126
Bate, Jonathan, 54
Bauman, Elizabeth Hershberger, 87, 135n115
BDSM, 33, 116, 121, 123, 127, 128
Beachy, Kirsten Eve, 130n33, 132n57
beauty, 27, 46, 54, 56, 108, 121
  and ethics, 5, 125–26, 127–28
Bechtel, Greg, 94–95, 96
  See also "Smut Stories"
Beck, Ervin, 7, 110, 129n5, 131n34, 143n61
  and Daniel Shank Cruz, 36, 131n36, 137n1, 144n70
Bellamy, Dodie, 146n21
Bender, Elizabeth Horsch, 8
Bennett, Jane, 12
Bergen, Jeremy M., 9
Birdsell, Sandra, 48
bisexuality, 4, 88, 90, 129n11
Blake, Nayland, 34
Body in Four Parts, The (Kauffman), 24, 33, 91–94, 100, 121
  queerness of, 92–94
  See also Kauffman, Janet
Bonzo, N. O., 109
bookstores, 31, 32, 88, 115
Brandt, Di, 22, 38, 44, 61, 104
  decolonization in, 49, 52–55
  feminism in, 48–52, 55, 58, 137n6, 138n39, 138n74
  poetry of, 48–56, 112
  theapoetics of, 48–50, 55–56, 137n6
  transgressiveness of, 6, 48, 138n43
Braun, Connie T., 9
brown, adrienne maree, 20
Brownstein, Carrie, 143n56
Bucher, Michael, 123

Buechel, Andy, 89–90
Buller, Rachel Epp, 19, 134n96
Burns, Stephanie Chandler, 18
Butler, Octavia, 141n3

Cain, Amina, 21, 32, 135n3
Carl-Klassen, Abigail, 2, 22, 57–58, 59, 60, 102
Carter, Terry Ann, 125
Cary, Lorene, 134n110
Cascadia Publishing House, 135n116
Chee, Alexander, 15
chess, 31, 32, 88
Cicero, Chic, 126, 127
Cicero, Sandra Tabatha, 126, 127
citation, 20–21, 33–34, 98–99, 133n77, 134n105, 134n110
climate change, 2, 3, 24, 99, 106, 142n28
  governmental inaction on, 15, 39, 59–60
  See also apocalypse
Coffman, John S., 140n23
Cokinos, Christopher, 107
Cole, Alicia, 21
Collins, Patricia Hill, 134n110
community, 13, 17, 32–33, 56, 59–60, 124
  failure of, 28, 35
  mutual aid in, 84–85, 107, 113–14
  shaped by stories, 23, 79–81, 90
  of two, 42, 106, 117
  See also literary community; Mennonite community; Mennonite literature (field): community of; queer: community
Cooppan, Vilashini, 20
COVID-19. *See* pandemic
Crawley, Ashon T., 135n3
Cruz, Daniel Shank
  archives of, 115–16, 127
  bibliophilia of, 3, 29–35, 88, 115, 131n36
  birthday of, 1, 33, 40
  cats of, 20, 107
  education of, 46, 89, 115, 128, 134n89, 134n96
  Ethics for Apocalyptic Times, 2–4, 19, 133n88, 134n96, 135n117, 136n21; haiku of, 124–26, 127; life writing of, 33, 118, 124–26, 127, 130n17; on queer Mennonite literature, 3, 21–22, 47, 103, 105, 110
  ethnicity of, 2, 15, 26, 64, 129n6, 131n34
  faith crisis of, 22, 36–38, 40, 43, 47, 48
  family of, 2, 35, 37, 46, 63, 87
  at Goshen College, 27, 34, 36–37, 48, 63, 142n42

intersection with queerness, 10, 47, 120, 130n17, 133n77
  living spaces of, 31, 34, 46, 64
  marriages of, 89, 117–18, 145n12, 145n13
  Mennonite prose, 36, 78, 95, 135n115, 139n11, 140n9; Mennonite poetry, 37–38, 40–41, 43, 60; queer literature, 24, 115–21, 136n9, 146n21; speculative fiction, 87–89, 95, 115–21, 123; sexuality of, 10, 90, 116–20, 129n11, 133n77; kinkiness of, 4, 116, 128; realization of, 34, 41, 116
  Mennonitism of, 19, 37–38, 46–47, 63, 116, 119
  pandemic and, 1, 20, 25, 30, 139n104
  reading experiences of, 31–32, 120, 127–28, 134n110
  spirituality of, 3, 19, 29, 33, 116, 124–28
  theology of, 2, 18, 89
  writing of, 15, 31, 115–18, 129n12, 133n77
  See also Beck, Ervin: and Daniel Shank Cruz
Cvetkovich, Ann, 136n9

Davis, Ray, 121
DeLaFleur, M. L., 1
Delany, Samuel R., 31, 115–23, 127, 141n3, 145n21, 146n21
  ethics in, 24, 80, 89, 117, 145n22, 145n33
  memoirs of, 116–18, 144n3, 144n9
  Surrealist Anabaptism of, 55, 95, 118–23, 145n15
  See also *The Mad Man*; *The Tides of Lust*
DeLillo, Don, 31, 32
Dentz, Shira, 137n5
Dickel, Simon, 123
disability, 12, 18, 89, 100, 117, 142n30
Divine, the, 25, 59–60, 90, 119
  feminist aspects of, 10, 55–56
  and Mennonite literature, 11, 22, 37, 39–45
  queer aspects of, 29, 33, 97, 119
  and theapoetics, 13, 105, 121, 123, 124–27
Dorsey, Candas Jane, 95
Dostoevsky, Fyodor, 31
Doty, Mark, 12, 13
Dueck, Lynnette, 47
Dula, Peter, 142n33
Dungeons & Dragons, 1, 32
Dungy, Camille T., 132n76
Dunham, Mabel, 8, 62, 131n39, 135n115, 137n8, 139n6
Dutch Blitz, 78, 140n9

INDEX   163

Eby, Benjamin, 139n6
Eliot, T. S., 127
Epp, Claas, 102
Erb, Paul, 131n36
eroscomix.com, 35
erotic joy, 80, 117, 121, 123
ethics, 20, 30, 39, 56, 59–60, 112
    in literature, 3, 13, 40, 48, 63–64, 78
    teaching of, 23, 53, 57–58, 76–77, 114, 124–25
    See also beauty: and ethics; Delany, Samuel R.: ethics in; *I Hear the Reaper's Song*: ethics of; literature: ethics of; Mennonite community: ethics of; poetry: ethics of; *Summer of My Amazing Luck*: ethics of; theapoetics
exile, 3–4, 28, 101–5, 138n37, 138n44
    See also Mennonite community: leaving

"Fallow" (Samatar). *See Tender*: "Fallow"
Fanon, Frantz, 121
feminism, 36-37, 79, 85, 97, 132n71, 144n66
    See also Brandt, Di: feminism in; the Divine: feminist aspects of; Kauffman, Janet: and feminism; Mennonite literature (field): feminism of; theapoetics: feminism of
Ferlinghetti, Lawrence, 8
Fisher, Elizabeth, 12
FitzGerald, Russell, 146n21
Fitzpatrick, Cat, 109–10, 143n59
Fournier, Lauren, 19–20, 31
Frankenstein (Shelley), 88, 99
Freeman, Elizabeth, 119
Friesen, Gordon, 8
Friesen, Lauren, 129n2, 130n12
Friesen, Patrick, 6, 19, 63, 104, 133n85

Gatchalian, C. E., 32
gelassenheit, 102
Ginsberg, Allen, 145n21
global warming. *See* climate change
Good, Merle, 6, 61, 62, 63, 65, 139n7
Goshen College, 27–28, 63, 103, 136n4, 142n42
    See also Cruz, Daniel Shank: education of: at Goshen College
Graham, Melva, 15
Gray, Lois Frey, 40
Gundy, Jeff, 3, 5, 13, 61, 63, 118
    nonfiction of, 9, 16, 17, 124, 130n23, 137n3
    poetry of, 38–46, 48–50, 137n6
    and theapoetics, 12, 40–46, 50, 90–91, 127
    See also "In Praise of the Lurkers"; "Manifesto of Anabaptist Surrealism"; *Rhapsody with Dark Matter*
Gurga, Lee, 124, 146n10

haiku, 25, 124–27, 146n4, 146n10
    See also poetry
Halberstam, Jack, 106
Herald Press, 5, 7, 36, 133n88, 135n115, 135n116
    didactic publications of, 6, 18, 35, 86
Herr, Hans, 129n6
Hershey, Barbie, and family. *See I Hear the Reaper's Song*
Hiebert, Paul, 131n40
Himmelfarb, Martha, 133n80
Hinchcliffe, Peter, 130n23
Hooley Yoder, Anita, 4, 9, 12, 56, 125–26, 132n57
"Honey Bear" (Samatar). *See Tender*: "Honey Bear"
Hossack, Darcie Friesen, 11
Hostetler, Ann, 11, 48, 55, 124
hymnals, 29, 101, 135n115
hymns, 41, 45, 68–69, 101, 124, 142n34

I Hear the Reaper's Song (Stambaugh), 23, 24, 60–75, 77, 79, 110
    critical neglect of, 33, 61, 66
    ethics of, 71–75, 112
    railroad in, 64–66, 69–74
    See also Stambaugh, Sara
"In Praise of the Lurkers" (Gundy), 22, 38–40, 43–44, 140n6
    Mennonite writers as, 39–40, 49, 65, 140n13
    See also Gundy, Jeff
"in the world but not of it". *See* Mennonites/Mennonitism: "in the world but not of it"

Jantzen, Grace, 9, 40
Janzen, Jean, 7, 131n34
Johnson, Chelsey, 108
Johnson, Julie Swarstad, 22, 60, 62, 139n107
Jordan, Mark D., 119–20
Juhnke, James C., 66

Kampen, Melanie, 11–12, 142n34
Kasdorf, Julia Spicher, 19, 40, 46–47, 132n57, 135n115, 139n107
    on Mennonite artmaking, 65, 140n13
    on *Mennonite Identity and Literary Art*, 5, 130n33

164 INDEX

Kasdorf, Julia Spicher *(continued)*
   poetry of, 22, 59-60, 129n8, 137n5
   See also "Sunday Morning Confession"
Kauffman, Janet, 22, 60, 62–63
   critical neglect of, 33, 61, 91
   and feminism, 36, 58, 91
   See also The Body in Four Parts
Kaufmann, Britt, 10
Kehler, Grace, 113, 144n69, 144n70
Kendig, Martin, 129n6
Kennel, Maxwell, 9, 11, 129n2, 132n53
Keogh, Theodora, 31
Khalifeh, Sahar, 132n76
killjoy survival kits, 99, 127, 146n2
   as queer, 29–30, 33, 115–16, 136n9
   See also Ahmed, Sara; objects
kink. *See* BDSM
Kirch, Claire, 82
Klaassen, Walter, 90, 141n6
Kliewer, Warren, 6, 8, 131n40, 139n3
Kline, John, 62, 139n4
Knippen, James Henry, 1, 133n79
Koestenbaum, Wayne, 30
Koop, Karl, 18, 142n34

Lachman, Becca J. R., 2, 22, 33, 132n57
   A Ritual to Read Together, 56, 109, 139n107
Lancaster County, Pennsylvania, 2, 23, 31, 44, 69
   See also Mennonites/Mennonitism: in Lancaster County, Pennsylvania
Lapp, Jessica W., 62
Lee, Li-Young, 44
Lerner, Ben, 14, 132n69
Lewis, C. S., 31, 87, 131n42
LGBTQ+. *See* queer
Liars and Rascals (Tiessen), 39, 61, 103, 137n8, 139n3
life writing, 19, 67, 89, 135n3
Lindenberg, Rebecca, 16
Lindsay, Nick, 103, 142n42
Lisowski, Zefyr, 20–21
literary community, 6, 45, 65, 109, 137n6
   See also Mennonite literature (field): community of
literature, 3, 8, 55, 99, 139n91
   as activist, 35, 96, 126
   ethics of, 3, 9, 11, 13, 15
   See also Mennonite literature (field); writing
LittlePuss Press, 143n59
Long, Geraldine, 142n29

Lorde, Audre, 13, 15, 19
Loveless, Natalie, 19–20

Mad Man, The (Delany), 24, 57, 95, 119–23, 145n22
   See also Delany, Samuel R.
Making Believe (Redekop), 4, 16, 129n12, 131n40
   See also Redekop, Magdalene
"Manifesto of Anabaptist Surrealism" (Gundy), 24, 119–23, 145n17
   See also Gundy, Jeff
martyrdom, 39, 51, 64, 100, 104, 135n115
Martyrs Mirror (van Braght), 44, 60, 78, 102, 142n38
   in personal libraries, 29, 135n115, 136n20
   as teaching text, 23, 62
Masthof Press, 135
memoir. *See* life writing
Mennonite community, 5, 6, 19, 37, 40, 68–69
   ethics of, 61, 89, 101, 110, 122
   as exclusionary, 11, 44–45, 51–52, 82, 101–3, 130n17
   leaving, 69, 104–5, 112, 140n13 (*see also* exile)
   See also Mennonites/Mennonitism
Mennonite ethnicity, 17, 63, 77, 94, 100–101, 140n5
   Russian Mennonite, 7, 110, 131n34, 138n44
   Swiss Mennonite, 7, 63, 110, 130n14, 131n34, 138n44
Mennonite Identity and Literary Art (Ruth), 4–10, 18, 98, 130n17, 133n88, 137n1
   writers' responses to, 6–10, 12, 48, 124, 130n23, 130n33
   See also Kasdorf, Julia Spicher: on *Mennonite Identity and Literary Art*; *Mennonite Literary Voices*; Mennonite literature (field); Ruth, John
Mennonite Literary Voices (Reimer), 6–10, 49, 61, 124, 130n23, 137n1
   See also *Mennonite Identity and Literary Art*; Mennonite literature (field); Reimer, Al
Mennonite Literature (college course), 36, 38, 137n1
Mennonite literature (field), 5–9, 17, 48–49, 91, 130n23, 133n88
   community of, 10–12, 38, 118, 124, 131n34, 140n13
   feminism of, 47, 48, 58
   first generation of, 56, 58, 60, 139n88, 139n107
   history in, 60, 62, 110, 139n5
   Mennonite/s Writing conferences, 11, 38, 46, 130n23, 132n55

Fresno 2015, 3, 47, 145n16; Goshen 2002, 46, 64; Goshen 2022, 2, 132n55; Winnipeg 2017, 47, 132n55
   pacifism in, 4, 60, 62, 65, 72
   and people of color, 2, 100–101, 130n17, 131n38
   second generation of, 56, 57, 60, 139n88, 139n107
   as secular theology, 2–3, 10–11, 78, 82, 85–86
   as theapoetic, 4, 9–10, 127, 141n10 (*see also* the Divine: and Mennonite literature)
   transgressiveness of, 3–5, 40, 140n13
   transnationalism of, 61, 131n38
   See also "In Praise of the Lurkers": Mennonite writers as; *Mennonite Identity and Literary Art*; *Mennonite Literary Voices*; queer Mennonite literature
Mennonite Starter Kit, The (Haas and Nolt), 131n34
Mennonite/s Writing conferences. *See* Mennonite literature: Mennonite/s Writing conferences
Mennonites/Mennonitism, 129n2
   ableism of, 18
   "in the world but not of it", 4, 8, 13, 38, 78
   and speculative fiction, 24, 27–28, 95, 99, 102–5, 113–14
   and Jews, 102, 140n5, 146n15
   in Lancaster County, Pennsylvania, 2, 62–68, 70, 129n6, 139n8, 140n31
   plain dress, 67–68
   queerness of, 17, 90, 110, 126, 133n86
   queerphobia of, 4, 18, 45, 74, 77, 130n17, 134n90
   racism of, 4, 18, 27, 74, 130n17, 134n90, 136n5
   colonialism of, 2, 49, 53–54, 62, 101, 129n5, 129n6
   secular Mennonites, 9, 11, 17, 77–78
   sexism of, 18, 23–24, 27, 44, 67, 74, 77, 111, 138n60
   theology of, 10, 62, 63, 67–68, 80, 145n17
   See also Anabaptism/Anabaptists; Mennonite community
Mennonot, 140n6
mermaids, 93, 141n16
Mierau, Maurice, 130n13, 133n85
Miller, Evie Yoder, 62
Moby-Dick (Melville), 8, 94
Mok, Annie, 118, 145n15
Mookerjea, Sourayan, 2
Moraga, Cherríe, 19

Morrison, Toni, 88, 141n3
Myers, Natasha, 129n3

narrative theology, 22
Neufeldt, Leonard, 138n43
New York City, 31, 34, 63–64, 89
   in literature, 67, 119, 122, 145n33
9/11, 2, 64
Nussbaum, Martha, 22
Nye, Naomi Shihab, 17, 56

objects, 31–32, 42–43, 45, 56, 85
   queer, 29–30, 127–28, 136n8, 136n9
   See also killjoy survival kits
obsession, 32–33
ordinary theology, 18, 124
   See also queer theology
the Other, 57–58, 64–65, 70–74, 79, 100, 106
outer space. *See* speculative fiction: outer space
Out in Culture (Creekmur and Doty), 34–35
outsiders, 10, 39, 73, 103–5, 110, 113
Oxford English Dictionary, 90, 113

pacifism, 17, 56, 60, 74, 113
   writers and, 16, 119
   See also Mennonite literature: pacifism in
Pandora Press, 135n116
pandemic, 1–3, 9, 17, 126
   emotional effects of, 3, 125, 127
   societal effects of, 15, 39, 88, 99, 100, 142n28
   "triple pandemic", 3
   See also apocalypse; Cruz, Daniel Shank: pandemic and
Perdomo, Willie, 15, 37, 56
Piepzna-Samarasinha, Leah Lakshmi, 3
plain dress. *See* Mennonites/Mennonitism: plain dress
Plett, Casey, 2, 63, 105–10, 143n44, 143n59, 145n15
   See also "Portland, Oregon"
poetry, 13–17, 36–60, 131n34, 137n1, 137n5
   activism of, 38, 54, 56, 58, 132n71, 133n79
   anthologies, 36, 56, 139n107
   ethics of, 9, 16, 22, 38
   function of, 14–15, 60
   "news" in, 14–16, 34
   poets as teachers, 36, 38, 103, 120, 124, 142n42
   queerness of, 37–38, 56, 89, 92
   as theapoetic, 37–38, 59, 91, 132n57
   See also haiku
Pollack, Rachel, 126–27
Pope, Simon, 19

pornography, 34, 115, 121–22, 144n2
Porter, Lavelle, 145n17
Portland (OR), 108–9, 143n56
"Portland, Oregon" (Plett), 24, 105–9, 114
    literary references in, 105–6, 107–8
Portlandia, 108–9, 143n56
Potok, Chaim, 31

queer, 12, 21
    activist worldview of, 11, 16–17, 110, 118, 122
    archiving, 29–30, 33, 110, 136n9, 143n59
    community, 28, 116, 122
    hope, 24, 108–9, 114, 130n17
    literature, 31, 35, 125, 128, 131n41 (*see also*
        Delany, Samuel R.; queer Mennonite
        literature)
    See also queer theory
queer Mennonite literature, 24, 47, 94, 105,
    138n37
    See also Mennonite literature
queer theology, 18, 90, 97, 119, 123
    See also ordinary theology
queer theory, 11–12, 18, 19, 36, 89–91
    activism of, 93–94, 113, 117, 145n12
    See also queer

Ra, Sun, 28
Redekop, Magdalene, 11, 13, 48, 114, 129n12,
    135n115
    on community, 17, 90
    See also Making Believe
Reed, Ken Yoder, 2, 62, 139n5
Reed, Sabrina, 135n117
Reimer, Al, 7, 59
    See also Mennonite Literary Voices
Reimer, Nikki, 12, 14, 15
Remer, Molly, 10, 12–13, 55, 56, 94, 132n49
"Request for an Extension on the *Clarity*"
    (Samatar). See *Tender*: "Request for an
    Extension on the *Clarity*"
research–creation. *See* autotheory
revolution, 15, 16, 29, 124, 132n76
Rhapsody with Dark Matter (Gundy), 33, 38,
    43–45
    See also Gundy, Jeff
Rich, Elaine Sommers, 131n40
Richardson, Suzanne, 1, 125, 127–28, 141n3
Robinson, Dawn G., 126
Rohrer, Jane, 139n8
Rosenberg, Jordy, 116, 120
Rosenstock, Gabriel, 125

Ross, Bruce, 124
Roth, John D., 130n13
Roth, Philip, 31, 32
Rozansky, Chelsea, 21
Rubin, Steven, 59, 137n5
Ruth, John L., 6–8, 19, 59, 61–62, 131n34, 140n23
    on Hershey–Barge accident, 66–67
    reading of, 130n14, 131n39, 131n40, 131n41,
        133n88
    See also Mennonite Identity and Literary Art
Ruti, Mari, 30

Salesses, Matthew, 133n77
Samatar, Sofia, 2, 31–34, 40, 139n107, 140n30,
    145n16
    and archiving, 26, 104–5, 135n3
    autobiographical elements in work of, 19,
        21–22, 26, 136n20, 142n28, 142n42
    lineage of, 63, 110, 130n17
    and other writers, 94–95, 105, 118, 129n5,
        135n3, 136n6
    queer elements in work of, 24, 89 90, 100,
        103
    See also "The Scope of This Project"; *Tender*
Sanchez, Melissa E., 33, 90
Sandor, Marjorie, 120
Schalk, Sami, 24, 87, 90–91, 117, 119–20
Schirch, Lisa, 136n5, 146n15
Schlabach, Theron, 145n17
Schroeder, Karl, 118
"Scope of This Project, The" (Samatar), 3, 100–
    101, 122, 131n38, 142n31
    See also Samatar, Sofia
secular Mennonites. *See* Mennonites/
    Mennonitism: secular Mennonites
Sedgwick, Eve Kosofsky, 136n8, 146n4
Sena, Marie, 127–28
Serano, Julia, 143n52
sex, 36, 43, 47, 93–94, 117, 121–23
sex work, 57, 105, 107, 143n47, 143n52
shunning, 102, 113, 120
Smith, Sidonie, 31
Smucker, Barbara, 87
"Smut Stories" (Bechtel), 24, 94–99
    See also Bechtel, Greg
Snaza, Nathan, 31, 32, 136n21
Snow, Cassandra, 30, 127–28, 136n17, 147n24
Solís, Migueltzinta C., 32
speculative fiction, 23–24, 87–114, 115, 117, 142n44
    definition of, 87, 90–91, 119, 141n1, 141n3
    genre hybridity in, 87, 89–91, 92, 94–96, 118

hope in, 96, 98, 106, 108, 114
marginality of, 88, 90
outer space, 27–28, 34, 87, 101–2, 129n5, 139n107
possible worlds in, 20, 96
queerness of, 34, 37, 89, 97, 99, 105
theapoetics of, 24, 87–91, 97, 120
Stafford, William, 17, 56
Stambaugh, Sara, 61, 65, 67–68
family of, 63, 139n6, 140n25, 140n28
See also *I Hear the Reaper's Song*
Steffler, Margaret, 144n66
Stenson, Esther, 15–16
Stockton, Kathryn Bond, 118, 145n13
suicide, 104, 139n104
Summer of My Amazing Luck (Toews), 24, 63, 75–87, 94
autobiographical elements of, 23, 79
ethics of, 77–78, 81–86, 121–22
See also Toews, Miriam
"Sunday Morning Confession" (Kasdorf), 3–4, 7, 39, 48, 61, 131n40
See also Kasdorf, Julia Spicher
superheroes, 24, 93

tarot, 25, 30, 124, 126–28, 146n21
Devil card, 127–28
ecumenical elements of, 126–27, 147n24
Tea, Michelle, 10, 107–8
Tender (Samatar), 21, 26–27, 135n3, 137n36
"Fallow", 24, 26–27, 101–5, 110, 113–14, 145n28
Mennonite elements in, 102–4, 106, 112, 143n61
"Honey Bear", 24, 99–100, 110, 142n29
"Request for an Extension on the *Clarity*", 21, 26–35, 102, 103, 114, 137n33
Afrofuturism in, 28–29, 34; narrator's books in, 27–30, 34–35
See also Samatar, Sofia
theapoetics
decolonialism of, 13, 22, 38, 57, 100–101, 131n42
feminism of, 10, 22, 48, 131n42, 146n21
hopefulness of, 16, 44, 58, 85
and literatures other than Mennonite, 17, 63, 78, 119, 124–28, 146n4
and personal experience, 23, 65, 118
everyday, 25, 110, 123, 125, 127, 132n49; as sacred, 10, 12–14, 18, 33, 94; as witness, 39, 57, 79, 110
queerness of, 10–12, 21, 29, 38, 57, 131n42

reading as, 28, 35, 37, 76, 95, 99
secularism of, 9, 124
theology of, 18, 61, 77, 89–91, 101, 119–20
See also Brandt, Di: theapoetics of; the Divine: and theapoetics; ethics; Gundy, Jeff: and theapoetics; Mennonite literature (field): as theapoetic; poetry: as theapoetic; speculative fiction: theapoetics of; Whitman, Walt: writing as theapoetic
theology. See Mennonite literature (field): as secular theology; Mennonites/Mennonitism: theology of; narrative theology; ordinary theology; queer theology; theapoetics: theology of
theopoetics, 8–9, 38, 131n42
Threadgill, Elizabeth, 1, 125
Tides of Lust, The (Delany), 115–16, 144n2
See also Delany, Samuel R.
Tiessen, Hildi Froese, 17, 76, 78, 79
See also *Liars and Rascals*
Toews, Miriam, 76–79, 106, 110–14, 140n9, 141n10
on function of writing, 76, 82, 114
prominence of, 88, 139n91
See also *Summer of My Amazing Luck*; *Women Talking*
Togane, Mohamud Siad, 129n5
Tolkien, J. R. R., 87
Tom of Finland, 34
Tucker, Jeffrey Allen, 122

Unger, Andrew, 11

Valente, Catherynne M., 33
van Leyden, Jan, 102
Viramontes, Helena María, 132n76
Visser, Piet, 131n38

Watson, Julia, 31
Waugh, Thomas, 34
Weinstone, Ann, 34, 88, 105
Welch, Michael Dylan, 146n10
Wenger, Amos, 66–67, 70
Wenger, Ruth Yoder, 143n64
Whitman, Walt, 15, 31, 119, 123, 133n77
"letters from God," 41, 136n14, 146n21
and lists, 57, 121, 145n31
and queerness, 12, 29, 145n21
writing as theapoetic, 17, 55–56
Wiebe, Armin, 101–2

Wiebe, Dallas, 6
Wiebe, Katie Funk, 139n3
Wiebe, Natasha G., 76
Wiebe, Rudy, 2, 7, 104, 139n91
   The Blue Mountains of China, 6, 36, 101–2
   My Lovely Enemy, 94, 141n19
   Peace Shall Destroy Many, 6, 8, 76
Willems, Dirk, 44, 78
Williams, William Carlos, 14, 15, 16, 34
Winnipeg, 23, 77, 108
Womack, Ytasha L., 28, 120
Women Talking (Toews), 24, 76, 78, 106, 110–14
   See also Toews, Miriam
Woodhouse, Reed, 123
Woods, Jamila, 132n71
Wright, David, 43

writing, 39–40, 44, 56, 59, 91, 132n49
   as archiving, 20–21, 114
   of literary characters, 103, 105
   as resistance, 58, 114, 132n76
   See also literature

xandria.com, 35

Yoder, Rachel, 139n7

Zacharias, Robert, 91, 102–3, 138n44, 145n28
   on field of Mennonite literature, 3–4, 11, 131n39, 133n88
Zambreno, Kate, 135n3
Zapruder, Matthew, 14
Zimmerman, Diana R., 135n3
Zoltan, Vanessa, 30

www.ingramcontent.com/pod-product-compliance
Lightning Source LLC
Chambersburg PA
CBHW022014290426
44109CB00015B/1167